Earl th‹

Earl the Twirl

My Life in Basketball

EARL CURETON
with JAKE UITTI

Forewords by Julius Erving and Isiah Thomas

McFarland & Company, Inc., Publishers
Jefferson, North Carolina

Frontispiece: Earl on a fast-break, dunking during a 1985 home game for the Detroit Pistons and showing his leaping ability.

ISBN (print) 978-1-4766-9383-5
ISBN (ebook) 978-1-4766-5159-0

LIBRARY OF CONGRESS AND BRITISH LIBRARY
CATALOGUING DATA ARE AVAILABLE

Library of Congress Control Number 2023053301

Front cover: Earl Cureton takes a shot as Kevin McHale (far left) and Larry Bird (far right) of the Boston Celtics look on in a 1982 NBA game (courtesy of the Philadelphia 76ers)

Printed in the United States of America

*McFarland & Company, Inc., Publishers
Box 611, Jefferson, North Carolina 28640
www.mcfarlandpub.com*

For Judith and Sari, my loves—Earl

For my father Karl and Aunt Betty,
two Michigan kids—Jake

Acknowledgments

The authors would like to thank everyone who helped make this book possible, including Minnie and Johnnie Cureton, who are no longer with us today, as well as the lovely Judith and Sari Cureton and Eva Walker. We would also like to thank basketball stars Julius Erving, Isiah Thomas, Muggsy Bogues, Derrick Coleman, Charles Oakley, Spencer Haywood, Sam Cassell, Bob McAdoo, George Gervin, Scott Brooks, Dave Bing, Mike D'Antoni, Dick Vitale, Rudy Tomjanovich, Greg Kelser, Rick Mahorn, James "Buddha" Edwards and Ben Wallace. An additional big thanks to those with the Pistons organization, like Mike Horan, Tom Gores, Kevin Grigg, Cletus Lewis, Chris Economeas, Erika Swilley, Alicia Jeffries, Nicolet Lewis, Aaron Smith and Arn Tellem. We would also like to thank John "Sunshine" Crawford, Dr. Gary Gilyard, Amy Slowik, Patty Jobbitt, Arnie Kander, Tom McLaughlin, Isaiah McKinnon and Rick and Carol Kaczander for decades of support. Finally, we would also like to extend appreciation for outlets like *Sports Illustrated*, the *New York Times*, the *Washington Post*, the *Guardian* and *Grantland* for their coverage of Earl's career over the years.

Table of Contents

Table of Contents

"When I think of Earl Cureton, I get a good feeling. Because he helped us win a championship."—Rudy Tomjanovich, two-time NBA champion coach

"Talk about an ambassador for HOOPS HYSTERIA! Earl Cureton's new book will make basketball lovers appreciate the efforts of a lifetime roundball fanatic. If you love hoops like I do, you will absolutely LOVE reading Earl's life story—it's AWESOME BABY with a capital-A!"—Dick Vitale, legendary broadcaster and coach

"I love the guy. I truly love him."—Arn Tellem, legendary sports agent

"I was lucky to play with Earl at the times that I did. I'm lucky to know him as a person now. He's just a sweetheart of a guy and a great player. He's won two NBA titles and that's never easy."—Mike D'Antoni, longtime NBA head coach

"The future dreamers that want to play in the NBA should all read this book because Earl is the blueprint of how to make it as a role player and how to stick in the league. He should be everybody's role model."—Scott Brooks, longtime NBA head coach

"I call Earl one of the best utility guys in pro basketball. That's what separated him. For me to see that, it gives me a great appreciation of the man, himself."—George Gervin, NBA legend

"He was very important to our championship run. We needed a guy who could play backup center, but who also had veteran leadership, who understood his role and how to play. Earl was old school!"—Sam Cassell, two-time NBA champion

"Everybody respects Earl—or should I say, 'Big Twirl!'"—Muggsy Bogues, NBA legend

"Earl has serious integrity. He's a good person, he cares. He has this heart. He wants the best for all the people that he's touched in his life. He leaves you a better person than you were before you met him."—Spencer Haywood, NBA legend

"He'd give you the shirt off his back."—Charles Oakley, NBA legend

"When I played against him in high school, he'd be knocking me down. But he'd also be helping me back up. He let me know *this* is what it's like up here at this level. He's always been that type of person."—Derrick Coleman, NBA all-star

Foreword

JULIUS "DR. J" ERVING

Whenever I think of Earl, it makes me happy. He's such a delight-ful individual. During the season, he'd always come in with the joke of the day and, like Bill Russell, after he tells the joke, he starts laughing. So, whether it's funny or not, if you're not laughing at the joke, you start laughing because *he's* laughing!

When I first met Earl at training camp, I didn't know anything about him because I really didn't follow college basketball. So, when he and Andrew Toney showed up as rookies, they were fresh faces, like deer in the headlights. For them, everything was 90 miles per hour. For instance, we got out there on the track to run—and we used to pace ourselves, to try and run the mile in six minutes. But they came out and did it in *five*. They were setting a whole new standard. Earl and Andrew were like that duo, Frick and Frack. Thankfully, they both stuck with our team and made sig-nificant contributions.

Camp was a couple of weeks back then and then you went through an exhibition season. Then once you paired down and you got your team, it was time to go! Our team was so unique in that we had four forwards, four guards and four centers. And then we had some guys who could be a lit-tle more interchangeable. But nobody else looked like us, had our type of setup. So, my first meeting with Earl was in that 1980 training camp. (In the off season at that stage in my career we took off to places like Europe, Asia, South America, wherever.)

Once we met, the conversation was always reflective; we often talked about the people we knew in common. There was a number of them, start-ing with Terry Tyler, Terry Duerod and the whole Detroit connection. And the Michigan connection, too, with Magic and the different people who'd come out of the state with Earl. Those were the people whom he idolized and who helped him at one time or another during his developmental stages as a player. I'd have to tell them they did a good job, too—especially

1

Earl's mom. He is so family-oriented. You could tell right away that Earl had a very, very good upbringing. That started with his mom.

I could tell I was one of his favorite guys, too, if I may say. With a lot of young players, that was the case. But guys can be kind of reluctant to talk about that because they're not going to do things that make them seem small in your presence. And to many I was bigger than life. But I knew—I knew I was one of his guys. Even though we didn't play the same position, every now and then, Earl would go and shoot a sweeping hook shot and I could just see him saying to himself, "Dr. J did it like that!" Those are the special moments you remember.

Practices were pretty intense back then for us. When you have a championship-caliber team like we had, and you got Moses Malone out there, you're going to work hard. Because Moses shows up for practice already sweating. So, Earl was playing—but we had four centers. And he knew he was going to have to fight for all the minutes he received. Even though Earl played two positions for us, he still had to fight for every minute. That was his role. And it was a dogfight in practice—we practiced hard. We played hard, too. But I never looked down on any guys who came off the bench. I knew from my early experiences with the Virginia Squires as a young player that there should be respect from the veterans, and young guys had to fight for time.

It would be a tribute to our guys on the bench if the starters could run up the score and we could get our rest in the fourth quarter and those guys could play the rest of the game. When I first went to Philly, Steve Mix was the guy backing me up and I told him, "Man, I'll bust their chops so I can get you more minutes tonight!" I remember on Steve's birthday I played the first quarter of the game, and I told the coach to take me out to rest and to let Steve go in and let him play the rest of the game. That's the type of thing that builds team chemistry, camaraderie. That's very important for you to ultimately reach the highest level of success. When a lot of those little things get done that way, that leads to winning. And Earl was great with that, too.

Earl and I hung out often. That first Thanksgiving in 1980—I was going back and forth to New York. Earl and Andrew Toney had just joined the team, so I took them to my home in Long Island and put them in front of my family to celebrate the holiday. My door was always open to them, and Earl took advantage of it many times. He was a single guy, and I had a nice little place out in Villanova near Philly where we had social gatherings and parties. I had a pool, tennis court and a big yard, so we could do cookouts and all of that. I generally was the guy hosting that stuff, which was always fun. And I loved having Earl and Andrew over.

But when we won the championship in '83 and Earl hit that hook shot in game two, that was a *big* moment—Earl coming into the game, hitting that shot as he did. The confidence he had running back down the court. It was important. It's cemented in there with all the great memories of that championship series. Then we swept the Lakers! Everybody got a chance to play a role in that series and some people's roles were bigger than others, but I would say that the celebration associated with Earl's moment was as big and as good as it got. Everybody was happy after that shot. Except Kareem!

The next year, though, seeing Earl leave the team was a blow. I was approaching the next season thinking if we could stay intact, then we would still be really good. But Moses ended up getting hurt and then later he was traded for Jeff Ruland. My last three years in Philly, we were never contenders again; we were just potential spoilers. But of course, I kept up with Earl when he went down to Houston and won his other ring years later with the Rockets. Earl is the type of guy who really doesn't go away, in that sense. We continued to have conversations about our kids, all the way up to his daughter Sari going to Georgetown.

And my son went to Cal-Berkeley. They both finished recently. I always thought it would be interesting if they ended up at the same school—got to know one another a bit better. But, of course, they went to fine institutions on their own, way different than where Earl and I went! Earl went to the University of Detroit, and I went to UMass. But that's what it's all about, right? Helping the next generation. Providing for the next generation to do even better than we did. That was definitely always part of our M.O. It's one of the many reasons I love Earl to this day.

—Julius "The Doctor" Erving

NBA icon **Julius Erving** *is one of the most dynamic players in league history. The Hall of Famer and member of the NBA's Top 75 Team helped the Philadelphia 76ers win the 1983 NBA championship. Today, Erving remains one of the league's most dignified statesmen.*

Foreword

Isiah Thomas

When I think of Earl Cureton, laughter comes to mind. Just in terms of his positivity. I also think of perseverance. Those would be the two words that I come up with—positivity and perseverance—when I think of him.

To be honest, I don't remember our first meeting, but I'm sure it was somewhere around the basketball court when I was with the Pistons. I played a lot in the city and for whatever reason, I just always seemed to be with Earl. The thing I loved about Earl and playing with him was his energy, his effort, which he brought to every single practice and to every game. You always knew what you would get from him out on the floor. He was going to play hard. He was going to rebound the basketball. He would set screens and he was a great teammate.

Earl wasn't a great shooter like Steph Curry, or somebody like that. But he was dependable and that's the thing that I loved about him. Being a teammate, you want people who you can depend on out on the floor who knew their assignments, knew where they were supposed to be and followed the gameplan. And Earl did that. The key phrase here is "glue guy." The team doesn't hold together without people like Earl. Everyone has their role, and everyone fits, it's really like putting together a puzzle. The pieces of the puzzle—everyone must understand their role and what they do. For Earl that was rebounding, running the floor and defending. That's the piece of the puzzle that he brought to the table. Oh, and *always* positivity.

When you talk about him as a "journeyman," being able to be positive and persevere and yet find a role within a team—how to help a team—that's what he was all about. That's why he was able to play in so many places with so many different personalities and so many different teams. That's not easy, but Earl did it.

We spent a lot of time together outside of the court, too. We were

4

great friends as players and as I retired, I knew I was going to another phase in my life in terms of being an owner and running a team. I wanted to maintain our friendship and our relationship. So, I said to Earl, "You have to grow for us to continue to have this great relationship and friendship that we have." I encouraged him to go back to school, encouraged him to finish and keep growing as a person, keep growing as a man. Because children and everything else are going to be on the way. To handle that, you have to keep maturing, have to keep growing. And he took that conversation extremely well. In fact, he not only took it well, but Earl set on a course to start pursuing it. I can't think of too many people that have persevered and worked as hard as he did with the limited amount of resources that he had.

Later in our careers, I always wanted to help him. And I saw that he was always trying for more. As a person, having experienced extreme poverty myself, you know that you don't get success without people helping you. But on the other side, you want to see people trying. And Earl was always trying. Therefore, I felt that I should and could help. The biggest thing overall was that Earl was trustworthy. You could trust him. You could trust him to try. You could trust him to be upstanding. You could trust his word, trust him showing up, to be on time, to be professional. He was trustworthy and worthy of all the opportunities he received.

When we were with the Pistons together, the Bad Boys, our team culture revolved around the things that I'm talking about. Positivity, perseverance, the trust and, I'll add a fourth: loyalty. At every building phase, there's a foundational phase and Earl Cureton was part of the foundation phase in terms of those building blocks that went into establishing our culture: how we interacted and how we worked together as teammates. All those playoff experiences that we had together, those losses that we had together, he was a big part of working through that. We definitely couldn't have achieved what we achieved without those building blocks being formed early and he was a big part of the team chemistry.

—Isiah "Zeke" Thomas

Isiah Thomas *is a two-time NBA champion, Top 75 player, Hall of Famer and league legend. The former "Bad Boy" Detroit Piston is considered the best six-foot point guard ever. Today, as a broadcaster, he remains one of the league's most recognizable faces.*

Preface

JAKE UITTI

The life and career of former NBA player and basketball coach Earl Cureton is a study in the payoff of perseverance. He is the Johnny Cash of the NBA. Truly, he's "been everywhere, man." Indeed, Earl, who was not born with other-worldly talent, can be thought of as the Patron Saint of Basketball Patience. He's the professional game's Job.

Earl, after a growth spurt that got him first to 6'4" and then to 6'9" as a young man, succeeded in the game in high school, at two different colleges, on seven NBA teams and a handful of others in countries abroad—from France to Argentina to Italy (twice)—and later he went on to coach successfully in several leagues, from the ABA to the CBA, USBL and WNBA.

Since, he has worked as a broadcaster, a team ambassador and even a strength and conditioning coach in the NBA. Earl boasts a list of long-time friends like Julius "Dr. J" Erving, Muggsy Bogues and Isiah Thomas. He was teammates with Michael Jordan, Moses Malone and Hakeem Olajuwon. He won two historic NBA championships, hitting a huge hook shot over Kareem in the 1983 Finals and providing much-needed backup minutes for Houston in 1994.

Today, Earl sometimes thinks of himself as a "Jack of all trades but a master of none." But that's not totally accurate. While he has a great deal of experience in basketball over many years, his subject of mastery is *hanging on* and not giving up. It's a lesson we could all learn from when it comes to our own dreams. We all know about the game's stars like LeBron James, Kobe Bryant and Shaquille O'Neal. But what about those who aren't as heralded—what are their lives like? That's exactly what this book is about.

In the NBA's golden era of Magic and Bird, Jordan and Dr. J, there was also Earl Cureton. But while those all-stars and MVPs soared over their competition with speed and shooting ability, Earl scraped and clawed with savvy and hunger to stay in the league for a dozen seasons, eventually winning two coveted championships some 11 years apart. Few people can boast two rings. But Earl can.

Earl is open-minded and affable. He's a great storyteller, able to remember detail after detail. And he's kept the faith throughout decades of ups and downs, what he calls his "rollercoaster" professional life and career in the game. It is fitting for someone nicknamed "The Twirl," given that title by legendary coach and broadcaster Dick Vitale. Indeed, perhaps more than any other, Earl's life offers a window into the universe of professional basketball, and it does so from angles rarely discussed. In this way, "Twirl" could stand for "The Winding Intersection of a Role-Player's Life."

Somehow, Earl has always known this book would come to exist. Even if he didn't know how, exactly. But that was no real concern to him in the moment. The continuance of a dream was all that mattered. Such is the lot for the Patron Saint of Basketball Patience. Earl has faith. It's his super-power. From his growth spurts in college to his call-up in '94 with the Houston Rockets just two days before the playoffs, his life is a working-class, professional-sports fairytale.

I was happy to help him tell his story—honored, actually. Earl and I met through the great point guard Muggsy Bogues. The two of them had met when Earl played for the inaugural Charlotte Hornets season in 1988, along with Rex Chapman, Dell Curry, and others. The team had selected Muggsy in the expansion draft and Earl, who'd signed with the squad in the offseason, helped the new franchise win 20 games that first historic season.

While Muggsy is an NBA star, just about as recognizable as any player in the history of the league (he is still the shortest ever to lace up sneakers, at 5'3"), the two were integral in stabilizing the team in its first year with the likes of Chapman and Curry. But the Hornets was just one of Earl's seven NBA teams in his career, along with the Philadelphia 76ers, Detroit Pistons, Chicago Bulls, Los Angeles Clippers, Rockets and Toronto Raptors. He's endured tryouts, cuts and playing overseas as he kept his career on track.

Today, Earl is known as a "journeyman." He's traveled the globe, as well as the United States. It's a life few could have succeeded at for as long as he did. But Earl, with the help of close friends and a loving family, made it work for well over a decade. If you turn to the correct page in the Merriam-Webster's dictionary, you might even see Earl's handsome smiling face where the word "determination" is listed!

Earl played at a time when there were some 300 elite athletes in the NBA. He was one among them. That itself is remarkable, considering the hundreds of thousands of high school players in America and elsewhere who play basketball each and every year. And among the fortunate few

who realize the dream of playing in the NBA, only a fraction
experience the joy of winning a
championship, let alone two. But
his accomplishments don't stop
there, as you will see in these
pages.

In 2022, controversial NBA
champion and multi-time all-star
Kyrie Irving wrote something on
Twitter. He said, "My Dad told me
at a young age, I had a 1 in 3,333
percent chance (.03%) of making
it to the NBA and that I should
have backup plans for my life
regardless if it happened or not. I
am grateful he told me the truth
because, with or without basketball, I know myself.... Is it true
there have only been a little over
5,500 total individuals ever (4,502
men, ~1,000 women) that played
in the NBA/WNBA at least one

Earl knocked on his butt mid-game,
1984, and observing what might happen next on the court.

minute? Our world attempts to downplay the fact that it's a RARE case to
make it to the league, let alone dominate. RARE AIR."

If this "rare air" is true for Irving today, it's even more so for Earl
decades ago, who played at a time with half-a-dozen fewer teams and that
many fewer roster spots. Keep reading here to find out the whole story, in
Earl's charming words.

Introduction

Earl Cureton

"Never heard of you." I should probably get that tattooed somewhere on my body; I've heard *it* so many times. "You ain't shit!" That one, too.

Yet, despite that—or perhaps because of it—I managed to play in the NBA for 12 hard-fought seasons. And between a few of those, I played internationally in countries like Italy, Argentina, Mexico and France. I've played with Magic Johnson all over the world on his famous touring all-star team, after he'd announced his diagnosis with HIV. I've played with stars like Michael Jordan on the Chicago Bulls, Isiah Thomas on the Detroit Pistons, Dr. J and Moses Malone on the Philadelphia Sixers. I've played in frigid Alaska with Planet Lovetron's No. 1 alien, Darryl Dawkins. I started in 141 NBA games, including playoffs (and played in a total of 728). I dunked *hard* on Patrick Ewing (look it up on YouTube). I also hit a hook shot on Kareem in the NBA Finals, helping to seal our sweep. I've won two diamond championship rings. I've even coached WNBA legend Brittney Griner, going up against her in practice in Phoenix. And still people—*kids*, even—tell me that I'm nobody.

It's funny to me now. Really, it is. Because to play in the NBA for a dozen years means you're at the absolute peak of your profession, for each of those years. The top of the top. The best among the very best. *Elite.* Sometimes it's too easy for people to forget that.

That's why this book is so important to me and to understanding the league. I don't know how many times I've heard someone tell me I wasn't special. Yet, as you'll see, it takes someone with a strong constitution and skills to survive what I've survived in and out of the league. To thrive in what I went through. From battles in the NBA, to staying sane at a time when the league was still in its rocky, formative days, to growing up in Detroit's inner-city during race riots. Sometimes, it felt like I was at odds with the whole (basketball) world. But I made it! I had a lengthy career, covered in outlets like *The New York Times, Sports Illustrated, Grantland, The Washington Post* and *The Guardian*. And to this day, I have lifelong pals in Julius Erving, Isiah Thomas and Muggsy Bogues.

Does that sound like someone who ain't shit? Nope.

In my career, I had to answer the bell more times than a phone operator. I fought through more adversity than Andy Dufresne crawling through that fetid sewer pipe at the end of the film *Shawshank Redemption*. But people don't have respect for fighters these days. Only so-called "winners." Yet, I was one of those, too. *Twice!* I've also been a coach in big developmental basketball leagues, from the USBL to the ABA and CBA (I must have run out of letters in the alphabet or else I would have coached more). I know how to talk to players, from starters to those who begin the game on the bench. I know how to spot and develop talent.

Stars have it easy, if you ask me. On the court, at least. If you've got great talent and a solid work ethic, you get to play 30–40 minutes a game. You get in your groove. For a bench player, you must accept less and still shine when your number is called. That's who I am. That was my role. My good games were 8 points, 7 rebounds, two blocked shots and a victory at the end of it. (But my great games were 20 and 15, just so you know.) It's important to have guys like me on your team. You can't win without us. Not long-term, anyway.

Most people think a player is successful only when he or she averages 20-plus points per game or manages double-digit assists or rebounds. Well, my career averages were 5.4 points, 4.7 rebounds, one assist, half a block, half an assist and zero three-pointers. Yet, I earned two priceless diamond-encrusted NBA rings. I also won a championship as a coach with the ABA's Long Beach Jam with players on the roster like Matt Barnes and DerMarr Johnson. My cell phone contact list is filled with famous names.

I've been a broadcaster and a team ambassador. I've been intertwined with the National Basketball Association since 1979. That's more than 40 years! But I've also had to fight for my place every day of those four decades. From backup plans to broken promises. I'm in the Hall of Fame at two different colleges *and* in my high school. Though I've never won an MVP award and I've never been an NBA all-star or an icon, I've tasted real success.

But most would rather see Steph splash three-pointers or MJ dunk from the free-throw line. And I get that. However, it's necessary to also understand the process of *making* the league, too. Teams are just that: groups of people working in unison toward a common goal. When I played in the NBA in the '80s and '90s, there were 250–300 players in the entire operation. Now, there's something like 450. To make a roster, you're in the top tier, the top percentile of your profession. It's more selective than doctors in major hospitals. If you make one NBA team, you're special. That's a simple fact. And I made seven of 'em.

"Ah, you ain't shit, Earl!" That's probably what you're thinking.

My stats make it easy for a person to think that. To think of me, in the parlance of the famous rap group TLC, as a "scrub." But that doesn't mean it's true. That's another thing I've learned on my journey. I had to be concerned with my career first and foremost. Not the thoughts and lives of others. Not the highlights and lowlights of others. People might think it's easy to be a journeyman, a backup. It's not. I had to make sure I was prepared, ready at a moment's notice, unsure of when or if I'd see the floor on a given night. But if I was called, I couldn't blow it. Or else I'd never get another chance.

Something I tell people often is to always have a backup plan. Sports shouldn't be your primary goal. Sports should be your secondary objective. The kids I speak to all want to be stars—the next Jordan, LeBron or Steph—but not everyone can occupy that role. Even if you make a league like the NBA, you're only going to be in it for 15 years—or maybe much less. Then what? You'll still have the rest of your life ahead of you. Maybe you'll be rich by then. Maybe not. I tell people: lay a foundation, get a degree. One day you'll be old. What's the plan then?

I was fortunate that sports led me to other careers in the business, like coaching, broadcasting, scouting and more. I was able to stay in the game thanks to the relationships I forged. But it's different for everyone.

In '94, I was called in at the end of the season to join the Houston Rockets on the team's championship run. To stay in shape, I'd been playing at a local YMCA. One of the guys at the "Y" later said to me, "Man, I was playing against you at the gym and a few weeks later, I look up and see you in the NBA Finals!" Pretty good, huh? After we won our ring that year, though, I messed up my leg so seriously that my doctor said I might not walk again. But I suited up 18 months later in Argentina with a young Luis Scola and I won our first game there on a buzzer-beater tip-in.

That's storybook stuff. And this is my storybook.

This memoir is all about overcoming what other people say that you can't do. It's about perseverance. It's about staying true to *you* and your vision. Taking control of your life and working hard, daily. Because you're one in a million, kid. You're somebody. Your story is worth telling, hearing. Trust me. That's the message I relay to everyone that I can. To those who listen—I can't wait to see what you become, too. What you do with your time. And when I see you later on down the line, I can't wait to say, "I'm proud of you."

From Detroit to doubters to diamond rings, this is my journey.

1

Houston: Champions

When the buzzer sounded, I looked for Judith. I tried to find her in the Houston stands amongst the thousands of people in the crowd. She'd come to every game. The woman I loved. The woman who had stuck by me for years as I struggled and scraped to stay in the NBA. She was my rock, my backbone. The mother of my daughter, Sari. My heart. I scanned the array of screaming fans for her warm face.

I tried to locate Judith as my Rockets teammates shouted in glee and as league officials handed out the 1994 championship hats. We'd won the Finals, victorious over the New York Knicks, the team that had cut me not long ago. Everyone was going crazy, from the nearly 20,000 spectators to everyone on my Houston team. Everyone but the Knicks, that is, and their pair of Patricks (Ewing and Riley), who were headed to the locker-room between bright confetti and streamers falling on their sweat-soaked heads.

I was ecstatic but I was also a bit reserved. I'd gotten to the team just two games before the regular season had ended, in something of a mad dash that didn't even allow me to get my luggage from baggage claim when I landed at the Houston airport after leaving my hometown of Detroit. I'd had to make the second-to-last game if I'd wanted to make the Rockets' playoff roster, officially. That meant leaving my luggage behind and racing to the arena to make game time. But it was all worth it.

My immediate reaction was to play it cooler than anything after the final buzzer, I didn't want to step on anyone's toes. But after a few moments, I was swept up in the electricity along with everyone else. I walked a fine line between respectful and exuberant. That's why I wanted Judith near me, to share it with her. She was the one I could celebrate with in full. The person who knew my struggle to even get here.

I'd contributed well to the Rockets during the postseason, playing a big role in the various playoff series leading up to the Finals. I'd been playing at the YMCA some handful of weeks before I got the call to join the team. But now I was here, my second ring earned. I'd also been writing a newspaper column for the *Houston Chronicle* throughout the postseason—"Earl's Pearls"—giving the details, the blow-by-blow, as our ultimate goal came to fruition.

Bill Russell had written a newspaper column during the playoffs for his final ring in 1969, too, when he was in Boston. And though his career was vastly different than mine, here I was. Doing the same as he had. Eventually I found Russell's heir apparent, the star of our team, Hakeem "The Dream" Olajuwon. We embraced as champions, grinning like kids. While I'd just got my second ring, he got his first. Men at the top of their profession.

For both of us it was the culmination of long, arduous lives in the NBA. His had begun in 1984 as the top pick in the draft (over Michael Jordan) and mine had begun five years earlier in 1979, drafted in the third round, unceremoniously. His started in Africa and mine in Detroit, Michigan. His was the life of a star's star, mine was the life of a career journeyman.

But here we were, together. Hugging in Houston on our home court wearing our white and red jerseys, having earned the final victory in the 1993–'94 playoffs. Only one team could say that, and we were on it. Hakeem was the Finals MVP, and I was the guy who signed with the team off the street just two games before the playoffs started. But as Dream later said, the Rockets would not have won the NBA Finals without me. And I believed him. I knew it even before the buzzer, the elated crowd mobbing our court.

Olajuwon's life in the league had been comprised of ups and downs, the result of sky-high (er, "Twin Tower") expectations when he entered the NBA ten years prior in '84 as a rookie, paired with Ralph Sampson, another center with big expectations. Mine was a rollercoaster ride, too, the story of someone working just to stay on a team's roster each year. A year later, after the Rockets repeated in '95, coach Rudy Tomjanovich would say, "Don't ever underestimate the heart of a Champion." But the phrase fit us like a glove in '94, too. We'd beaten the Knicks in seven tough games. Now, it was gleefully all over.

Some 11 years earlier, I'd had another big moment in the NBA Finals. I'd hit a critical skyhook, ironically over the man who made the shot famous, Kareem Abdul-Jabbar, to help my 76ers team win game two on our way to a four-game sweep of the vaunted Los Angeles Lakers, in the '83 series. That's when Dr. J and Moses Malone got their first NBA Finals hardware, too. Dr. J said after that shot, I wouldn't "be able to walk the streets of Detroit" without being surrounded by fans. That felt good.

In between those Finals, I'd been on four more teams (with a fifth to come later) and several more squads abroad (with more ahead, too). It was the best of times, it was the worst of times, to quote Mr. Charles J.H.

Dickens. But in that moment in Houston, after the O.J. Simpson white Bronco car chase that interrupted one of our telecasts, after enduring New York, after the gritty seven-game series, I was at the top of a tall, tall peak with a team full of future legends, from Kenny Smith to Robert Horry to Sam Cassell, embracing the man we called Dream. The metaphor wasn't lost on me.

When I finally found Judith, we looked at each other and embraced. She didn't mind my sweaty body, my tired face. We'd done it. I told her I loved her. She told me she loved me. And it was all that mattered in that very special moment of euphoria.

Memory Lane: Sam Cassell

"I met Earl when we were looking for a backup center. He came to the Rockets at the end of the season. And his home locker was right next to mine. We were already friends because he'd played in Charlotte with a good friend of mine, Muggsy Bogues. Muggsy used to talk about me to Earl all the time, how I was going to be the next one out of Baltimore, out of Dunbar High School, to be a pro. So, by the time Earl got to Houston, he knew everything about me!

"It can be difficult to come into a new team during the season. You have to be mentally tough, not just talented. I remembered Earl had that running hook shot against the Lakers in the NBA Finals. Now he was sitting right next to me! It was so fun being around him. When he got to know my personality and I got to know his personality—you know, these guys were grown men. I was just 21 or 22 and Earl was 34 or 35. Earl was a grown man. But we got to the point where we were really close. He helped me a lot.

"He was very important to our championship run. We needed a guy who could play some backup center, but who also had veteran leadership, who understood his role and how to play. Earl was old school! Every shot that went up, he boxed his man out! He couldn't jump as high as he used to, but he could box a player out and check guys off the boards. He'd come from that era of physicality, man, with Dr. J and the Pistons. He had toughness in him. We needed that.

"As a rookie, I needed someone to help me understand the league. I remember we were playing the Knicks in the Finals and Derek Harper was one of the best NBA guards in the league at hand-checking. That's when you could hand-check. Earl said, 'Man, listen.' He looked at me, 'You take your fucking fist and as soon as he puts a hand on you, smack it as hard as you can. You got to control that part of the game.' Once I did that, I think I got some respect from Derek Harper!

"Earl is an awesome human being. It's hard to describe somebody like him who is just always looking at the brighter side of things. But that was Earl. If I had two or three turnovers, I'd come back to the bench and I'd be pissed off. But Earl would say, 'Look, hey, we're going to have another chance. We need you out there. You'll get another chance. Keep your head up. It's just one game!' Hearing that from a veteran who'd won a championship as a young guy, that this man, this O.G. veteran has got a lot of confidence in me—that was awesome."

2

Hello, My Name Is Earl

I know what World Championship champagne tastes like. How the bubbles tickle your nose and tongue with every big, grateful swig. I know how it froths out of the bottle and sticks to your face and shoulders as your teammates pour it on you in celebratory victory-style. I was on two NBA teams that put the *champ* in the champagne, if you can forgive the pun—in '83 and '94. I still have both diamond rings to prove it. They read, "Fo Five Fo" and "Clutch City."

When you win an NBA title, you don't ever want to take your uniform off. You keep it on for 24- or 48-hours, or even longer. Sometimes you sleep in it, champagne smell, stickiness and all. That's how good it feels to win the final game of the NBA season. When we won, it was before those big goggles that players get now. The bubbly got all in our eyes, reddening them. That *good* sting. We didn't mind it. We were world champs.

But my start in the game of basketball could easily have never happened. I could have died in the poverty-stricken streets of east Detroit. I could have gone crazy trying to figure out the world around me. I could have never found the sport at all. Indeed, I came to basketball later in life. I was already 12 years old before I picked up a ball and shot at a (makeshift) hoop. Some of the NBA's biggest names also began late, like me. Hakeem Olajuwon, my former champion teammate, started at 15 years old, in Lagos, Nigeria. He grew up playing soccer. He had the best footwork in the history of the NBA. Him and Kevin McHale, that gangly guy from Hibbing, Minnesota. I played against him, too, banging elbows with that droopy-eyed Celtic. Joel Embiid started late (15 in Yaoundé, Cameroon). Tim Duncan, too (14 in Saint Croix, U.S. Virgin Islands). And Dirk Nowitzki (13 in Würzburg, Germany). But none of those big men, many of whom have statues in front of their home arenas now, grew up on the rough east side of the Motor City, known for its deteriorating neighborhoods and violence.

That was my home. And this is my story, one of average skill and exceptional hard work. But it's also the story shared by most of the NBA players, in one way or another. Those men I talked about above were all born with superior skills. For the rest of us, who were not imbued with such celestial talent, to make the league and remain in it, we had to work just as hard as the legends simply to be average. Heck, some guys with top talent don't even make the league—like New York City playground legend Earl "The Goat" Manigault. It's that difficult. People like me must work that much harder. And that lesser-written of, more trodden path is what my life is all about.

I was lucky to (eventually) grow tall, finally shooting up to around 6'9". But with all the rollercoaster rides I had to endure throughout my career, I could easily be in a straitjacket by now! There was seemingly a crazy loop-di-loop every season for some 16-plus years. But everything, thankfully, made me stronger. Perhaps that's my superpower: *Perseverance.*

Growing up, I lived on the east side of Detroit, amidst drug houses, corner prostitutes and violent gangs throughout my childhood. But I do want to stress that it wasn't *all bad* back home. There was a lot of good. Where I grew up obviously wasn't *great*, compared to some glistening suburbs, but bad experiences can help you just as good ones can. The area molded me. And most people from there, including myself, are proud of where we came up. I'm still tight with a lot of folks from the east side today. The area was my homebase until I went to college and eventually to the NBA, where I'd play with teammates like Michael Jordan ('86–'87), Olajuwon ('94), Muggsy Bogues ('88–'89, '91), Julius Erving ('80–'83), Norm Nixon ('87–'89), Moses Malone ('82–'83), Mike D'Antoni ('83, '89–'90 in Italy) and many more.

But I wasn't ever one of those guys with a long-term guaranteed contract. I was never firmly in the plans for any of my teams' futures. My nails are probably still somewhere in half-a-dozen basketball courts, I scratched and clawed so hard to stay in the league. When I hit the NBA in 1980 as a rookie, it was still very much establishing itself, in the awkward stages of the path toward the global, iconic business it is now. And today, I'm proud to say, I *still* work in the NBA, as a Community Ambassador for my hometown (and former) team, the Detroit Pistons. Yes, I also played with Isiah Thomas ('83–'86). But I left Zeke and them right before Detroit won their two rings, right before Rodman showed up and cemented the Bad Boys. (More on that later.)

As a kid, my family moved around to two or three different places in Detroit, but we always stayed on the east side. Familiarity, I guess. The first place we lived was known as "Black Bottom." It's where Ford Field is now, the current home of the NFL's Detroit Lions. As the name suggests, the historical locale at the time wasn't very well thought of, a poor Black neighborhood in the city. That's where we lived when I was an infant, though I remember nothing much about it. Then we moved, and from age three-to-four years old, we lived on Hart Street where we had a coal furnace. My first friend there was a white kid named Tommy. We were both three years old. We'd catch butterflies and play outside. When I was five, my family moved again, to 3740 Mount Claire, into a red, yellow and green house we rented from Mr. and Mrs. Jones. It was a two-family flat and we lived on the lower floor. I went to St. Claire Elementary School for kindergarten and first grade.

Then we moved again, this time to Mack and Bewick, a notorious neighborhood in the city where Black people were able to get by. I went to Krolick Elementary school in second grade on East Canfield Street and then back to St. Claire for third-through-sixth grade. In seventh grade, I enrolled at Hellen Newberry Joy Junior High. Everything on the east side seemed to have holes in it, from windows to cars to rusty chain-link fences. By the time I was 12 years old, I'd seen it all. I was eventually introduced to the game of basketball by my next-door neighbors, the Davis family. They were one of the more tightly knit families in the area, along with the Weatherby family, the Olivers, Mixons and the Fosters.

Little did I know then that basketball would, decades later, take me outside of the U.S. to Toronto to play for the expansion Raptors, or to leagues in Italy, France, Venezuela, Mexico and Argentina—truly, around the world. Baseball has the movie *Bull Durham*, the NBA has me! When I started playing, I didn't know I'd grow to be 6'4" and then later to be 6'9" or that I'd get recruited by the legendary University of Detroit coach Dick Vitale, who gave me my nickname, "The Twirl." Indeed, I've played with the best athletes in a game that already boasts the cream of the crop: from Jordan to Olajuwon, Isiah to Dr. J, and Muggsy Bogues. That 5'3" guy's legs were made of springs and cinderblocks. He was the best athlete I ever saw.

Basketball didn't come to me early, nor easily. I had to find it and work at it. But once I did, I never let the game go. I was born on September 3, 1957, first entering into the world on Jefferson Avenue in Lakeside General Hospital. At the time, the east side of the city was somewhat integrated. The place was a hodgepodge of people, all working hard trying to raise kids and make ends meet. But then as the '60s unfolded, it became mostly, if not entirely, Black. At the time in the mid–'60s, it was the eye of the tornado of the Detroit auto industry. Every man within a ten-mile radius seemed to work in the business.

Cars built Detroit. Michigan, too—along with the mines of the Upper Peninsula. The city was a major metropolis in the early- and mid-20th century. Then everything changed, as it always does. But when I was a kid, the city *revved*, you could say. I lived in the hard part of town at a time when things were good in some areas miles away—if you had a car, that is. On my street, there were a lot of families living day-to-day, getting by. There were a lot of kids running around, sharing bikes and playing games on the sidewalks. Mothers stayed home, fathers went out to provide. Everyone worked hard.

Auto plants were cash cows for their owners. A lot of Black families had moved up from the south to work them, trying to find a better life in the Motor City. Many dropped out of school to take a job in the plants. For most Black folks, it was either the plants or the army. Or sports, for the lucky few. I remember when my brother Junior went to the service, to Korea. He was the sibling I was closest with. I remember crying my eyes out when he left. By then in the late '60s, Detroit was a heated place. Scary, even. There were race riots by the time I turned 10 in 1967, a conflict that many called one of the most deadly and destructive in U.S. history: five days, 43 people killed, 342 injured and 1,400 buildings burned. My current friend, Detroit police officer Isaiah McKinnon, who is Black, was also intentionally almost murdered by a racist white fellow officer. That rocked the city on top of everything else happening. The National Guard and U.S. Army were both brought in, some 7,000 soldiers parading through town. Detroit was damaged by violence and looting. Many residents fled. Black Americans were fighting against severe racial profiling and violence, along with unemployment and prejudice.

Then, during the summer of 1968, the Detroit Tigers won the coveted World Series 4–3 over the St. Louis Cardinals and helped bring our city together. That's the power of sports. My father had played baseball. Growing up, he wanted me to play, too. But it wasn't the game I fell in love with. Nevertheless, he and I would listen to the Tigers on the radio, hearing the din of the crowd, every pitch and the crack of the wooden bat. When the Tigers won, it was big for us and our city. Every person could get behind the Tigers. I can still remember the victory parties, the pictures of the players in the papers. Thank God for that team.

Where I grew up, families lived on every block. Not all of them were solidly built, but more were than you might imagine. My father, Johnny Frank Cureton, worked, and my mother, Minnie Mae Turner, stayed home. I had a lot of half-brothers and half-sisters, too. My mother, who was originally from Homer, Louisiana, never got past a third-grade education. Her father, whom I'd never met, died at 101 years old, born a slave. A sharecropper, my mother's boss wouldn't let her get an education, she was allowed merely to till the earth. She had seven adult kids from her first marriage (four girls and three boys) and my father had another two. In total, that made a family of 10 children.

When she and my dad, a construction worker from Georgia who

never learned to read or write, who used to sell liquor as a kid, hooked up, I was the only child they had together. But they did a good job with all their kids; it was a miracle, really. All of us graduated high school, and some, including me, even went to college. The closest sibling in age to me was my sister Valencia, who was some seven years older. Everyone else was at least a few years older than that. I wasn't an outcast within our family, per se. But I also wasn't *not* an outcast, either. My father, who was 6'5", was taller than all my half-brothers and half-sisters. They were barely, at their best, around six-feet. I was different.

What's funny is everyone in the neighboring Davis family was short, around 5'6" or 5'7". I used to hang out with my friend Lee Davis. He was older than me by a year. But Lee was one of my best buds growing up and one of the few kids I spent time with that didn't go the gang route. Sadly, many of my friends took that darker path. But Lee's whole family was into sports. The Davis family played football, basketball, baseball—everything. They invented games when they didn't have others to play.

My father left my mother when I was nine. When I started to play basketball around 12, he'd already moved out of the house. My parents' relationship didn't end badly, they just had their differences. I understood that even at nine years old. My mother, who'd had me at 40, raised me, as a couple of brothers and sisters hung around the house. By that time, she'd started working and I was almost always on my own. Homework wasn't a big priority, unfortunately. But I got my first job passing out sports equipment at the Krolick Rec Center as a young kid. Then at 11 years old, I began working in a luggage shop. I remember being underage getting $15 a week in a manilla envelope there, working 3–8 p.m. every day. I cleaned bathrooms, moved boxes. A year later, I got a job as a stockboy at a grocery store, working eight hours a day at the notorious Mack & Bewick Market. There, you could get anything, from insurance to narcotics. They paid me 50 cents an hour: $27.50 a week; less if I ate snacks. I heard later they got involved in a lawsuit for paying people too little, but I wasn't involved in that.

The neighborhoods collectively raised the kids. Any parent had the right to discipline any child. Ms. Davis, Ms. Weatherby, they all knew they could tell me right from wrong. And us kids would help them if they needed a hand carrying groceries up to the house. My mother worked afternoons and evenings, and I'd go and meet her at the bus stop and walk her home every night, locking the door finally, well after 11 p.m. My mom, who'd spent her youth picking cotton and not going to school, would sit in the living room, and we'd put the television on as the streetlights buzzed outside. She was a great mother. She never drank or smoked and always cared about us. Back then if you didn't come from a two-parent home, some families wouldn't want you around. I suspect it's the same way today. So, when Lee Davis invited me over to his house one afternoon, I wondered if he had one of those strict families who might turn me away. Leery of me, a kid without a father at home. Lee's folks were still together. Would they wonder if I was a *wild child?* But thankfully they let me in and treated me very well.

On that first day I walked inside, I saw the family's display table covered in 50 trophies from all the sports they played. I was taken aback. My eyes darted, staring at the glistening awards. Until that point, I was hanging out with a different kind of crowd. I wasn't playing sports. I was into other things I shouldn't have been. There was one rough house in the neighborhood—that's the house I'd learn to get away from. There, I was exposed to drugs early on; I saw naked women before I hit puberty. I kept a cigarette pack rolled up in my shirt sleeve. In that house, we'd make our own "fun," including some things that weren't toys so much as they were actual weapons. Back then, kids knew what the term "zip-gun" meant. A zip-gun is a *real* gun made from a door latch, a long pipe and a bullet. The spring in the latch is so small and wound so tight that when you click open the latch, it shoots and can do real damage. One day, we fired that zip-gun, and the police were called (no one was hurt). I'd hid the thing under a bucket I sat on as the police searched the garage. Thank goodness, they never found it. That bad house later got torn down. A baseball field went up in its place.

As kids, we'd also make horseshoes out of water hoses. We'd play football in the streets. If a wagon broke, we'd turn it into a go-kart. We made bows-and-arrows out of branches. We were industrious. By the time I hit 10 years old, I'd seen a lot that your average 10-year-old didn't get to see. In the '60s in Detroit, Motown was huge. Its music everywhere. You could hear songs in the streets, on the radio, in shops and restaurants. My brothers and sisters were always talking Motown, Stevie Wonder and the Temptations. Skating rinks were big then, too. Lots of people would hang out at the rinks (or in their parking lots). Black people wore processed, wavy hair; everyone had their hair done, me included, even at 11 years old! My half-siblings were 10-plus years older than me and I watched what they did. Back then, heroin was popular amongst people, too. My siblings weren't criminals, nor were they into drugs. But everyone knew it was around the city, around where young people spent time. In a way, people didn't know any better. In another, it's all we had. As such, I was headed in the wrong direction. A knucklehead. Until I found basketball.

There were no playgrounds around Lee's house. So, he and I would go into the nearby ally between buildings to shoot at a makeshift hoop. That's where I learned about the game. That's where I fell in love with basketball. I watched Lee, who was left-handed, and some other guys play, and it made me want to join in. Lee began to teach me. He showed me what dribbling and shooting were, traveling and defense. He showed me how to play one-on-one and then we got into bigger games, five-on-five. If that wasn't enough of a change, around that time something very personal and very significant happened to me. I stole something from my sister and got caught! I'm ashamed to say it now, but as a kid I stole money out of her purse. It happened one afternoon. I took the cash to the nearby Edgewater Park. It was something like $12–13. I gave some to a friend and we had a good time. Then, later that day, I took some more from her. That's when my sister began to suspect. Not long after, while I was outside playing hoops, I heard my mother's voice. "Earl!" she shouted. "Get in here!" I knew I was caught. I put the cash I'd taken into my underwear and went home.

There, my mother asked, "Boy, did you go into your sister's purse?" Immediately, I lied. "No, what are you talking about, mom?" My mother went into my pocket and patted me down. Somehow, she knew. She pulled down my pants and the money fell out to the floor of our house. She proceeded to give me the worst beating I've ever had in my life. We had company at the house, too! But she didn't care. She put it on me that day. Though I was already in 7th grade, there was nothing I could do to stop her. I had to take it. I honestly thought she was going to kill me! She took out a vacuum cleaner cord and told me, "I brought you into this world, I can take you out of it!" Nowadays, someone might go to jail for how hard she beat me. The plug on the end of the cord caused bruises on me everywhere.

She then told me to take the money I'd stolen and go down to the barber and get my processed hair cut off. My mother thought because I was wearing a popular hairstyle of the time, that it was a sign I was headed in the wrong direction, pulled more by fads and fashion than by what's right in the world. It was the longest walk I'd ever had to make it to that barber. And I got my whole head shaved that day. The entire time, I tried not to shed a tear for what I'd done, for how I was hurting. But the lesson stuck forever. Since then I've never, ever, ever taken anything that didn't belong to me. So much so that, about a month later after my buzz cut, I saw a guy getting out of his car and saw that he'd dropped his wallet. I picked it up and ran it back to him. Still with my mother's beating in the back of my mind. *Yeesh.*

That's when basketball started to mean even more to me. It was a real turning point. Once I started, I became hooked on bettering myself through the game. I now had something I *wanted* to do all the time, not just something that I *would* do to pass the time. I had ambition even before I realized it formally. I looked for every chance to engage with the game.

I spent a lot of time at Lee's house, as a result. He had two older brothers. One played on the Finney High School football team in Detroit. Alfred would come home after games and I couldn't wait to talk to him. He'd show me the paint chips on his helmet from banging heads with other linemen. Billy, another brother, went to Cass Tech. And he was the first person to take me to a University of Detroit basketball game. I fell in love with the school. I knew I wanted to play for the Titans (now the Mercy) as soon as I was old enough.

It was then that I began to go to the local rec center. Countless NBA players, from stars to scrubs, have the rec center in their hometowns to thank for giving them athletic direction. Kids in New York City, Baltimore, Washington, D.C., Philly and Detroit, among many more. And I was one of them. We went as often as we could—after school, on weekends and in the summer. I played so much that I quit working at the Mack & Bewick Market. Thanks to the local Brewer Rec Center, I would later fly over oceans on planes headed for new, glistening basketball cities. That combined with the tutelage I received from an early coach, Marty White, who taught us kids all about structure, from zone defense to wearing uniforms properly. But it all began for me at the rec center, coincidentally, with swimming. I swam laps in the Brewer pool as I got familiar with the layout. Later, I started to play basketball. And even a little baseball.

Initially, I was scared to dive into the pick-up games at Brewer. The people at the rec center were all acquainted with each other, which also was the case at another city rec center I played at sometimes, Brewster-Wheeler. Adults. Groups of them, cliques walking together who could mean-mug you, could block your shot, strike you out, pin you to the floor. In other words, beat you. I was just 13 years old. But day by day— every day—I got used to playing there against them. People began to learn my name. All Lee and I wanted to do was get better. We'd wear sweats, run with ankle weights. I would go left with the ball often because I'd learned the game from Lee, who was left-handed. At the Rec Center, to get into a game, you had to call out that you were "next." But I had a hard time with that, at first, which makes me laugh now. I was so nervous! The initial couple of games I only called "next" to myself, under my breath.

Lee was there one time and when it was supposed to be my turn another team got up to play. Lee said, "Didn't you have next?" I said, "Yeah." And he replied, "Why didn't you take your game? Next time you miss your game, I'm going to hit you in the jaw!" So, I started being more vocal, aggressive. I became more confident. At that same time, there was a popular Detroit neighborhood basketball program. It didn't cost anything to sign up. And you could build your own team with friends. I was sold. I set my sights on the league. I put together my team. But sadly, we were horrible! I got a bunch of guys I hung out with. A lot of them were street guys, into different stuff. Basketball wasn't their number-one priority. I realized I had to be a better general manager. I had to find guys for my next team that wanted to *play*, who cared about doing well. Things were beginning to make sense.

Lee was my example on and off the court. He had a paper route. And I wanted one, but I could never get one. So, Lee let me go on his with him occasionally. I remember one morning we went to a house, a two-family flat connected by a staircase inside. Lee opened the door to the stairway to throw a paper in and we were met with a double-barrel *shotgun*. We both threw our hands up and backed away quickly. That's something he and I always talk about now. That dude with the shotgun scared the shit out of us! But that wasn't the only scary event we experienced. Another was even worse: one day, Lee knocked on my door to get to the rec center but for some reason I wasn't home. When I eventually made it to there to meet him, I asked around looking for him, but some guy told me the police had him. I said, "What are you talking about?" Apparently, a white woman had claimed Lee had raped her on the playground outside, not far from the center. You had to cross a field to get there, and Lee and I had crossed it many times to go play ball. That's where the rape had happened, she had said.

But I just knew Lee couldn't have done such a horrible thing. The woman had been raped and when she told the police about it, they went to the rec center and found Lee changing in the locker room. The woman, shook up, pointed to him and the cops took him away to the precinct. It was the one day I wasn't with him, and they snatched him up. Mr. Chapman, who ran the center, went down to the station to help Lee, saying it couldn't have been him. Thankfully Mr. Chapman looked out for everyone there. Thankfully, too, the police eventually let Lee go. It wasn't my friend who did that horrible thing, but we were scared out of our minds for a while, thinking he'd be found guilty for something he didn't do. It wouldn't have been the first time someone incorrectly accused a Black man like that, we all knew that much.

The police later found the guys who did it. They were grown men. It wasn't Lee. Once we got over it all, we went back to playing ball—our salvation. That wasn't the last of our run-ins with crazy times, either. One day, Lee, Tony Jamison and I went into a store, one of those candy shop and record store places. We went in there for snacks and candy. A minute or two later another guy came into the place and started to rob the joint! He said, "Anyone that tries to walk out the door in the next five minutes is getting shot." We waited, stone still, while he did what he came to do and got what he needed. He took the money from the shop owner and ran. It's moments like this that make me remember how tough it was to grow up in Detroit. How much of a strange adventure it was, too.

In my seventh-grade year, I didn't play for my junior high school. I just played at the rec center. Like I said, I had confidence issues. I was still new to the game. But I remember asking a coach there, Alonzo Littlejohn, if he thought I could hang in the school leagues. Littlejohn, a local legend known for spotting talent, told me, "I don't see why not." That simple single little comment meant the universe to me in that moment. It made me want to take my game seriously and try out for my school team the following season. So, the next year, I went out for the 8th grade team simply based on what Coach Littlejohn had said.

That year, after trying out, I made the team! Coached by LeVert France, we were strong. Lee was on the squad, too. He was in the 9th grade, and one of the better players. Most of the guys on that team went onto play in high school and college. The east side of Detroit was stacked with guys like Eric Money, Coniel Norman and Tony Jamison to name a few. And there were superstars from the area, too, like George "Ice Man" Gervin and Spencer Haywood (who also went to the University of Detroit before leaving early after a difficult year). Both were 20-point-plus scorers in their day in the NBA—all-stars. Legends.

It's impossible to overstate Gervin's influence on Detroit, let alone the basketball landscape of the 20th century. Today, he's a Hall of Famer. The man was so famous in the '70s and '80s that he *still* does Gatorade ads today. He was a 12-time all-star, seven-time All-NBA (and 2-time All-ABA). He led the NBA in scoring four times, had back-to-back 50-point games, and was the all-star game MVP in '79–'80 (the same year the NBA brought in the three-point shot, taking it from the ABA). But more than that, he was an icon in the Motor City. His mere presence let kids like me know we could make it one day. And Gervin would often come back to the city, even years into his career, to give Detroit some of his time. Whenever he came home to play in a local gym, the place would be packed. This was before social media and text messages—word-of-mouth ran through the streets and people ran to the gym to see George. The funniest part about it all, though, was in those games, you couldn't foul him! If you did, 10 guys would run up onto the floor and let you know you'd messed up. Gervin was that prized, that protected. He was skilled, the master of the finger roll. The Ice Man, as smooth as his name implies.

Haywood was the first "hardship" case in pro basketball. He was the first person to get to join the pros—in his case, the ABA—without spending four years in college. At the time, Haywood wanted to turn pro after his sophomore year, but the NBA only allowed four-year college graduates into their league. The ABA, too. That's when the executive Mike Storen came up with the hardship clause (aka the Spencer Haywood Rule), which later brought billions into the NBA, much to the chagrin of the NCAA. Haywood's mother was raising 10 kids while picking cotton for $2 a day in Mississippi. So, Haywood met the new "hardship" criteria and entered the league with the Denver Rockets in the ABA draft. That later opened the NBA to players fresh out of high school like Moses Malone, Kevin Garnett and Kobe Bryant.

And since so many of these guys like Gervin and Haywood were from the city, it made me believe I could be something, too. So, I worked. Hard. But my junior high school team was stacked with good players. So, I sat at the end of the bench. I'd just barely made the squad, wearing the number-13 jersey. Lee was our co-captain along with Tony Jamison. We won the division championship in the 1970–'71 season. But the following year, when that class graduated and went on to play in high school (Lee played for Cass Tech), there were a lot of holes left on the roster. That meant room for me to shine. That is, if I could get my grades straight.

While my basketball dreams were coming into focus, life was still rough. I once saw a guy get shot within 20 feet of me with a .22 on the playground as a kid. He didn't die, though, he just ran, with two bullets in him. Rough stuff. Many days after school, I was chased home by different gangs, like the Black Avengers. But back then, it was different. Gangs would just beat you up. Guns weren't prevalent. Few were simply shot and killed. My fear was getting the piss kicked out of me. I was smaller then, skinny as a rail, and I'd sit in class pondering ways home to avoid them. That's one reason I got so fast as a runner later in my career! Basketball practices helped, too. By the time I got out after practice in the evening, the streets were somewhat safer to walk on. It's not that the neighborhood was all bad, it's just there were distinct bad elements, which forced people to make hard choices. This is all to say, it wasn't ever easy to focus on school work. But I did what I could, and I played well on the court, too.

As I got older, I began to think I wouldn't be safe around home. So, for high school, I decided not to enroll in my local neighborhood school, Southeastern High School. Instead, I bussed to Finney. My first year, Coach France got an associate head coaching job there. And I went with him. Ray Pierson was the other varsity coach. To me, Coach France was like a father figure. He even let me drive his car sometimes. I'd applied to Cass Tech to be with Lee, but I wasn't admitted because of *one* failing grade. So, Finney it was. When the year started, it took me an hour each way to get to Finney, which was 60 percent white at the time. They'd just started bussing in Black kids like me to school. I attended Finney starting my 10th grade year. It was there that I began on the junior varsity squad under Coach Clifford Aitch. I'd met Coach Aitch at Helen Newbury Joy

Junior High, but he'd recently become the junior varsity coach at Finney under Coach France.

I didn't get a lot of playing time on that team right away. I was still growing, height-wise and in just about every other way, too. In the summers between school, I played at home in the Detroit neighborhood basketball program. I worked on my game. I dribbled a basketball everywhere I went—I was one of those kids. I shot on a bicycle rim welded to two hooks that you could hang on a backboard and remove at night. Telephone wires were everywhere. I learned how to shoot up, over and around them. There are always obstacles. You had to do what you could. At night, the rim came down, so as no one would steel it. Each year I got better playing on rudimentary hoops, developing skills I didn't even know I was developing.

It's here I'd like to give a shout out to the neighborhood players, of which there were many where I lived. There were the Harmon brothers, William and Kenny. William and I played in the local Salvation Army league. Our coach, Danny, would take us out in a van on weekends and we'd play teams from all around the region, sometimes upwards of an hour away. William and I later played in junior high school together before he went on to a different high school. In the Salvation Army league, we'd play white kids who didn't care about the game as much as we did. Kenny later played at Eastern Michigan and William played at the University of Minnesota with Mychal Thompson (father of Klay Thompson) and Flip Saunders. I had another friend, Greg Guy, a 6'8" forward who got drafted later the same year as me; he went to the Pacers in the sixth round. There was also Terrance Watson, a super-skilled player who could barely get himself out of bed in the mornings. But when he did, he tore it up. There was Calvin Justice, who went to play at Eastern Michigan. We played together in high school. And Tony Fuller, Bubba Hawkins and Carl Jameson, who was a rec legend and later played D-1. These guys were all in the neighborhood. I learned from all of them.

By this point, I was scoring around 30 points in youth games, surprising people. Tony Fuller and I were kicking butt in the city summer league under Coach George Gatty. Later, Tony was drafted by the Pistons and he'd go on to coach at Pepperdine University, where he played as an undergrad. (He's also cousins with Dennis Edwards from The Temptations.) As kids, we got our pictures in the newspapers. We'd tried out for an important youth team and made it, too, but a day or two later we were cut in favor of some other, better neighborhood boys. I was 15 years old, and I was pretty upset about it. But whether I'd made that youth team, or not, I knew I was getting better. When I went back to my high school team at Finney as a junior, I knew I was ready for the big time. *Varsity.* It was 1974 and I was in 11th grade now. But just because I knew I was ready didn't mean everyone else knew it too.

When I got back to school for the new year, Coach France took me aside and said he wanted me on junior varsity that year. He wanted to see how I'd do on JV. But I looked at him right in the eye and said, "Coach, you're making a huge mistake." I'd been playing well all summer, scoring in big summer league games. I'd grown to be about 6'3". He could see the confidence in my eyes, hear it now in my voice. Coach France thought for a moment and replied, "Okay, I'll put you on varsity, but if you don't play well, I'm sending you back down to JV." I'd finally earned my chance! I began the season with a slight hamstring injury, but about six or seven games in, I was finally starting on the varsity team, and I never looked back. My star rising.

Playing for Coach France, I worked my way up, game by game. By my senior year I grew to be 6'4" and I became *the man* on our basketball team. Finney wasn't known for hoops. We were good at football and baseball. But my senior year was the best year in the history of the school. I scored 28 points in one half (in a loss to Kettering). I became arguably the team's top player. My friend David Cochran (who was 6'5") and I each averaged 20 points per game. I scored 29 points in my final state tournament game, matched up against Bruce Flowers, who later played for the Cleveland Cavaliers. But we lost that one, too, sadly. Nevertheless, I was thriving. When high school ended, I'd made all-city third-team in 1975—that was a big deal given all the talent Detroit had to offer. After my high school season, I kept improving.

One of the ways I did so was by going down to play at the St. Cecilia Gym on the west side of the city. St. Cecilia, which is located in a sleepy residential neighborhood, was where the best players in the city met to ball. It was and is the Mecca for the game in the Motor City, a positive place during significant strife. Basketball, invented by Canadian James Naismith in Springfield, Massachusetts, has long had a relationship with churches. Back then, physical education was thought of as just as important as intellectual education, part of a communion with God. So, thanks to places like St. Cecilia and various YMCAs, the game spread like wildfire in the United States and beyond.

The St. Cecilia gym, itself, opened after the riots in the late '60s. It was a melting pot of all races. Unassuming and supremely important. George Gervin played there. I watched him when he came home during the NBA off season in the summers. Haywood and future city Mayor Dave Bing, both local legends and NBA all-stars, played there. And I played there, on the same court. Amazing. Spencer used to roll up to the gym in this big Cadillac. It drove everyone wild to see this hometown guy doing it! To this day, he talks about how the best of Detroit could beat the best in any other city, including The Big Apple.

Basketball fans know the Rucker League in New York, it's where the best players in the city go. In Detroit, it was St. Cecilia. The city's proving ground. If you wanted to scout the city's best, go to that little hallowed hot box of a gym on the weekends. Later, big Detroit players like Jalen Rose, Chris Webber, Derrick Coleman and Glen Rice would make their names at St. Cecilia. Even Marvin Gaye stopped by sometimes (he could sing better than he played). So did Magic, Isiah Thomas, Kevin Willis, Darryl Dawkins, Gus Johnson. B.J. Armstrong, Vashon Lenard, Steve Smith, "Tractor" Traylor, Scott Skiles, Rudy Tomjanovich and Jalen's father, NBA player Jimmy Walker. (Later, Sam Washington, Jr., ran the place after his father died in 1988.) I was on a team there once that played against the Junior Russian National Team, along with traveling teams from New York and other cities. St. Cecilia was big time. Central to the city's basketball legacy.

I'd be at the St. Cecilia gym from 8 a.m. to 9 p.m., watching games and shooting. Playing at the next level in college was all I thought about. I loved Detroit and my mother, of course. Yet, I knew I needed to get away from home for a while. But I wasn't one of those guys with piles of recruitment letters. I wasn't a *star* star. Greg Kelser, an opponent of mine in high school who I've known since 15 years old (and who now is a mentor for my daughter), went to Michigan State and he paired up with Magic Johnson. Greg would go on to be the fourth pick by the Pistons (he's been a team broadcaster for decades). Greg had a solid career, albeit hampered by some knee issues. William Mayfield went to Iowa and played for the Golden State Warriors. Larry Knight went to Loyola and played for the Utah Jazz. And there were more. But me? I wasn't getting a lot of big time looks. My grades weren't great; I never had a knack for hitting the books, though I was surely smart enough.

At the time, I was dead set on playing for the University of Detroit. The Titans. But I was only being recruited by smaller schools like Oakland University. And even then it wasn't anything real serious. Dick Vitale was the coach at Detroit. He recruited all the best players around. But he didn't give me a much of a look at first. I was floating around after my senior year, unsure what would happen next. But at the St. Cecilia Gym, my life changed. I went up there a lot after my senior year. Hoping just being around the game would influence my future. I didn't have the grades in high school, so I didn't have much of a plan moving forward. But I shot jumpers, worked out as often as I could. Then one day Sam "The Godfather" Washington, Sr., came in. He ran the place, the athletic director. His sons were getting offers to play in smaller colleges. Sam Washington, Jr., had just won the state title at Brother Rice. Sam, though, had gotten sick and big colleges had cooled off on him.

But one day Sam Sr. introduced me to Coach Cleveland Edwards, who asked if I'd be interested in playing basketball for Robert Morris College, which was also recruiting Sam Jr. To Coach Edwards I said, naively, "What is Robert Morris College?" Cleveland told me it was one of the top two-year junior colleges in the country. It was also my only real hope.

Robert Morris was in Pittsburgh, Pennsylvania, some 300 miles away from Detroit. Sam Sr. told me I should go visit. At the time, I'd never left Detroit. And Pittsburgh seemed *light years* away. Cleveland, who was later supposed to get the head job at Robert Morris but never did, said they'd fly me in for a visit. I said, "*Fly?*" And so, I went. Until then, I'd never been on an airplane. Sure enough, they got me a ticket and I hopped on the quick 40-minute flight to check out Robert Morris. I still remember that plane ride. I pretended like I knew what I was doing on the plane. But the whole time, I sat completely still. When it finally touched down and everyone was getting off, I just sat still. Sam Jr. laughed at me and said, "You can get up now, we're here." I got up and prepared myself for the next experience: walking on a campus.

Robert Morris had a great junior college program. It was a four-year business school at the time, but had a two-year basketball program, led by Coach Gus Krop. There was talk of expanding the program in years to come, but I didn't pay any mind to that. On campus, there were *maybe* 20 Black people. I'd come from a predominantly Black neighborhood. But Detroit's Finney High School, which I'd graduated from in 1975, was more of a mix. I was somewhat used to multicultural places. Robert Morris was the other extreme—almost *all* white. I felt that same trepidation when I first started going to the rec center. Who was everyone? Where did I fit in? *Did* I fit in? Nevertheless, I told Coach Edwards and Coach Krop that I'd enroll to Robert Morris to play for them. I didn't have another choice, really! The coaches said they'd take care of me, help me get my books, acclimate. It was on.

Back at home, my old friend Coach LeVert France, who was a proud Black fellow, pulled me aside one day before I left for Robert Morris and told me not to mess up my one chance. If I did, he said, "They'll buy you a bus ticket, a comic book to read and a banana to eat and send your monkey-ass back home to Detroit." I told him I wouldn't *ever* let that happen.

Memory Lane: Spencer Haywood

"My surrogate dad who adopted and raised me was a famous high school coach. He was the first Black coach in NCAA Division-1 history,

Will Robinson. He was also the assistant to the General Manager and scout for the Pistons. So, when Earl went to the University of Detroit, it was nothing but big love for him because we had such a belief system that our great talent should stay in the city and rebuild Detroit."

"I was in the '68 Olympics and I had over 300 offers to go to whatever school I wanted to. I chose to come back to Detroit. We had just suffered through a riot in the city, a lot of things were destroyed, and our city was burning in '68. So, I had to try to come back and rebuild and reestablish our city. And to see Earl, who is like me, the descendant of cotton pickers, sharecroppers, follow me in that program was just—I was so elated."

3

Big Man
on Two Campuses

Every time a coach called me into his office at Robert Morris, I was prepared for them to give me that bus ticket home. I thought a ride out of there was always just around the corner, perhaps the ticket would even be hanging from my locker when I opened it. Thankfully, it never came. At Robert Morris, Sam Jr. and I became close friends. Prior, we'd known each other, but not particularly well. We were roommates now. We hung out in a group of seven or eight guys. There were two white guys, Tom and Jesse Hudson; Lavelle Joyner who had lost both his parents prior to coming to school; the stoic Paul Jones; and a few others. I got off to a good start. In my first game at Robert Morris, I scored 33 points. I thought, "Well, maybe I have a chance to stick around here." My first year of college, in 1975–'76, I measured 6'4" and then shortly after, I grew to 6'6" and kept on growing. I got to be 6'7" and then 6'8" and, finally, 6'9". (Like me, Boston Celtics center Bill Russell grew five inches in college at the University of San Francisco, and Giannis Antetokounmpo grew three or four inches when he made the NBA.) My height helped me become a better rebounder and scorer.

Sam's father was happy we'd gone to play together in Pittsburgh. We had a good team, too. I came off the bench my first year and we won our fair share of games. Robert Morris wasn't yet a Division-1 team. So, our first game was in a junior college tournament. Ahead of the trip, Sam had gotten hurt. He stayed in the dorms and listened to the games on the radio, cheering us on. In the first game, as I mentioned, I had 33 points off the bench, and I played well in the second game, too, scoring 16. I played so well that I made the All-Tournament team. After the tournament, the coaches said they'd find a way to get me in the starting lineup. And I didn't let them down, averaging 14.5 points and 8.1 rebounds for the whole season.

When you grow like I did so quickly, your knees hurt like hell. Mine

33

ached. I wondered what it was at first, but then I realized it was just my body growing. I was a late bloomer. I outgrew all my clothes, shooting up some five inches at Robert Morris. I remember Sam looking at me one day, seeing how tall I'd gotten, and saying, "You know, you might have a chance to make the NBA." Sam was shorter, around 5'11", and I told him that if I ever made it, I'd look out for him. Though, sadly that turned out to be a debacle. Sam Jr. and I would later have a falling out. I still can't believe it. But for now, that was years down the road.

In the summer between my freshman and sophomore years, I went to the prestigious Five Star basketball camp in Holmesdale, Pennsylvania. The legendary scout Howard Garfinkel, who ran the camp, made me a counselor. The counselor games, which included the likes of Hollis Copeland and Pat Cummings, were legendary at Five-Star and that's where the coaches saw the best amateur players in the country go at it on the court. A young Coach Mike Fratello was there, running things, the future NBA head man for the Atlanta Hawks with Dominique Wilkins and Doc Rivers and, later, the Cleveland Cavaliers with Mark Price and "Hot Rod" Williams. He even blew the morning bugle to wake us up every day. At Five-Star, Dick Vitale began pitching me on the Titans. He'd seen how tall I'd gotten. We kept in touch after camp. He'd call me and I'd call him almost every day. "YOU'RE GOING TO BE NEXT, EARL! YOU'RE GOING TO BE MY GUY! COME HOME, BABY!"

Growing up, my school coaches always told me to stay humble, so I took it all in stride and kept working. Humility is a skill worth mastering. Back in Detroit, recruiters were talking to Sam Washington, Sr., about me. Now that I was taller, bigger and had already made a name for myself in the college ranks and at Five-Star, they were interested. Turns out I wasn't the only one growing. Between my first and second year, Robert Morris made a big jump, too. The school went from a junior college to a bona fide NCAA Division-1 program—the first of it's kind. And they wanted me to stick around and be one of the better young players on the team during my sophomore year, their first in the new class, to get the revamped program off the ground. But once I shot up, I wanted to test my skills against even better competition. I wanted to go play for the Titans. That had always been my dream.

Vitale knew I was a Detroit product and told me I belonged at his school. He'd call and shout into the phone, "EARL! YOU'VE GOT TO COME HOME TO DETROIT, YOU'RE NEXT!" But in the end, I decided to stay for my sophomore year at Robert Morris in 1976–'77. (Fun fact: University of Kentucky head coach John Calipari's mother used to be a cafeteria worker at the school.) I wanted to give it one more go and I was grateful the school had taken a chance on me so I wanted to repay them. One more

year. Robert Morris, which brought in a new coach that season, Tom Wei-
rich, now my second coach in as many years, had scheduled 18 away games
my sophomore season. We played Division-1 programs week-after-week
and my game continued to grow. I could dribble, run, pass, rebound and
hit mid-range jumpers.

I'd first learned to play as a guard, like Lee. So, when I grew, I kept
those same skills and added new ones. At Robert Morris, for some reason my teammates called me "Cornbread." To this day, if I hear someone
shout, "Hey, Bread!" I know it's someone from the old days. I had this play
the team would run for me freshman year that would often get everyone
on the bench excited. At the time, the dunk was still illegal in the NCAA.
But I'd start at the foul line, and someone would set a back screen for me.
I'd come down the lane, catch a pass mid-air and just drop the ball into the
hoop. I wanted to slam it home but that was against the rules. The crowd
always got hyped on that one though.

One of the opposing players I matched up against in college was
Wayne Cooper at New Orleans, who later went to play for the Denver
Nuggets and Portland Trailblazers. I remember I had 28 points against
him one game. I also played against Gerald Henderson at Virginia Com-
monwealth, and Norm Nixon, the future L.A. Lakers great, when he was
at Duquesne University (also in Pittsburgh). Norm had the key to the
gym at Duquesne and I'd meet up with him there sometimes and we'd
play one-on-one. Later, when we both suited up for the L.A. Clippers, we
became good friends. During my sophomore year, I played against Larry
Joe Bird when he was at Indiana State. Ever heard of him?

After a failed year with Bobby Knight at Indiana University, Bird had
gone back home to tiny French Lick where he worked in the sanitation
department. He'd later enrolled at Indiana State and was killing it there,
the star of the team and of college basketball. Indiana State famously
played and lost to Michigan State and Magic Johnson in the NCAA final
game in 1979, a grinning Magic cutting down the nets. That game practically created the modern college basketball boom ("March Madness" anyone?). Larry was always in the middle of the big games.

I remember when my coaches at Robert Morris gave me the scouting
report on Indiana State ahead of our matchup in the annual Indiana Hall
of Fame Classic my sophomore year. Indiana State had DeCarstra Webster, Harry Morgan and some other strong players. I remember being worried about Webster, in particular. When I stepped on the court, though,
I saw Bird. There was something eye-catching about him. At one point
in the game, he had the ball in the corner and pulled up for what would
have been a three-pointer, had the arc then been a part of the game back
then. *Swish*. Next time he got the ball, he up-faked, put the ball on the

floor, drove and dunked it (the shot was now legal in college). Next time, he threw a no-look pass. I said, "Damn! Who the hell is this white boy?" I still have photos of me and Bird going at it on the court that day. Indiana State ended up beating us 78–65, but I made the All-Tournament Team, along with Bird and several others.

At the end of the tournament, Bird had 57 points and 33 rebounds in just two games. I'd notched 25 and 21. That was my introduction to Larry Legend. Later, Indiana State recruited me to join him. If I had, I would have played against Magic in that famous 1979 NCAA Finals! But I declined. Indiana State had wanted me so bad that I actually had to lie to them. I said my mom was sick (she wasn't) and that I wanted to stay around Detroit for her. Indiana State even went as far as to call my home and talked to my mother, telling her they'd move her down there to help. When she told me about that, she said, "What have you got me into?" I didn't go with the Sycamores. If I was to leave, it was always going to be for the University of Detroit.

At Robert Morris, I also played against Sly Williams at Rhode Island—he later suited up for the Knicks. While we played in these big games, we only won about a handful of contests that second season, our first in D-1. We finished 7-19. We only had about nine home games. But for our first home one, Robert Morris pulled out all the stops. They hired a helicopter to take the team from campus to the Civic Arena in town. It was about a 40-minute drive, but with the choppers, it was a quick hop-skip-and-a-jump. We landed in front of the arena in style.

It was around this time, too, that a big film crew began shooting in the city for the Dr. J–led movie *The Fish That Saved Pittsburgh*. It was one of the first in now a long string of wonderful basketball movies like *Blue Chips*, *Space Jam*, *Hoosiers*, *He Got Game* and *White Men Can't Jump*. But that Dr. J was in this one got me excited. He played Moses Guthrie, the star of the team. Big name ballers and Hollywood-types were all over the city as a result. Pittsburgh was hopping! The movie, which came out in 1979, included Kareem Abdul-Jabbar (who also had a big role in the 1980 comedy, *Airplane*), Spencer Haywood, Bob Lanier, Harlem Globetrotter legend Meadowlark Lemon, Norm Nixon, Phil Ford, Cedric Maxwell, Jerry Tarkanian, Connie Hawkins, announcers Marv Albert and Chick Hern, and many more of basketball's royalty. It was a surreal mix of disco and hoops, a true one-of-one work of creativity.

That year, Robert Morris was paying its dues. But I was the star of our team and I'd worked hard for it. Some of my teammates even thought I was crazy. I'd pick up some evenings and just go out running, in the rain, sometimes even to the airport miles away. And all the while, Vitale kept his eye on me, calling me, telling me about his campus, how I'd fit in on the team. "EARL! COME TO DETROIT, BABY!" Back home, Sam Washington, Sr., was saying I didn't have to go to U. of D. He said Michigan and Michigan State were also interested. But my heart was set on the Titans. It felt good to be wanted. Hell, it felt good to have anyone paying attention to me and my game. Suddenly, I was recruited like a big-time blue-chipper. I had a lot of eyes on me, and I was putting up numbers as a sophomore. During my first year at a D-1 college, I averaged 17.2 points on 47 percent shooting, along with 10.5 rebounds (landing as the top rebounder in school history with 274 that season).

Now, I had options heading into my junior year. Pitt, Duquesne, the University of Southern California, Indiana State, Michigan, and Michigan State all wanted me. But in the end, I chose Vitale. How could I not? We'd talked almost every day. And Vitale convinced me with that signature infectious energy. Robert Morris didn't want me to go, of course. They offered me a lot of things to get me to stay, but I declined. I was headed where my heart had always wanted. I'd earned my way. I wanted the chance to go pro, and I knew Vitale could help. The University of Detroit had sent several guys to the NBA, which made me believe I could be next. As a young basketball player, I idolized Dr. J. In fact, I had his posters hanging in my room. Every college English essay I wrote had to do with Dr. J, his nimble game at UMass, his early days in the ABA for the Virginia Squires, dunking on everyone. How the Nets bought his contract when he came to the NBA. His afro. And how he flourished with the 76ers.

He was mythical-yet-still-living-and-breathing. I wrote about him so often that a professor bought me two more Dr. J posters simply because she knew I loved him so much. I tried to dunk like him every time I could. I thought of myself in the University of Detroit uniform dunking on people like him as Vitale drew up plays. There was just one holdup. Because of the rules at the time, I had to sit out a year after transferring from Robert Morris. The rule was designed to keep people from leaving schools, dissuading them from changing teams. It didn't dissuade me, though. I knew once I made my choice, I had to forego games for the entire 1977–'78 season as a "redshirt"—not to mention about a dozen credits U. of D. didn't accept. But Coach Vitale ran a good program and promised it would be all right. I believed him and went for it. I had to live my life and do what was right for me, in the end. I knew in my heart I'd made the right choice.

Vitale's team had gone to the Sweet 16 the year before in the 1977 NCAA Tournament. They'd upset the powerhouse Marquette University to do so. Vitale says if I had been there and not at Robert Morris, his team would have gone further, maybe even won the NCAA championship. "We could've dominated," he said. But once I enrolled in U. of D., I had to sit out a calendar year. My third college season was the first time I couldn't play regular games since I started in that alley behind Lee's house. Nevertheless, I worked every day. I wanted to make the NBA badly. Larry Bird had sat out for a year when he transferred from Indiana University to Indiana State. If he could do it, then there was hope for me, too. That next year, Bird came back and dominated before going pro to play for the Boston Celtics. Why couldn't I do the same? During my redshirt year, I had to sit back and watch Michigan State beat Detroit. Magic notched a triple-double. I knew I couldn't have helped. Maybe with my defense and rebounding, I could have swung the game.

There was another issue, though. The following year, the year I arrived at U. of D., Vitale left the team. He'd been there with us throughout the preseason. I'd gone to all the practices with him as the coach. He'd told me I could do everything with the team except play on game day. I got a uniform with my number on it, a locker, all that. Even early on, Vitale was big on making the players feel valued, even to the point that he made the NCAA salty about it. I remember our uniforms hung out the back of our shorts, showing our names, which we thought was cool, but the league thought it was uncouth. I did everything with the team, went wherever they went. I

went up against the best in practice, including Terry Duerod, John Long, Joe Kopicki, Jerry Davis, Wilbert McCormick and Terry Tyler, who would block my shot constantly until I figured out how to avoid his massive hands! It was great. Like everyone with U. of D., Terry and I had a special bond. But before the season started, there was drama: Vitale resigned somewhat mysteriously. We all knew something was up—maybe he'd gotten another job offer in the league? Something must have happened.

David "Smokey" Gaines, a former Harlem Globetrotter, took over, the university's first Black head coach. Three or four weeks later, the Detroit Pistons announced that they'd hired Vitale as their new head man. Greener pastures, I guess!

Earl at halfcourt taking a team photograph, 1979.

Earl all smiles in 1978 as teammate and best friend Terry Duerod checks out the action.

I couldn't be too mad; I would have done the same thing. Heck, I just had, leaving Robert Morris. After Vitale was hired by the Pistons, he called me up and told me he'd be looking out for me in the pros, not to put my head down, to keep working on my game. I'd get my chance, he said. He told me he'd maybe even draft me in the later rounds (he drafted Terry Tyler and John Long the next year). I'd be eligible for it the season after my redshirt year, he said. That gave me confidence. Even if I was taken in the ninth round, I'd have a *shot*. But that's not all Vitale left me with. It had been him who gave me the nickname that would stick with me for the rest of my career, "The Twirl." When I first got to the University of Detroit, John Long and Terry Tyler were called "Thunder and Lightning." And Terry Duerod was "Sweet Due." So, Vitale said to me, "I've got to come up with a nickname for you. We got 'The Pearl' already [Earl Monroe]. So, we're going to call you... 'The Twirl.' EARL THE TWIRL, BABY!" And the name has been with me ever since. My best friends still call me Twirl, from Muggsy Bogues to Charles Oakley. It's a great nickname and I'm proud of it. Strangely, it matches my rollercoaster of a career, too. Always spinning with ups and downs.

In the summer after my redshirt year, John Long and I played one-on-one many nights on the outdoor courts by the dorms. He wanted to get ready for the NBA and was always working, preparing for the next step. It was incredible playing against him. That helped me lay the groundwork for my *official* junior year. I'd lived at home with my mother during my redshirt year, but she'd eventually kicked me out, saying I needed to live as an adult. So, as a junior, I now had my own dorm on campus. The dorms were fun, but I was always thinking about when the games would start.

My junior year, I averaged 11.7 points and 9 rebounds for the season, leading the team to a 22–6 record with big wins over Oregon, Georgetown and Marquette. But I remember one matchup against a smaller school where things didn't go so well. A few days before that game, Coach Gaines had given me a pair of dress shoes, which was probably a petty NCAA violation. But I played so poorly in the game that he took them back! "Give me my goddamn shoes back," Gaines said, angrily, after the game. But I began to play much better. I scored 32 points and grabbed 23 rebounds against St. Bonaventure, pleasing our coach. My teammate Terry Duerod played well, too. Me and Terry were fast friends (I'd later be the best man at his wedding). It was good to have a buddy on the squad.

Earl in 1979, accepting the team MVP Award for the University of Detroit after a successful senior season.

Our team went to the NCAA Tournament that year—one of 32 invited— but we lost in the first round to Lamar, sadly, 95–87. We got our butts kicked. I had 16 and 11 but the guy I guarded outdid me, notching 32 points and 19 rebounds. It was a bad showing by everyone involved, from the coaches down to the players. And me, especially. Yet, the Titans finished the season ranked No. 20. Though that was a solid showing, I was still disappointed. I'd averaged just over 11 points. But at Robert Morris, I'd averaged around 17 points and 11 rebounds. The good news was, however, I was now eligible for the NBA draft. Even though I wasn't a senior, I'd been out of high school for four years and I could enter my name in for consideration. I'd put my name in, but I'd resolved to go back to school for my senior season either way. I wanted one more year of refinement with the Titans.

That summer, I went to work to make some money before my final college season tipped off. I was stripping floors. The acid I used to do the job got on my skin. It ate your skin. I was using drills, working the midnight shift. The whole time I was thinking about the NBA, though. When I went home, I stared at my Dr. J posters. And at night, I went back to stripping floors. One night, though, at about 2 a.m., one of my coworkers came in and said, "Earl! You got drafted!" I said, "Shut up! What are you talking about?" But he told me the Philadelphia 76ers had taken me in the third round. I said, "Man, get the fuck out of here." I didn't believe him and so I just kept working with the acid. He must have been messing with me, I thought. After work, though, I went back to my room and sure enough, I found out it was true. I'd been drafted! Pat Williams of the Philadelphia 76ers had taken me in the third round of the 1979 draft on June 25, 1979, with the 58th pick. Terry Duerod was picked ahead of me at number 48 by Vitale in Detroit. (Terry would later win a ring with the Boston Celtics before becoming a respected fire fighter.)

I was in another world once I found out for sure. Pat later called me, and the team sent me over a contract. The 76ers had my draft rights and the team had also drafted Bernard Toone that year. But we agreed I should stay in school for my fifth year, my senior season. The 76ers gave me a standard, nonguaranteed contract for $30,000. And I put it in a desk drawer with my coaches to keep safe. But now my confidence was through the roof. I found it hard to focus on anything, school (my sociology major) or my job stripping floors. All I wanted to do was get in the gym and work on my game. I'd had a handful of coaches in a handful of years but now it was time to evolve again. I wanted into get in the *league*. To show off and show out. So, during my senior year at the University of Detroit, now with my fifth coach, Willie McCarter (Gaines had gone to San Diego State in the summer, becoming the first Black head coach of an NCAA Division 1 school in California), I averaged 19.9 points on 52.7 percent shooting, along with 9.1 rebounds—both led the team.

An article in the University of Detroit media guide my senior year called me, "An explosive, exciting front line performer who is the Titans' No. 1 rebounder." I was known by some scouts as the "quickest forward in the country." I was 6'9" and 215 pounds. And I could dunk with the best. We finished the year at 14–13 and I was named the Robert Calihan Team MVP and Honorable Mention All-Midwest. In one big game, I'd scored 32 points with 20 rebounds against Oral Roberts. The 76ers called me after the

Earl, shown here in 2017, speaks at teammate Terry Duerod's jersey retirement ceremony at the University of Detroit. Former coach Dick Vitale is just behind him.

season and asked me to sign a new contract. But by now I knew I had more options. I could reenter my name into the draft to see who might want me. Maybe I'd be picked higher or by a team that would put me in their starting rotation? At the time, the league was much smaller than it is now. Only 24 teams, with something like 250–300 players. The 76ers wanted me to sign but said they couldn't guarantee the contract (a soon-to-be recurring theme). But if I signed, they'd give me a $10,000 bonus check. It was 1979. I was a kid in college with nothing. Getting an offer with a $10,000 signing bonus was like winning the lottery. I agreed and the team flew me to Philly to sign it.

The 76ers were playing the Lakers that night when they brought me in. Magic Johnson was a rookie. He was from Lansing, Michigan, originally, not too far from Detroit (just 90 miles). He'd won the championship the year before at Michigan State as a junior, defeating Bird. Now, Magic was starring in the NBA. On his way again to win the NBA 1980 championship with the Lakers that season. That night he had something like 42 points and 15 assists against Philly, beating the 76ers. I wasn't even on the team yet, but I felt the sting of the loss. The 76ers brought me into the locker room after the game. I met my idol, Dr. J and I instantly thought about watching him in the old ABA dunk contests with Gervin! I met

Doug Collins, the former all-star and #1 pick of the 76ers. I met "Chocolate Thunder," aka Darryl Dawkins. With all these stars, I wondered why the team drafted me? *What the hell am I doing here?*

Suddenly, the world of the NBA seemed too big. My heart began to pound. But I put my John Hancock on the contract's dotted line and put my faith in the team. The next day, I flew home and went back to practicing my game so that I'd be ready for training camp with the 76ers. I wanted to be as ready as I could be. In my two seasons at the University of Detroit, after my redshirt year, I led the team to a 36–19 record. I'd been

Earl at the University of Detroit in 1978, flying through the air and about to dunk on his opponents.

selected in the 1979 draft and once 1980 came around, I was ready to start my pro career in earnest. Though the 76ers said they couldn't guarantee my contract, they still wanted me to come to camp and see how I faired. And that was good enough for me. I wouldn't let any obstacle discourage me.

At the time, my thinking went, the 76ers team was among the cream of the crop in the NBA. And they had my idol, Dr. J. I could have taken a chance in the draft to reenter my name. San Antonio was sniffing around, so was Seattle. But I also knew that if I didn't make the 76ers roster, because Philly was so well-respected, one of the other 24 teams would likely scoop me up for their team. So, I went with the 76ers, and my gut. If you're a star player, you don't have to go through these ups and downs. But I wasn't one of those. So, I knew I had to earn it one day at a time.

When the morning came finally came for the first three-day rookie camp with Philly, I was prepared. Salivating. I'd flown to Philly a few days

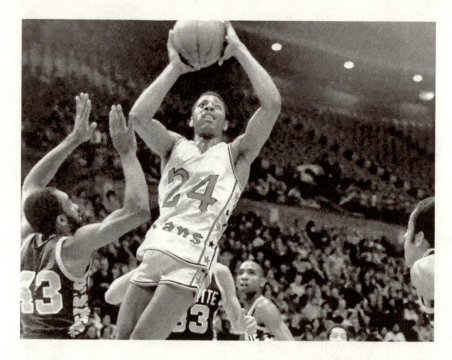

Earl rising up for a shot against Marquette in 1978.

beforehand. But then I heard the news that the team had signed Monti Davis out of college. He was the nation's leading rebounder and the 76ers had signed him for about $80,000 the first year and $90,000 the next—all guaranteed, of course—after drafting him that summer, less than a year after they'd drafted me. Suddenly, I felt like the 13th man on a 12-man roster. Outside looking in. My nose pressed against the proverbial glass. But out of all the rookies the team had drafted in the myriad rounds of the NBA draft, I felt I had the only shot out of those with nonguaranteed contracts to get a spot on the roster. The 76ers already had stars like the all-world defender Maurice Cheeks, big man Bobby Jones, Dr. J, Caldwell Jones. Now Monti Davis. They'd also drafted Andrew Toney that year in the first round with the 8th pick. That's a lot of big names, including *three* promising rookies. What did they need me for? That's what I hoped to show them.

There I was with a non-guaranteed contract on a team that didn't seem to need me. But any opportunity I had, I knew I would have to go for it, full bore. To rookie camp I went. And you know what? I showed OUT at camp. I had a great tryout. Andrew Toney wasn't there the first few days; he was in a contract dispute while finishing his master's degree in Louisiana. But I would find myself at times in the same locker room as Dr. J and I didn't know if I should talk to him, shake his hand, tell him what he meant to me. Or just keep my mouth shut. *Shit!* How far I'd come in such short a time. One of the ways I stood out in 76ers camp was my speed. Coming out of college, people called me the fastest big man in the country. I really could run. So, when the rookies had to run a mile to start veteran camp for the team's annual Magic Mile race, I knew I could stand out. In high school, I'd run cross country. At camp now, when the whistle blew, I took off. I ran the mile at camp in five minutes and seven seconds.

Andrew Toney, who had made it back to camp, and I virtually tied, beating out the rest of the 18 guys. Andrew must have been charged up because when he came back, Pat Williams, who'd drafted both of us, had told him I was looking the best out of all the rookies! It was a highlight for me to do so good in the mile, and the local newspapers even wrote about it. The 76ers had never seen rookies run so well. Back then, if you were over, say, 6'6" you were supposed to be a plodding big man. Magic Johnson was the first to break out of that mold at 6'9". But me? I was quick *and* tall. I hadn't yet totally filled out, so I was still sleek. In fact, at 220 now, the coaches wanted me to put on more weight. To encourage that, the team and Coach Billy Cunningham, a former 76er all-star and "sixth man" who played on the last squad to win a ring for the city in '67 along with Wilt Chamberlain, had me match up against Darryl Dawkins. He was huge and

Retired University of Detroit legend Earl Cureton at the podium for a team press conference in 2020.

one of the best dunkers in the league. He used to name his slams. I was supposed to be intimidated, but I didn't let it affect me.

Dawkins gave his dunks long, crazy names like "The Chocolate-Thunder-Flying, Robinzine-Crying, Teeth-Shaking, Glass-Breaking, Rump-Roasting, Bun-Toasting, Wham-Bam, Glass-Breaker-I-Am-Jam." He was good but he didn't put me to shame. I was quick enough to hang with the small forwards. And I was strong enough to pound with the bigger guys down low now that I had grown to be 6'9". My height and speed made me versatile. The scrimmages at camp, which took place on the nearby Franklin & Marshall campus, were amazing. The fans came to watch us in full. But no matter what, I kept wondering what would happen to me if I played well. There wasn't a roster spot for me, it didn't seem. Yet, I put my head down and kept working. Back then, they could cut you in the middle of camp at a moment's notice. You'd leave practice and go up to your hotel room and the phone could ring and it'd be your end—perhaps a bus ticket, a comic book and a banana would be waiting for me.

Every day could be my last in the league. I knew I had to be the first guy at camp and the last to leave. To bust my ass. I couldn't have any bad days. Not one. There were about 19 of us at camp, from Doug Collins (who wasn't long for the 76ers, thanks to bad ankles), to Dawkins, Dr. J, Monti, Toney and Bobby Jones. But as each day passed, more players dropped. Somehow, I kept surviving. The 76ers then put us in a team facility. My roommate was Monti Davis, the first-round draft pick. If I made the team, he was the one I'd have to beat. We were neck and neck in the preseason. Not only did I have to deal with all that, but we had to endure rookie hazing. Rookies would have to get food for the veterans, carry their bags. But Monti, on the other hand, couldn't handle it. He couldn't handle the hazing. He wasn't playing well. He wasn't worried because he had a guaranteed contract. I saw weakness in him—even though I liked him as a person. I knew I could battle him and win.

Monti was a nice guy, but he couldn't take all the stress of the pros. In the beginning, we'd get to our room and just go to sleep. But as camp went on, he was on the edge of the bed, drinking beers and smoking cigarettes. One day, I came back to the room and all his stuff was gone. When I saw him later, he said, "Man, I'm getting out of here." I asked if he was going home. He nodded. I sat down with him, and we talked. In fact, I talked him *out of* leaving camp. This guy was ahead of me on the depth chart. If he left, I would have made the team outright. But I talked him out of bolting. Monti ended up staying. The damage, however, had been done. I could tell that, even though he'd stayed, his head was done. I felt I had the edge coming out of training camp. I was playing well. Defending, rebounding, running the floor and scoring. Still, though, I wondered what the chances

The 1983 Philadelphia 76ers team photograph. Earl (front row, third from left) sits beside his idol Julius Erving.

were of me staying for good. My contract wasn't guaranteed, but I never gave up.

It was either Monti or me. The week before the start of the season, Monti and I were still living together, competing. In fact, I depended on him to get to practice every day! I didn't have my own car. He had a Chevrolet Monte Carlo, complete with a turbo button, purchased with his big, guaranteed contract. He was often going 90 miles per hour on the highway in that thing. I was nervous as hell every single day going to practice. It was like he had a death wish. Finally, though, with camp over, I got the news. I got a call from our assistant coach Chuck Daly. Chuck would later go on to coach the "Bad Boy" Pistons in the '80s and win two NBA championships in Detroit in '89 and '90. He'd also be the Dream Team head coach in 1992, the greatest team ever assembled. But when he called me up as a 76ers rookie, he was an assistant.

Chuck said, "I'm coming by to get you." I thought, "Oh, shit. It's over for me." When Chuck pulled up to pick me up, he was driving a yellow Audi 4000. His hair was perfect, slicked back, as usual. I got in the car, and he didn't say a word. I said, "Where we going?" He replied, "The baseball game." I said, "The *baseball* game?" We drove that night to see the Philadelphia Phillies. When we got to the stadium, we went up to a suite. In there, I met 76ers owner Fitz Dixon. To this day, Fitz' name is on every No. 2 pencil—check it out when next you're holding one. And when I walked into that suite, he looked up at me and said, grinning, "You know what? You fucked up our plans, Earl!" I was worried, unsure what would come next from his mouth. He continued, "We didn't plan on keeping you. We wanted to keep the best players. But you know what? You're one of them. We're keeping *you*, Earl!"

I damn near fainted. I wanted to stay calm, but I couldn't help myself. I broke down in tears right then and there, right in front of everyone. All the emotion came flooding out. When I finally had a chance, I went out and found a phone and called my mother back in Detroit to tell her I'd officially made the NBA. I was a Philadelphia 76er! And while I knew nothing was guaranteed (including my contract), I'd found a home. For at least a little while.

Memory Lane: Dick Vitale

"Having been able to say that I saw Earl in the infancy of his hoops career makes me so PROUD. To see how, through mental toughness and determination, he has put together a career that many who have laced up sneakers would dream of is AWESOME BABY with a capital-A. Earl has become a popular player with the stars of the game due to the RESPECT he earned from his work ethic and unselfishness. He was about doing whatever it took to HELP teammates get to the winner's locker room. That's Earl!"

4

Playing Alongside My Idol

Against all odds, I'd made the 76ers roster. I'd signed a contract for $55,000 for the first year and, with it, I'd earned the trust of my coaches. Or so I assumed. I thought I'd get minutes. I thought I'd grab rebounds and start the break with Dr. J and Andrew Toney, my roommate on the road who was also coming off the bench, running the wings. But during my first year, which was the NBA's 35th season (and expansion Dallas Mavericks' first, for those counting), I didn't even get into a game for about a dozen games. Finally, I made my NBA debut on October 10, 1980, wearing my number-25 jersey.

Throughout the season, I mostly rode the pine. I don't think our coach, Billy Cunningham, a future NBA top-75 player (my career was filled with them), even really knew I was on the team, waiting to play. Coach hardly ever talked to me. I didn't even get into scrimmages in practice. Only the top 10 players got to do that. Coach Cunningham liked to hold shorter practices, "shootarounds" they were called. I stayed on the sidelines, running, during them, the 12th man, just trying to keep a sweat going. So, even though I'd made the team, I was constantly worried. I also endured some rookie hazing: the veterans would make us sing at team dinners in front of the players and coaches (Barry White was my artist of choice). Of course, rookies also carried veterans' bags.

My contract wasn't guaranteed for the season until December (around the time of the annual team Christmas party). So, I kept thinking to myself I'd get cut sometime before Thanksgiving. I didn't want to go back to stripping floors, to the acid that ate up my skin. So, I rededicated myself. I had to be better, work harder than ever. I made sure I gave my all, one 24-hour period at a time. I got my start in the league and I wasn't going to blow it now. I knew that much.

Let's take a second here to talk about "The Doctor." Just as it's impossible to overstate George Gervin's effect on Detroit, it's impossible to overstate Dr. J's impact on the history of professional basketball. He's a Hall of Famer, a 16-time all-star. In a way, professional basketball, as we know it, starts with Julius. Dude could palm two basketballs at once and dunk each in the same mid-air jump. It was Dr. J by himself who essentially forced the NBA and ABA into a merger in 1976. Julius, who got his nickname, "The Doctor," way back at Roosevelt High School in New York City, came up in the era when white people were scared to give Black people formal power in the game. The dunk was illegal then in the professional game, which in effect negated something many Black players could do, and many whites couldn't. That rule kept Kareem from dunking in college, which indirectly led him to mastering the skyhook (there we go again, turning tragedy to triumph).

So, Julius took his style and swagger to areas like the famed Rucker Park, where he wowed fans. He was the first person to dunk leaping from the free-throw line. The first time he'd done it, he was a junior in high school, a bench player. But after his coach saw that, he started every game. Dr. J turned pro in 1971. He went to the ABA, thanks to Spencer Haywood, who should be a top-75 NBA player, having already broken the "hardship" case barrier. Julius hadn't finished college, hadn't gotten his degree yet, which kept him from the NBA since the league required one for entrance. Julius played for five years in the lesser-watched ABA. But at the time, the ABA was more expressive. There was dunking, three-point shots, gigantic hair. A red, white and blue ball. His legacy grew through word-of-mouth and the occasional glossy magazine feature. Wilt and Russell were giants. But Julius had *wings*. Back then, college basketball was more popular than the pros, although Julius was changing that one game at a time. He dunked from the free-throw line in the 1976 ABA all-star game. He was a bolt of lightning.

Some more history: in 1970, after Haywood got into the ABA with the hardship rule in '69, he along with Seattle SuperSonics then-owner Sam Schulman launched an antitrust lawsuit against the NBA to let hardship cases into the National Basketball Association, too. And he won, which helped pave the way for Julius to enter the league when the NBA and ABA merged. Today, everyone remembers Magic and Bird from the '80s (their relationship did well for the league and race relations), but it was Dr. J who paved the way for their stars to shine. He was the reason the NBA and ABA combined and the reason the NBA took on four teams from the American Basketball Association (the Denver Nuggets, Indiana Pacers, San Antonio Spurs and New Jersey Nets). But upon that merger, the question remained: who would Dr. J play for in the league? He was under contract with the Nets at the time (after first playing for the Virginia Squires out of college). But the Nets were in severe debt as part of their entrance to the league. Not only that, Julius needed a new contract.

Without the funds, the Nets sold The Doctor's contract to Philly. Pat Williams made it happen. (Years later, Pat Williams would draft Shaquille O'Neal first overall for the Orlando Magic, among many other stellar career transactions, including drafting me.) The 76ers made the NBA Finals in The Doctor's first season, 1977, but lost to Bill Walton and the Portland Trailblazers. The following two years, Washington and Seattle each earned Finals rings. Dr. J was the league's MVP in 1981, the first non-center to win the award in 17 years. In 1980, his 76ers lost to the Lakers and rookie Magic Johnson. That's the series that showcased one of Julius' greatest shots, the reverse, behind the backboard, switch hands in mid-air layup that's still shown on league highlight reels today.

But more than a player, Julius was a businessman. He had deals with Coke, Converse and many other big companies. He created jobs for Blacks in bottling plants. He was an icon, a pitch man. The first athlete, in many ways, to break the color barrier in American advertising (take *that*, Don Draper!). He was even a movie star, the lead in *The Fish That Saved Pittsburgh*. I watched everything he did, from the clothes and shoes he wore to the car he drove (a sleek-yet-solid Mercedes-Benz 6.9). He carried himself like the deity he was on and off the court. He'd won two rings in the ABA already and now, as I landed on the team, he was looking for his first NBA ring, the one that would solidify his legacy as a professional basketball legend. I was only happy to help any way I could.

In the 1980–'81 season, my rookie year, I was listed as a center. I was 23 years old and over the course of that full season, I played in 52 of the 82 games, spot-starting in six during the season and averaging 10.2 minutes per game over the course of the year. I averaged 4.2 points and 3 rebounds and played solid defense against all three frontcourt positions. I notched my season high 16 points on January 16 against Cleveland. Dr. J, who won the league's MVP award that season, averaged a whopping 24.6 points per game. It might seem easy or cliché to say, but we should have won the championship in '81. The 76ers had gone to the NBA Finals the season prior, beating the Celtics in the Eastern Conference Finals. But the team lost to the Lakers in a matchup of run-and-gun offenses. In the '80 NBA Finals, the Lakers trapped the 76ers and forced the team out of its game. That's when Magic famously jumped at center in the series' clinching game six with Kareem hurt and finishing with 42 points and 15 boards.

Now, one year removed, during my rookie campaign, we thought we had our chance as a squad to win it all. We finished the 1980–'81 year 62–20, tied with Boston and Milwaukee for the best record in the league. But had we beaten the Celtics on the final game of the season, we would have been alone at number one, home court advantage throughout the East playoffs. We also finished fourth in offense and first in defense that season, which historically leads to good outcomes in the postseason. In the playoffs, we went against the Celtics and my old college foe, Larry Bird. We went up 3–1 against Boston and could almost taste the Finals. But we ended up losing to the Guys in Green. They won 4–3, advancing by beating us three games in a row. Heartbreaking stuff. The Celts beat the Houston Rockets in the NBA Finals 4–2 and Bird got his first ring, grabbing 21 rebounds in each of the first two games of that series. Even the Rockets made history that season, finishing the year under .500 (40–42), yet still making the Finals.

Houston's stoic Moses Malone was the playoffs leader in points and total rebounds that postseason, one of the best in the NBA by any calculation. But we felt that if we had beaten the Celtics in the Eastern Finals, we would have beat Houston, too, despite Moses' potential for heroics. Houston had a good team, to be sure, but we knew the winner of the Eastern Conference Finals would be the eventual champion. Once we lost, me and Andrew Toney were distraught. We wept. Somehow, we got our hands on a couple of Miller Lites and we just sat in the famed Boston Garden trying to drown our sorrows. But the story of that season, for me, was just scraping by and making it through. Though the team had taken me in the third round of the 1979 NBA draft, I didn't play my first pro game until late into 1980. After those first dozen games, a few guys on the team started to get injured. You never want your teammates (your friends) to get hurt. It's never good. But with guys out, that made room for me, and I wasn't going to let the open opportunity pass me by.

Earl in 1982, shooting as Larry Bird and Kevin McHale look on.

Injuries meant more minutes for those of us who rode the bench. And I was ready. Coach Cunningham came to me one afternoon my rookie year and said, "You're starting tonight, Earl." I said, "*Starting?*" But that was the beauty of my role. As a bench player, you must always be ready. If your number is called, you must contribute—instrumental in the team's success, without being a star on the stat sheet. Some people might think being a bench player is the best job in the world—let me tell you, it's tough. There's so little time for practice during the season—you must always be prepared. And do it largely on your own.

Coach Cunningham, who preached hard work constantly, knew I stayed ready, which is why he eventually leaned on me in big moments when the starters weren't cutting it. It's why he felt comfortable spot-starting me or putting me in during the fourth quarter of a big game. He knew I'd been watching the whole contest closely, that I knew what was needed of my positions at any given moment. The game I started, we flew to Indianapolis to take on the Pacers. I was shaking in the locker room ahead of the matchup. We had a lot of good players my first year, from Maurice Cheeks to Darryl Dawkins, Dr. J, Lionel Hollins, Bobby and Caldwell Jones (both of whom would make the All-Defensive team that year). I was pacing. Andrew Toney, who'd replaced Doug Collins in the rotation, said, "Sit down, Earl!"

That night I got 15 points and 14 rebounds. I played great. And after the game I was thinking, "Now I'm going to get some regular playing time." But I stayed on the bench for another 15 games, or so. *Oh well.* I continued to accept my role. I had no other choice. We were a team of skilled veterans, largely, and that meant waiting my turn. It meant I could learn a lot from the guys in practices, but it also meant I was at the end of the bench during most games. In the playoffs that season, we beat the Pacers and Coach of the Year Jack McKinney in the first round. Then we beat the talented Milwaukee Bucks in the second round. Coached by Don Nelson, the Bucks had big names like Sidney Moncrief (who was in my draft class), Marques Johnson and big Bob Lanier. They always worried us. That victory didn't last long, and we lost to the Celtics in that heartbreaking seventh game of the Eastern Conference Finals, leading to me and Toney's Miller Lites. But I'd gotten through my rookie season and played nine games in the post season, averaging about a point and a rebound per postseason contest.

The next year, the 1981–'82 season, was my second in the NBA. Thankfully, I was invited back to the 76ers. My nonguaranteed contract for my second year was for $65,000, which was $10,000 more than the year before. Ronald Reagan was President at the time and Uncle Sam took about $25,000 from my checks. But if we made the playoffs again in my sophomore campaign, I knew I'd get most of that back as a playoff bonus. At training camp for the 1981–'82 season, I had to prove myself again. We had another standout roster, which included Cheeks, Dawkins, Julius, Hollins, Bobby and Caldwell and more. Henry Bibby, too, but he was cut later on. Personally, I wasn't given anything, let alone a secure roster spot. That's never been my lot in life. I had to make the roster, day by day. Monti Davis was back again in the preseason. He still had $90,000 owed to him with his *guaranteed* contract (sadly, for him, he didn't make the roster). I was faced with the same situation as the year before. I had to beat guys out.

But now, I'd been around the pros for a year. I wasn't going to let that be my only one. So, I went into camp and kicked butt. I had purpose. I was more experienced, knew the guys. Today, a few stories come to mind. Of course, when you're in proximity of Darryl Dawkins, chances are you're going to walk away with a story or three. The big man broke his first backboard in the NBA on November 13, 1979, shattering the glass into a million pieces in the middle of

Earl boxing out the Celtic great, Robert Parish, in 1982.

a game. (Two games before, I'd scored my season high 23 points against the Rockets.) The NBA knew it had to do something about the rim. Players were only going to get bigger and stronger, so they had to protect the backboards and not cause a large delay in games if someone like Darryl destroyed one. So, the league eventually came into our training camp practices to test out new, collapsible rims.

At first, the league tried rims that, if too much weight went onto them, they'd just snap down and hang loose. One day during practice, I was going against Darryl, and I got the ball open in transition on a fast break. It was just me, Darryl and the rim. So, what did Darryl do? Instead of trying to stop me, he jumped up and snatched the rim down, leaving me hanging in mid-air with no goal! Dawkins was something else. He was Shaq before Shaq. I loved having him as a teammate. He was larger than life. He was one of the funniest guys I'd ever met. He told everyone he was from "Planet Lovetron." He was *out there*, man. We spent a lot of time going at it in practice. He was rough in practice, too. He was jovial off the court but on it, he tried to intimidate you. He'd say, "Don't foul me, bitch!" And I'd say, "Ain't nobody scared of you! You know where I'm from?"

Earl shooting a hook against New Jersey, 1982.

After one heated practice, I wasn't sure if we were still cool or not, if we left the gym on good terms. But that day, I went home and when I pulled up to my building, I saw Dawkins there in front waiting for me. We'd had our skirmish that afternoon and when I saw him, I got a little nervous. When I got out, though, he held out his hand and shook mine. We started talking and from that day on, we were good buddies. In fact, Darryl later came to my home back in Detroit. He stayed at my mother's house on the east side with us. The Mack and Bewick neighborhood went NUTS seeing him there. My mother gave him my room and cooked for him. He teased me about that later. But we developed a great friendship. (When he passed away too early in 2015, I was there at his funeral.) Dawkins was one of several guys I invited to Detroit, including my buddy Norm Nixon.

Darryl was ahead of his time. He wore gold chains—he had a whole backboard-shaped medallion, with diamonds on each corner. He used to rap in the locker-room. In fact, Stevie Wonder gave him his nickname: *Chocolate Thunder.* He and Coach Cunningham used to go at it, too. There was one time when they were off in the corner during practice, talking for 30 minutes. When they were done, Coach turned around and Darryl stuck his foot out and tripped him! "God damnit, Dawkins!" Coach yelled. "You're never serious about nothing!" (Years later, I saw Coach tell that same story on NBATV, which made me smile.) But perhaps to some surprise, Darryl didn't go out much. People would always bother him. So, he stayed in his hotel most of the time. He used to call me Pitbull. He'd call me up and say, "Pitbull, come to my room, let's get some room service!"

Darryl loved room service. One time, I went over, and we hung out for a while and when I left, as I was walking out the door, he pushed me out into the hallway and said, filling the hallway with his big, booming voice, "Get out of here, bitch!" All of a sudden, I was stumbling into the hallway, totally off-guard. There were a bunch of people in the hall, staring. I was embarrassed as he watched the whole thing through the peephole, laughing and laughing! But that was Darryl. Always joking. Always entertaining.

My second year in the NBA, I made the 76ers roster again—I wouldn't let myself lose out to anyone in camp. But making the roster wasn't enough for me this time around. I wanted to make the *rotation*, to get real and regular playing time and continue to make my name in the NBA. The practices were hard during the 1981–'82 season. I played my butt off. Still, though, I wasn't making the dent I wanted to on the roster. The coaches focused on the same eight or nine guys who they thought they could win with day in and day out. So, I came up with a new idea. It was simple: I'd make a name for myself with the *fans* by showing out in the layup lines before each game. Then the coaches would *have to* acknowledge me and get me in. Warmups were now my time to shine, and I was going to turn those layup lines out. I'd make them my own personal slam dunk contest if I had to. I'd dunk every way I could. I got to the games early and I stretched ahead of layup lines so that I was limber enough to bring *wows* to the open mouths of the onlooking spectators.

When warmups started, I did 360-degree windmills. Rock-a-baby-to-sleep dunks that I learned from watching Julius. I did this whole big routine every game. Like a maniac. My teammates later pulled me aside and asked, "What the fuck are you doing? What the fuck is wrong with you? Why are you doing all this in the *layup lines*?" I told them, "The layup lines are my game time! This is the only time I get a chance to show myself off. This is game time for me, y'all!" They looked at me like I was crazy. But I didn't care. It was my career I was worried about, not theirs. And the fans loved it. Finally, Coach Cunningham started to pay attention, too. In the NBA, the last few minutes of a game that's long been decided is known as "garbage time." Coach Cunningham began to put me in during garbage time more frequently. And during those stints, I shined.

The 76ers also had this give-away promotion for fans. For McDonald's breakfast sandwiches: "McMuffins." If we scored a certain number of points and got the win, the whole crowd on hand would get free McMuffin breakfasts the next morning. So, when I got in for garbage time at the end of games, I made sure the whole crowd walked away with free McMuffin sandwiches. Philly is known for its rowdy fans. They can be unforgiving at times. But also, euphoric. So, I gave my thanks to them by earning a lot of free breakfasts over the course of that season. It happened so often that the local Philadelphia newspapers began writing about my garbage time hustle. It was like *The Gladiator* film years later. *"Are you not entertained!"* I won over the fans with my layup line dunks and my McMuffin victories. They cheered loudly. To my surprise, Coach Cunningham started to sub me in during the game more, even *before* garbage time. I played hard defense and rebounded my butt off. I scored when I could. My second year in the league, I officially earned my way into 66 games and started eight of them. I averaged 14.5 minutes per game, along with 5.3 points and 4.1 rebounds. All my stats and averages were inching up. *Mama, I made it!*

Let me mention something hard here: sadly, it's hard to talk about the NBA in the 1980s without mentioning drug issues. The league did have a substance abuse problem, and while I stayed away from the stuff (drugs never interested me), there were some who fell prey to their demons. The league didn't have a strong drug policy coming out of the 1970s and that didn't help. Those who ran the Association didn't know how to handle the epidemic. They were dealing with cases on the fly, like whack-a-mole, rather than being proactive. Cocaine was running rampant in America and, of course, it seeped into the NBA. Not to single him out, but I remember one time when I was in Philly when the great point guard John Lucas was visibly taken over by his addiction. He was one of the guys who went off the rails bad. He was with Washington at the time and during the game, John came out of the locker-room and he was out of it. He stood at the halfcourt line just saying, "The Doctor! The Doctor!" Screaming out Julius' nickname. We didn't know what was going on at the time, but John was in the throes.

John is and was a great man. Everyone loved him. Thankfully, he's since turned his life around. That season, though, was a low point. Others in league history have succumbed to addiction even worse, like Chris Washburn, Roy Tarpley, Michael Ray Richardson, David Thompson, Lloyd Daniels and John Drew, who was suspended from the league for life. John Lucas later created a substance abuse clinic in Houston to help many of these folks. Another one of us who turned tragedy to triumph.

The 76ers had big goals that season. After some heartbreaking years, we wanted to prove we were as good as the Lakers and Celtics. Sure enough, we made the NBA Finals again, which felt incredible. We'd beaten Boston and Bird in the playoffs and got to the promised land. It was in that series, after we went up 3–1, that the Celtics came back on us *again*. They put a good scare in us *again*. But in the seventh and deciding game, which we won handily, their fans gave us extra support, cheering us in unison, "*Beat L.A.! Beat L.A.!*" Winning that year marked my first time in the Finals! Even though I was getting in

Earl defending the rim against Washington during the 1982 season.

more, I played sparingly throughout the season compared to the team's stars, cheering for my teammates when I was on the bench. In the play-offs, I played in a dozen games, averaging more than two points and two rebounds in each. But in the Finals, I got in more and battled with the best.

It felt so good to beat Boston in the series prior that we almost forgot we had another series—against, yes, the Los Angeles Lakers. They were our opponent for the second time in three years in the Finals. The Lakers had skill and height. The 76ers needed me to help defend big guys, like the star of stars, Kareem Abdul-Jabbar. The Lakers had a number of big names, from Magic to Jamaal Wilkes, Bob McAdoo, Norm Nixon and Kurt "Clark Kent" Rambis, who was often dripping with blood from his hustle plays. But Kareem was literally and figuratively the biggest of them all. The Lakers also boasted the now-legendary coach Pat Riley. It was a star-studded matchup and the first year in recent memory that the Finals weren't on tape delay, played sometime late after the nightly news. In 1982 they were finally broadcast live, thanks to Magic, Kareem and Julius.

It was Game 2 of the Finals when I got the call from Coach Cunningham. I went out onto the court in the first half and matched up with Kareem. At that point, he was probably the best player ever to suit up in the NBA (he was also one of the most enigmatic). Magic and Larry were still solidifying their legacies. Michael was still in college at UNC. Bill Russell had won 11 rings in the '60s but for all his greatness that was when the league had just eight teams. George Mikan was a product of a bygone era. But Kareem was the new Gold Standard. The tall center from New York City, the multi-time college champion from UCLA. I knew he stood between me and earning more minutes. He wasn't King Kareem to me, not in that series anyway. How could he be? He was just another guy I had to beat out. And I knew, even though he had me by about four inches, I could use my strength and quickness against him.

I'd like to pause here a moment and talk about Bill Russell and what he meant to the social fabric of the NBA. While Kareem may have had bigger on-court stats, Russell has always been one of the most important players in league history. Bill passed away on July 31, 2022, at 88 years old. His old team, the Celtics, was the first team to ever put five Black players on the floor together. But in the '80s, there were few teams, if any at all, who did that. Social problems like racism can happen in waves. In the '80s, the world was in a downswing, sadly. In fact, in the 1978–'79 season, after putting five Black players on the court, the New York Knicks were called—in a hometown newspaper—the New York "Niggerbockers."

It was around this time that the NBA was thought of as "too Black." With the 76ers, we didn't have five Black players on the court ever. Mark Iavaroni was our Kurt Rambis. The talented white guy who found himself with four Black guys on the floor. The white guy who, through no fault of his own, sometimes took a Black guy's spot in the starting lineup, skin color breaking the possible tie. Nothing against Mark or Kurt, who both worked hard and were talented, but it's part of the league's history. Kurt is a good friend of mine and Mark would even sleep in his car in the parking lot to be near practice, if he had to. But it was against this general, prejudiced behavior that Russell fought for us all. The league will *forever* owe him a debt.

Against Kareem in Game 2 of the NBA Finals, I played well. Darryl got into foul trouble and Coach called my number off the bench. In the second game of the Finals, I scored eight points, had five rebounds and blocked three shots. I was ready. I'd watched the series closely and

Earl getting up for the ball against the Nets in 1982.

knew where I could make my mark. So, I showed everyone from Philly to L.A. that I belonged. I'd come a long way, from layup lines to garbage time to McMuffins to now earning stats in the NBA Finals against Kareem. In the end, though, his Lakers beat us, and they earned their second championship ring in just three years. We lost the series 4–2. But I knew I was on my way. I belonged at the highest level. I could contribute and make a difference in any game against any opponent. I'd proven that.

Toney and Dr. J played well for our side, each scoring about a ton of points. But in the end, it wasn't enough. Going into the offseason, the 76ers knew they needed something else to get over the hump. The team didn't want to believe the window was closed. We'd come *so close*. For three years in a row, the team had come up *just* short of champions. Now, an infusion of talent was needed. To make the final leap, the 76ers management decided to make a big, big move. They traded Darryl to the New Jersey Nets for a first-round draft pick. Then the team made an even bigger move.

The Sixers signed Moses Malone, the former MVP, to a huge contract that, they hoped, would make all the difference.

Memory Lane: Norm Nixon

"Earl was a 6'9" guy who played out of position—he played a lot of center—but he could do it. He could use his ability to compensate for his lack of size. His transition ability, getting down court. His leaping ability. He wasn't the biggest guy in history. But he could rebound, outlet to a guard, block shots. He was a guy that just *worked hard*. He was a great guy. A guy that played 12 years coming off the bench, which takes a whole different mentality to be able to do, and to do successfully. That speaks a lot about his character. Earl was a guy who put in the work. No complaining. That's what I've always respected about him."

5

The '83 Championship Team

The next year, my third, the run of close calls ended for the 76ers. *Almost* would become *finally*. The 76ers signed Moses Malone to a six-year contract ahead of the season and that was a big reason why we propelled far forward. I remember calling Andrew Toney after I'd heard the news and said, "We're going to win the championship this year!" As I've explained, I idolized Dr. J. And I don't know how many hours I spent staring at posters of him with his big hair soaring through the air. But I also wore number 24 in college, which was Moses' number with the Houston Rockets, in honor of the talented big man. Moses was a beast, and I couldn't wait to battle him at practice in Philly, learning the Art of the Rebound from the big fella. Each of our biggest rivals were earning rings—the Lakers and the Celtics—and we were always the team that couldn't quite get over the hump. Always the proverbial bridesmaid. Yet, we remained hopeful for the new season because we had Moses. Yes, 1982–'83 would be our year.

Kareem had beaten us in previous attempts, but with Moses, who would end up being the MVP of the 1983 season, we had a new chance. In between the 1981–'82 and 1982–'83 seasons, I went back home to Detroit for the summer to refocus myself. I worked out in the hot months at the St. Cecilia Gym, sweating. While it was good to be back home, I got myself into a little bit of trouble. Not with the law or anyone in the city, of course. That wasn't my style. Instead, I got injured. I fractured my foot while playing in the gym. I broke the fifth metatarsal ligament in my right foot, to be specific. I cursed loudly when I felt it break—all of Detroit probably heard me. I was about to enter the final year of my three-year, nonguaranteed contract and now *this*. I hoped the injury wouldn't end my time in the NBA. I had the option of surgery. But if I took that route, I knew I'd miss training camp and put myself behind the 8-ball in a major way. If I missed camp, I'd likely miss the whole year.

Doctors at the University of Detroit looked at my hurt foot and X-rayed it. Then they put me in a cast. That's when Philadelphia called and told me to come in and show them the damage. They needed to see me *now*, they said. In Philly, their doctors took the cast off, X-rayed me again. They told me I should get surgery, that they'd put screws in my foot. But if they did that, I knew I wouldn't be able to play for a significant time and, thus, I would likely not make the team. If I didn't make the team, where would I be? I could be out of the league entirely—just like that! So, I declined surgery. I refused to go under the knife, even though the doctors said I should. Instead, I flew back to Detroit again to rehab it ahead of 76ers training camp. With fingers crossed. Philly wasn't happy about it, but it was my body. I took a chance and bet on my ability to heal. In the end, I was lucky it happened so early in the summer. Time was on my side.

In Detroit, doctors put an electronic device on my foot that sent stimulations to it while I slept. In the meantime, I worked every day on my upper body. I rode a bike with my cast on. I had eight weeks to get right before camp. I rehabbed for hours a day. I knew the only thing that would be hampered would be my conditioning once I got back on the court, but that had never been hard for me to recover. If I was lucky, I'd just barely squeak by and make the team again. When I eventually got to camp, I saw all the guys I had to beat out to get playing time. The 76ers had brought in four or five guys at my position that year, including Marc Iavaroni, to whom the team had guaranteed a $100,000 contract. All-star Bobby Jones also played power forward. Russ Schoene, too. The team drafted the 6'11" Robert McNamara. And there was Moses, of course. Here we go again, I thought.

I wasn't 100 percent going into camp, given my foot. But I worked my way through it, somehow. I had two years of experience, and I had a strong sense of how to navigate the early parts of the job. I knew I could play three positions: small forward, power forward and center. I'd guarded Kareem in the Finals. I'd done well, made a name for myself with the crowds, scored in the championship series. The team didn't have anyone like me, no one as versatile (or hungry). Still, though, I figured they'd cut me and do so without remorse. I ignored every article that said I'd be gone before the opening tip. At camp, I was in pain. But I fought through. There would be no days off for me. It was a struggle, a nightmare, really. My nonguaranteed contract hung over me like a dark cloud comprised of ready-to-fall acid rain.

There were so many guys looking to take my minutes and my spot on the roster. It wasn't personal but it was a fact, nevertheless. Show me a competitive basketball player and I'll show you someone who thinks he should be playing more time over people on the team. It's just a reality. The majority of the power forward minutes belonged to Bobby Jones, our five-time all-star forward. When you're young and in the middle of a career, you feel you should get everything you want. I thought I could play in Iavaroni's spot. But in the end, I learned to accept my role. Not only was I competing against players on the roster for time, but I was also competing against my injury. As usual, I just barely squeaked by.

That year, ahead of the start of the season, we played several preseason games. We'd gone 6–0 in the first stretch and in the seventh and final game, I didn't get in until the waning minutes. I sat there, waiting. But Coach Cunningham didn't play me. Yet, with just a few minutes left, he told me to enter the contest. He wanted me in there for rebounding in a close game. It was a one-point affair in the final ticks. And we were down. A bucket would win it for us. During a time out, Coach drew up a play for guard Andrew Toney. When the game started back up, Toney got the ball, found an opening, and put up a shot. It missed, caroming off the rim. But I was underneath for the board. At the right place at the right time. *Boom!* I caught the ball and dunked it through the net, sore foot and all. I won us that game with the go-ahead basket. Joyous, we all ran into the locker room, celebrating. I shouted at the top of my lungs to anyone who could hear, "You can't get rid of me! You can't get rid of me!"

It was a big moment. It was another chance. Though I'd made the team again, I didn't have much seniority. That was evident in several areas, most of all on plane trips from city to city. On major commercial flights back then, there were usually eight first class seats for players. And each of those went to veterans like Dr. J or Moses (the proto–Shaq-and-Kobe). If you were a rookie or a player on your first contract, like I was, you most often had to sit in the back in coach. Our trainer at the time, Al Domenico, had been with the team forever. Through the 9–73 season in '72–'73 and into our winning years. But he was a piece of work, to be sure. He'd been with Billy Cunningham for years. Al used to love playing jokes on rookies. In the airports, he'd do all kinds of crazy things. His pranks ranged from the humorous to the dangerous. Sometimes he'd give the rookies movie passes instead of their actual plane tickets and when they tried to board the aircraft, he'd laugh his head off. One time, Maurice Cheeks was reading the newspaper and Al set the paper on fire!

At one point Al got himself into trouble with the team's owner, though. He started to take the first-class tickets meant for the veterans and trade them in for coach tickets, pocketing the money. The team owner, Harold Katz, caught wind of this and approached Al about it. Katz loved Al. But he had to confront him about the tickets and the money Al was pocketing. *What was going on? What happened to the money?* Al tried to dance around it but then finally admitted to what he was doing. Then, he asked Harold, "Want to split the cash?" That was Al, for better and for worse. That guy used to threaten me sometimes. Before games, I would come in to get my ankles taped. He'd say to me, "Earl, why are you getting taped? You're not going to play! You're wasting our time and our tape! I'm going to tell Harold you're wasting his dough and he's going to cut you!" I got mad at him and said, "Al, you're going to tape me up before every fucking game whether I play or not. Now do it!"

He also had this collection of heads in his office. Not real ones, of course, but heads of players he cut out of the team photos. Every time a player would get cut from the 76ers, Al would cut his head out of the picture and tape it on his wall. By the end, his wall was covered in our big ol' heads. I'll always remember Al, that crazy, lovable jerk.

If you like those silly situations, get a load of this one: as I mentioned, Andrew Toney and I were roommates on the road together. We'd come into the league as rookies, and we had a good relationship. We got along well. To this day, we're still best of friends. We talk two or three times a week. Well, one day, he came back to the room after just seeing Julius. At this time, we were both in our 20s. We idolized Dr. J. He was smooth as butter on and off the court. He was the league's No. 1 ambassador. And, well, he played the part. Toney had gone to his hotel room one day while we were on the road. He knocked on the door and when it opened, he saw Dr. J there in a smoking jacket and house shoes and behind him, Toney said, was a table as big as our room. The man knew how to get comfy. It was like he was Hugh Hefner. To this day, I don't know what the table was for. But maybe I actually *don't* want to know!

That third season with the 76ers, we went 65–17, winning our division (despite losing three of our last four games). Moses and Dr. J (who was the MVP of the all-star game that season) both averaged more than 20 per game and Andrew Toney averaged just under. Moses and Doc also both made first team All-NBA. I'd made the 76ers, earning a $75,000 salary for the year. I was thrilled to stay on the roster. The lasting image for the regular season was Dr. J soaring through the air in January when he rose against the Lakers' Michael Cooper with his now-famous "Rock the Baby" cradle dunk mid-game. He must have earned frequent flyer miles he was in the air so often for us that year. We won a lot of games in '82–'83, went on so many long winning streaks. But whenever we lost one, Coach Cunningham would come into the locker-room and scream at us. No nonsense, Coach would cuss everyone out. I remember after one loss, even his wife even said, "I'm not riding home with him! I'm going to catch a cab!"

There was another funny story that year having to do with Mitchell "J.J." Anderson. He was a rookie during the '83 season. Mitch only played for us for 13 games that year, but that's because he got cut early on by Coach Cunningham. Andrew and I used to make him drive us everywhere. We had Cadillacs and since Mitch was our rookie, picked in the second round 36th overall out of Bradley, he was our de facto chauffeur.

Mitch played small forward, backing up Dr. J and, so, he barely got any playing time. But during one game, Coach called for him to go in. Mitch wasn't used to that, though. He only played about four minutes a game for us. On the bench, he was always singing the song, "Tell me have you seen her?" by the Chi-Lites. He crooned, *But now I go for walks / To the movies, maybe to the park / I have a seat on the same old bench / To watch the children play, huh / You know tomorrow is their future / But for me just another day.* It still cracks me up!

So, when Billy called for him to go in, it took Mitch seemingly *forever* to get his warmup sweats off. By the time he'd loosened each button one by one, Coach Cunningham shouted, "Mitch! Take a seat!" and his butt was back on the bench. Billy cut him the next game and Mitch was just gone. Those are the breaks in the NBA. Later, Mitch landed on the Utah Jazz and he played for two more seasons, averaging about 5 points per game in Salt Lake City. We ended up picking up center Clemon Johnson to replace him.

Later, when Billy called for me to get in the game, I tore my sweats off so fast I almost hit him in the face. I wasn't going to mess around. Coach Cunningham was a perfectionist. During the year and especially in the '82–'83 season, he wouldn't let us lose focus. Billy knew we'd been through a lot, that the team had been through a lot. Losing in the '80 in the Finals to L.A., losing to Boston in the Eastern Finals in '81, losing again in the Finals to the Lakers in '82. It would take precision and focus to get to the Finals again in '83. He was right.

In the locker-room, I was stationed next to Caldwell Jones. Dr. J was across from me. Another nearby was big man Steve Mix. Steve was a funny guy. One time, we were down 30 and Coach called to him to get in the game. Steve walked to the scorer's table past Coach and asked him, "What do you want me to do, Billy? Win it or tie it?" Steve was on the 76ers for seemingly forever (nine years, officially, with his lone all-star season in '74–'75). He landed on the team starting the year after the 76ers won just 9 games. But he left just before we won it all. Steve went to the Bucks, then to the Lakers in '83—sadly for him. In fact, I still have a big, framed painting of Steve coming into the 76ers locker-room and pouring champagne on my head after we won (an image later used in a 2022 Netflix documentary, *Flagrant Foul*). He and Billy Cunningham had played together in the mid-'70s. Steve was a good guy, a vet I learned a lot from in my years.

We won the Atlantic Division title during the regular season. Then in the playoffs we swept the New York Knicks in the first round. Coached by Hubie Brown, the Knicks were good but not great, especially when compared to our squad. Big Moses went to work on them. Hubie even said after the sweep, "Moses Malone was absolutely awesome. They cannot pay him enough." And Coach Cunningham called Moses, "Something special."

Going into the '82–'83 season, people wondered if Moses and The Doctor could get along together on the same court, two big names, two big sets of hands that needed the lone ball. But the whole thing was seamless. In the next round, we played the Bucks. We almost had them in a sweep, but they took Game Four from us. Sidney Moncrief, Marcus Johnson and big Bob Lanier were a little too much in that one. But we took Game Five and sent them packing for good. Bobby Jones was big for us that series, quiet off the court and havoc on it. After we beat the Bucks, their coach, Don Nelson said, "Without any question this is the best team I've seen in 10 years."

Out west, L.A. was rolling through the playoffs. They beat the Portland Trailblazers. Then they took out the San Antonio Spurs and their big stars, George Gervin and Artis Gilmore. In the Finals, we matched up with L.A again. The celebrities were out. Jack Nicholson in L.A., Elliott Gould and Mia Farrow in Philly. Again in the Finals, I matched up against Kareem, goggles, bald spot and all. By now, he was a six-time MVP and three-time champion (combining his awards in L.A. and Milwaukee). My friend, Laker Norm Nixon, called Kareem the "Player of the Century." But, to me, he was merely an opponent. Someone I had to hang with, outdo if I could. In Game 2 of the Finals, Moses Malone got in foul trouble. After he earned his fifth, Coach subbed me in. The Lakers looked to attack me, but in the end, it was the other way around. They got stagnant. At the same time, I rebounded well and I slapped the ball away from Kareem a couple times, leading to fast breaks.

I even gave Kareem a taste of his own offensive medicine, a skyhook, sinking the shot over the big fella from the right block. That gave us an important cushion and led to a win in the second game of the Finals. It was the biggest shot of my entire life. My teammate Maurice Cheeks said of that make, "[Earl] threw a skyhook on Kareem, probably because he saw so many of them, he knew how to do it, himself!" The reporters laughed. And Dr. J said, "Earl Cureton is not going to be able to walk the streets of Detroit and have people wonder who he is. They're going to know. *There's Earl Cureton! Give me a dollar!*" The reporters chuckled at that, too. Years later, Norm Nixon told me that I had a "stretch that controlled the game." No matter what anyone wants to say, I was just happy to contribute. In an article from June 6, 1983, *Sports Illustrated* wrote of the matchup:

> … *Abdul-Jabbar had spent enough time on Malone to pick up his fourth foul with 6:17 to go in the third quarter, and as soon as he went to the bench, Philadelphia brought the ball right to the heart of the L.A. defense, scoring three straight layups to go from five points behind to one ahead. The Sixers held a four-point lead by the time Malone drew his fifth foul with 7:58 left in the game, and as Cunningham sent in 6'9" backup Earl (The Twirl) Cureton, he was "very concerned." But during the next five minutes and 34 seconds something*

remarkable happened, and Cureton, who played Abdul-Jabbar very well in last year's Game 2, deserved some of the credit. Not only did Cureton throw down a skyhook over the shot's creator, but he presented an irresistible target for the L.A. offense. Soon the Lakers were funneling everything into Abdul-Jabbar, who at 7'2" has a five-inch advantage on Cureton, and before long the rest of Los Angeles' glittering offense had shut down. No Laker other than Abdul-Jabbar scored while Malone was on the bench, and no L.A. starter except Abdul-Jabbar scored a point during the fourth quarter, the lot of them going 0 for 9. Nixon, who was 4 for 13 in Game 2, later conceded, "In the fourth quarter I was nowhere to be found."

The Lakers' 13 possessions after Malone went to the bench resulted in three baskets, and they turned the ball over eight times. The 76ers played a swarming, help-out defense in the middle, and with Cureton batting two balls loose, Bobby Jones two others and Cheeks a fifth, the Sixers had a 95–87 lead when Malone returned. By then the game was, in effect, over.

Sadly for L.A. (but not for us), they were without James Worthy and Bob McAdoo for the series, both out with injuries. Nixon and Andrew Toney, who was an all-star that year, got into a head-on collision during the Finals, too, which knocked Toney out for Game 1. But we were just too talented, too good all around. We couldn't be beat. It didn't matter who the other team put on the floor. With Toney out, Coach Cunningham put in role player, Clint Richardson, who had the game of his life and sealed Game 1 for us. After that contest, Lakers coach Pat Riley, who was always crouching on the sidelines, said, "If I have to devise a defense to stop Clint Richardson, we're in trouble."

Yes, they were in trouble. We played the first two games against L.A. in the Spectrum in Philly, on our home turf. The Lakers may have had Magic "the Magician" but we had Julius "the Physician." That was a common TV tagline. We were confident, though. Largely, because of Dr. J and Moses. They were unstoppable and the L.A. finesse strategy was no hope against Moses' power and brute force. The year before, Kareem was too much for us. Not this time. Now we held the balance of power. We won games 3 and 4 in L.A., too. Moses continued his dominance. Dr. J called him a "blessing." With the Laker girls shaking their stuff, and big-name actor Walter Matthau in the stands, we took the energy out of the Great Western Forum.

In the deciding Game 4, the Lakers led at the half. Kareem had 18 points in the first two quarters. Our defense tightened in the second half and Los Angeles' lead dwindled. Dr. J took it home for us in front of the Lakers' 18,000 fans. And after we won, Coach Cunningham kissed practically everyone on the cheek he was so happy! He'd known we could do it. He'd kept us together and it worked. Moses led every game in rebounds, averaging 18 per. And he'd led each in scoring, except the final contest.

We won every game by an average of 10 points. Moses won Finals MVP. We were kings—finally. Moses later told reporters, "The more they push me, the stronger I get." He was like the famed Yankee catcher Yogi Berra with his wisdom. Our Finals win that year marks the only non–Lakers and Celtics championship from 1980 to 1988. And it marked Doc's victory over both Bird and Magic in the same season. A rare feat.

We'd had such a good record during the regular season ahead of the playoffs that when a reporter asked Moses how we'd do in the postseason, Moses offered his now-famous response, "Fo' fo' fo,'" meaning we'd win all three playoff series in the minimum four-games. We were dominant and he was confident. In the end, it was "Fo' five fo'" with one loss to the Bucks in the Eastern Finals, but the message was clear. And "Fo Five Fo" would later be imprinted on our '83 Championship rings, which I still wear to this day.

After we'd won, the champagne flowed. Like I said, we didn't have those big goggles players wear now, so the sticky bubbly stuff got in our eyes and ears and noses. It burned in the best of ways. We didn't care about the sting. We'd won and we celebrated like our lives depended on it! We were a well-rounded team. One of only three to that point that had won the title with no more than four people averaging double-figures in scoring for the season (along with the '58 Hawks and '75 Warriors). I didn't take my uniform off for seemingly a week, though it was probably more like just 24 hours. We'd won in the Fabulous Forum in L.A. so there was no confetti or balloons. But we partied in the arena until we'd had our fill. And then we continued late into the night and into the next morning.

Many today think the '83 76ers is one of the best teams ever, right up there with the '96 Bulls and the 2017 Golden State Warriors. Everyone on our 12-man roster contributed. We all had talent. Many years later, Kareem and I were playing in a charity game in the mid-'90s. George Gervin was there, Tiny Archibald, and many others. Kareem was a guy I didn't know well, personally, even after playing him so often in the NBA. Kareem hardly spoke to anyone, truth be told. But at one point, during that charity game, we struck up a conversation. I remember talking some good-natured smack to him, saying, "There were two guys who dominated you in '83!" Kareem turned to me and said, "*Who?*" And I said, "Me and Moses! Moses for 40 minutes and me for eight!" We laughed about it. Everyone knew he was amazing. He was well over seven-feet with an unstoppable shot. My only hope, when I guarded Kareem, was to try and slap the ball before it got over his head. If he got it up above me, I was toast.

But in the end, Moses was the best player in the world at the conclusion of the '83 season. He was special and had earned that title, like a boxer or wrestler earning a championship belt. Moses, to his credit, never wanted to be treated like a superstar. He was always a teammate. He didn't drink, but he liked to go out to be around people. He was a regular guy who just happened to be amazing at playing basketball. Losing Darryl Dawkins before the '82–'83 season hurt us on several levels, but it was made easier with the addition of Moses. He was a quiet fella with the media, but he opened up more around his teammates. He was the kind of guy that, when he was invited to be honored before a game, he'd always want his team there with him. He wanted everyone to come and enjoy the spotlight.

Moses was terrific. He could have been a coach; he was so smart. That guy knew basketball. I remember one time talking with him later in life. He was headed to a surprise birthday party for our friend, Muggsy Bogues, who played with Moses on Washington early in Muggs' career. The party ended up being a surprise wedding for Muggsy and his wife, Kim, on Muggsy's 50th birthday. I couldn't make the event, but Moses told me he was going, saying, "I'm going to go to Little Pimp's party!" I couldn't help but belly-laugh at that one. We were friends until the day he died in 2015.

After we'd swept the Lakers and flew back home to Philadelphia, we were greeted by a swath of fans at the airport. Later, some 60,000 of them cheered our Finals victory at Veteran's Stadium in the city, too many even for our home arena, the Spectrum. Our fans were incredible. They were always there for us, and always pulled for us. They cheered when Dawkins used to cuss out a ref and applauded when Julius slammed home an electrifying dunk. It was a great time to be a Philadelphia fan. The Phillies were winning (they won the World Series in 1980 and played in another in '83), the Eagles were winning (they made the Super Bowl in '80), the Flyers were winning (making the Stanley Cup in '80, '85 and '87). But after our win in '83, we were the tops in town.

Yet, it was bittersweet for me. Now that we'd won, my three years with the 76ers were officially over. Somehow, I'd been in relative purgatory with nonguaranteed contracts, but I had made the most of it. I'd come out the other end all right. A champion, in fact. No one could take that away. Every time my number was called, I responded, even in the Finals. Though I wish it had been called more often, of course. Now that I'd established myself as a contributor in the league, my goal was next to earn a fully *guaranteed* contract on another squad. It would be easier said than done, though. Such was the life for journeymen.

Earlier during my third year, I remember one battle with big man Rick Mahorn. He was with Washington at the time, and we got into a game during garbage time. He was so big and nasty, I thought he was just out of jail! He looked at me and said, "If you score, I score. We got to earn some playing time!" We laughed at that one but we both knew in the back of our minds it was a dog-eat-dog league. Rick would later win a ring with the

Bad Boy Detroit Pistons. That's the thing, when you're in the league, all these giants become normal people. As a teammate of Dr. J's, I couldn't think of him as an idol of mine, either. I couldn't think about the posters. I had to be his peer. When I was a rookie, Coach Cunningham warned me about that. He said, "You are coming to compete for a job, don't be in awe of anyone."

What was great about Dr. J, though, was he was always available. I could ask him anything. Julius was always surrounded by fans. Everybody wanted to see him play. And people *always* asked things of him. Sometimes we'd be at the airport at 6 a.m. and fans would ask him for autographs. Yet, he was always courteous. So, I didn't want to be one of those guys tugging on his sleeve. I tried to give him his space and be respectful. He was in such demand. I remember we had to wait for him on the bus often because to move from the hotel to the team took him hours. Just to get through the throngs of fans. He was Michael Jordan before MJ. I remember one day in practice playing against Doc. He'd been hurt for a few games and was ready to come back. He'd missed a few practices, a few games and one day after a shootaround during my rookie year, he looked at me and said, "Come on, Rook."

Dr. J took me to one side of the court and, standing with the ball, he said, "Young fella, I'm going to go to the corner, put the ball between my legs, behind my back and dunk. Try to stop me." I hadn't been in the league at that point more than a cup of coffee, but I said, "Okay." True enough, Doc went down to the corner and did just what he said he was going to do. And *BOOM!* He dunked it on me. He could control his body with precision, even in the air. I played him better as the years went on, but he was just the best. He had one move, where he'd dribble drive and then hide the ball behind him as he came up towards you and the rim. All you saw was his chest coming at you.

But off the court, he was an open book. He led by example. He rarely yelled. Just a calm, cool, compassionate killer with his game. Dr. J noticed everything, too. His awareness was off the charts. He never let his teammates go astray. If he saw you talking to the wrong person, he'd say, "Come on, let's go," and pull your ass onto the bus. Julius was always dressed impeccably. He had the cleanest suits. He'd give Pat Riley a run for his Armani. He was a pro, whether speaking to the media or talking to fans. Always well-spoken, always kind. There was a certain air about him. He owned whatever room he was in.

After the '83 Finals victory, we took a trip to the White House on June 8 to meet President Reagan. We were all in suits, from Moses and Dr. J to Maurice Cheeks and Coach Cunningham. It was a nice, sunny day. The birds were chirping. We brought the Championship trophy and a signed basketball for the President, who shook each of our hands. "It's a real pleasure to play host to a team, a basketball family, that have come to symbolize America at its best," said the President. "You've given new meaning to the spirit of '76." I stood right behind Reagan and right next to Doc as the President spoke. "Thank you for a thrilling season," he told us.

To get to the White House, Andrew Toney and I took a limo! It was all style. I didn't let the President know I was still upset with all the taxes he was taking from my check, but maybe I'd have another chance next year. After all the formalities, the team partied some more. *What happens on the road stays on the road* was a common refrain. There was a parade for us in the city's downtown. Philly went crazy. As we rode down Broad Street, people were hanging out of windows, shouting, waving. They were starved for a basketball winner and we satisfied the craving. Now, whenever the '83 team gets back together for an anniversary, Philly still goes wild for us! But after the championship festivities were done, I had to figure out my future. The time had come. To do so, I leaned on Doc to help with my options. I was a free agent, and it didn't look like the 76ers were going to keep me, even though I wanted to stay with the team. So, I talked with Doc.

We were together in Detroit for an all-star charity game, and he told me, "You got to do what's best for you and your family, Earl." He was a star, but he was also supportive. I knew I was probably going to leave the 76ers, but Doc helped me put my best foot forward. He was my friend. That counted for a lot. Now at that time I had to face my greatest NBA nemesis: the right of first refusal.

Modern NBA fans don't know much about the right of first refusal. But let me tell you, it was a bullshit rule that almost ruined my career several times over. I had to negotiate it—or circumvent it—if I was going to join another NBA team. I knew I might even have to leave the country to get around it. In 1983, as I'd mentioned above, the 76ers were owned by Harold Katz. He'd purchased the team from Fitz Dixon in July 1981. Shortly after, we won the NBA title in '83. I always felt bad for Fitz for not being around for that. He'd always wanted a ring but had just missed out. Katz, who sold the team 15 years later in 1996, was pretty good to us as players. During the '83 season, we didn't have a team bus on the road because Katz had gotten us team Cadillacs, a dozen of them, three players to a car. But he must have spent all his money on rides because there wasn't any left over for my contract after '83. Most of the championship team, from Andrew Toney to Doc and Moses, stuck around for the '83–'84 season, and beyond. But not me. I had to fend for myself.

During my three years in Philly, I'd lived by the airport. A bunch of us did. My contract wasn't huge, so I wasn't like Doc or Moses, living in a nice place downtown. Instead, I stayed in a complex called The

Cobblestones with guys like Maurice Cheeks, Caldwell Jones, Franklin Edwards and Andrew Toney. Darryl Dawkins lived in New Jersey. Coming out of college, I had a sweet girlfriend for a while, Edith Rice, and we stayed together after I got to Philly. But once I was in the league, that didn't last long, unfortunately. I spent time with several gals over the years. Certainly not 20,000 like Wilt Chamberlain claims he did, but I had some suitors. I met another in Philly, and we spent some time together, but that eventually ended, too. When you're in the NBA, people tend to be around often, for better and for worse. They stand by the bus; they come to bars and restaurants. You have to be careful. But there wasn't any social media or cell phone pictures back then. It was an easier life. I sometimes feel bad for the NBA players now.

Now, though, I had to find new surroundings. New relationships. A new team! It's difficult to be a professional sometimes. But I owe a lot of my ability to be one to Dick Vitale. My journey to the pros really started with him. I'd grown at Robert Morris, for sure, but it was the program and the tools Vitale instilled in me during my redshirt year at the University of Detroit that really helped me to become an adult. He knew how to grow pros practically from scratch. He'd instituted a running program at U. of D., for example, making us run five miles a day, which helped make me become faster and helped me show out in 76ers camp during the mile race. Vitale had instilled in me mental toughness and a belief that I could make the NBA. That I belonged there. He always talked about life outside the game, how developing skills to be in the everyday world was crucial. He made me better.

That's what I leaned on in Philly to make an impact. Coach Cunningham built on that, too. Coach got me a membership at a nautilus club in Philly and told me to get stronger. I put on 20 pounds of muscle thanks to him. I spent a lot of time lifting. Between seasons in the NBA, I played in summer leagues. It wasn't like then it is now where rookies, right after they're drafted, are sent to Las Vegas to play. In the '80s, you had to make your own way and you were expected to handle it with maturity. I'd always come back in shape before camp. Not everyone else would be so lucky. In Detroit, I played in two summer leagues. One at St. Cecilia and another known as the Baker League, run by a guy named Sonny Hill. I won championships in those leagues during the summers. Sonny was a legend in town. He was one of the first Black sports broadcasters. He's still around today, too. I also ran, biked, swam—anything for an edge.

Thank goodness for the St. Cecilia gym. Today, I'm on the Board trying to revitalize it. Word has it the Pistons might even wear some retro jerseys honoring the place in an upcoming season. We don't want it to close. It's so important to me and the city. But not everything from that time in my life was so positive for me. Nope. Remember when I talked about all those rollercoaster rides? How my career has been full of them? Well, I was about to take another wild ride. Along with summer leagues being different in the '80s, so was the concept of free agency. I was a free agent after '83 and I wanted a better contract with the 76ers. I felt I'd earned it. But the negotiations didn't go like I'd wanted. My future with the 76ers quickly became more apparent—meaning I didn't have one—and I had to navigate the NBA's idiotic right of first refusal. It hurts my head to even talk about it now. And back then it took all my willpower not to let it drive me crazy.

The right of first refusal isn't a part of the NBA anymore, thank God. In a way, restricted free agency has taken its place in modern negotiating. But RFA is nowhere near as bad. Today, restricted free agency means a free agent (a player whose contract with a team has expired) can get a deal with another team. But the team he just played for has the right to "match" that offer and retain him. It's not quite as "free" as unrestricted free agency, in which a player can take any offer he's given, but it's nowhere near as awful as right of first refusal in the early '80s. (Free agency, it should be noted, came about in the NBA thanks to Oscar Robertson, who sued the league for the right to move teams in 1970. NBA players owe a debt to Oscar for that one. Rick Barry also had an important role, challenging the "reserve clause" in the '60s.)

With the right of first refusal, if another team wanted to sign me after our win in '83, the 76ers, who plainly didn't want me on their roster anymore, still had the right to demand compensation in return. Say, if the Detroit Pistons wanted to sign me outright, they'd have to pay me AND give the 76ers compensation for me—a player or a draft pick, or two. For someone like me who was a marginal backup, it was unlikely a new team would sign me, pay me and give up assets. Which meant I was stuck. Lost. Up a creek without a paddle. It's a rule that made no sense then and cost many people their careers and freedoms.

But I was determined to find a way out, even if the 76ers wouldn't help me. I would find another way. I was a champion, after all, and I knew that I wouldn't give up. But the question remained: How much further would I have to go? How many oceans would I have to cross to get what I wanted?

Memory Lane: Bob McAdoo

"Earl was playing on the front of Kareem, who was behind him. Kareem was probably the best, most talented center. Him and Moses Malone. But Kareem, once he got into his move for the skyhook, you should forget it! But Earl was so quick, he would get in front of him, butt-front him, and we couldn't get Kareem the ball half the time. Earl was aggressive with him, defensively. Kareem's main focus was Moses, but when they took Moses out, Earl would come in and he would do a hell of a job on Kareem.

"Earl was upbeat, energetic. That's just how he was. That's how he probably stayed in the league, at least in part. He wasn't a high draft pick like me. Earl had to battle for his job every year he was in the NBA because of that. Many third rounders don't make an NBA team. That shows you his resilience. We used to joke around—I tell him the only reason why they won in '83 after we won in '82 was because we got hurt. Most of our team was hurt! I got hurt. James Worthy got hurt. Norm Nixon got hurt. We had 50 points gone from our lineup with all the injuries we had. They swept us that year because we had all those injuries!"

6

What Now? Italy?!

I didn't want to leave Philadelphia. We'd just won a ring, the team was great, Doc and Moses were still foundational pieces. But somehow, I was the odd man out. Despite my performance, despite always being ready, it was my name placed squarely on the proverbial chopping block. No matter what I did, I was in limbo, at least for the time being. I tried to negotiate with the 76ers' owner, Harold Katz, but he wasn't budging. The team offered me a contract, but I didn't think it was the right amount of money. I didn't think it was fair for all I'd done to that point. They'd offered me a three-year deal for $125,000 the first year, $125,000 the second and $125,000 for the third, but that final amount would be deffered for three years to 1989. NBA careers are short, even at their best. So, to give up three prime years at below market value wasn't an option for me, especially as someone who wouldn't ever make the big, big bucks. So, I grit my teeth and I declined the team's proposal.

At the time, I was looking for a three- or four-year *guaranteed* deal with more salary than the 76ers were offering. Toward that aim, I'd been getting help from someone with experience in the NBA, a friend who'd become my de facto agent. I don't want to mention his name here, but he'd played in the NBA before taking a job on the collegiate sidelines. Sadly, this person turned out to be a horrible representative for me. He was also "helping" my former teammate, Terry Duerod. But we found out later the guy was stealing from both of us. We trusted the wrong guy. Back then, agents took 10 percent of your salary for negotiating your deal. But since players were often allocated into salary slots, I didn't think I needed an official agent. Boy, was I wrong. That's exactly what I needed. Live and learn.

Dr. J was known then as the "Six Million Dollar Man," because he'd signed a six-year, $6-million deal with Philly after leaving the Nets. Dr. J wore a number-6 jersey (same as the great Bill Russell) on the 76ers to commemorate that fact. Moses had signed a big deal, too. As for me, after I declined the team's paltry offer, I had to wait and see what would happen next. Maybe someone would sign me, maybe a team would give the

76ers what they wanted in the face of the right of first refusal. But the summer was going by fast, and nothing was happening. I hoped another team might try and snatch me up, but with each passing day that seemed less and less likely. I knew, however, that if I waited too long, there would be no options for me. And as a bench player, not joining a team for the '83–'84 year could be career suicide. In the NBA, it was "out of sight out of mind" all too quickly. I didn't want to hold out for the whole year without a team or league to play for. I'd heard the 76ers were asking for a first- *and* second-round pick for me as compensation. If that was the price, I knew I was doomed.

It was then, late in the summer, that I found a solution. I became aware of a loophole. I'd found out that if you left the United States for a year and played abroad, then your previous team would no longer keep your free agent rights and, thus, would no longer have the right of first refusal over you. You'd be a bona fide free agent. At the time, going overseas wasn't a popular option. Few did it. But it was a viable one for me to keep my career on track. Players weren't flocking to China, Greece or Italy in the mid–'80s, hardly anyone left to go overseas. But it seemed like the best path forward for me. As gung-ho as I'd been to make the NBA, I was feeling angry at the way I was being treated. I'd had to make the 76ers every season. I'd had to navigate nonguaranteed contracts. All that weighed on a person. I'd been constantly worried, overly stressed. If I'd gotten hurt in a serious way, even more than I had with my foot, I could have been up a creek without a paddle. I wanted more stability now that I was in my mid–20s. I deserved it.

So, I decided to leave America. I told myself that if I left and played well, I could come back and negotiate a fair contract a year later with another team. So, I resolved to do just that. With my de facto agent "helping" me, I negotiated a deal with a team in Pesaro, Italy. Scavolini. They'd come to my rep and offered a two-year deal worth about $500,000 total. A solid number. So, I went for it. But that's when things began to quickly get out of hand—cue up yet another rollercoaster ride. I took the offer back to the 76ers for one more last-ditch effort to re-sign with Philly. I told the team I thought I deserved better, but again Harold Katz didn't budge. I remember sitting in his office. He puffed a cigar, tore off a piece of paper and wrote his offer down to me, which I quickly declined. I told him I didn't want to leave and what I thought I was worth to the team. But he said he couldn't help. I told him the offer the team had given me wasn't acceptable. That I'd put a deal together to go to Italy. He didn't believe I'd leave the country, but I assured him I would. And I did.

Truth be told, it was a sad moment for me. I didn't want to leave my friends, my teammates, the city of Philadelphia. But when they say the

NBA is a business, they're not lying. Not only that, but I'd also be leaving America, the only country I've ever known. There was, of course, no internet. At best, you could reach people via phone. I didn't speak Italian. I was just 26 years old, and I'd never even been out of the country before. Remember my first plane ride from Detroit to Pittsburgh? Well, that would pale in comparison to the trip to another continent! It would be my first journey out of the country, and I didn't know anything about the place. But I did know that I was willing to fight for myself, fight for my rights and professional freedom. So, I made a bold move. I left everything behind. And I signed with Pesaro.

Gulp.

Before approaching Harold that final time, I'd taken a covert trip across the Atlantic to visit Pesaro and check out the lay of the land. Their season didn't start until September, but they'd asked me to come visit in July and I soon found out why. In July, Pesaro is idyllic. It's a beach town and when I went over to visit at the height of the warm weather, it was an oasis of sun, waves, vendors and bikinis. It was truly one of the most beautiful places I'd ever seen, and that fact made it that much easier to sign. What I didn't count on, however, was that wasn't what the area was like 12 months per year. So, when I flew back to start my life there in late August before the September season, the place was dead. A ghost town.

Thankfully, I wasn't alone. I'd been seeing a woman at the time named Diana. I'd met her while playing in Philly. When I told her about my upcoming move to Italy, she surprised me and volunteered to make the trip with me. It was sweet of her. She said she'd quit her job and join me. I was nervous because I didn't want to go to the place by myself. But Diana had said, "I'll go with you!" I said, "Really?" She nodded. So, we went, along with her pet poodle. It was good to have someone with me because as soon as I got to Italy, that's when things began to get out of hand. It turned out Diana wasn't the only familiar face I'd know in Pesaro. Duerod was also coming to play for the team. He'd left Boston where he'd won a championship in '81 but now he was without a team, like me. So, he and his wife came to Italy. That made me more at ease. For a little while, at least.

At the time, I wanted to make it clear to the team that Terry and I weren't a package deal. It was important for me to keep my independence. There were other Americans in the Italian leagues but few with the profile we had. There was at least one big name who'd tried Italy out before us, though. Detroit's Spencer Haywood, a gold medalist and former standout pro who'd also battled drugs and had been suspended from the Lakers during the '80 Finals. Later, he tested his luck in the Italian leagues. Spencer's rookie year in the ABA was 1969–'70. He'd made the all-star team that year. He'd later won a ring with the '79–'80 Lakers, even though he didn't finish the season with them. He was a five-time all-star (four in the NBA) and an eight-time 20-point-plus scorer (seven in the NBA). After his expulsion from the Lakers in '80, Spencer went to Italy before coming back to the NBA to play two more years with Washington before retiring. I think it helped that he was married then to the famous fashion model Iman. But they divorced in '87 and she got together with singer David Bowie a couple years later. Nevertheless, he was a role model for players and especially those from Detroit.

The summer Haywood retired from the NBA was the summer I went to Pesaro. Once I arrived over there, the team began to train. The season didn't start for a while. It was late August. I was in a different city, a different country, a different continent. Everything was different. I couldn't help but think about Philly and what I was missing back there. Located on the east coast of Italy in the northern part of the country not far from the city of San Marino on the Adriatic Sea, Pesaro has sandy beaches and blue skies and lots of umbrellas. It's a postcard town, especially in the summers. Picturesque. It was a far cry from the bustling City of Brotherly Love or the Motor City. But to be honest, I wasn't particularly thrilled to be there. Yet, since the pay was fair, I thought I could do it for a year and then get my NBA career back on track. It was my biggest gamble so far.

When I landed in Pesaro, it wasn't long until they took us up into the mountains outside town to begin practicing. We rode 10 hours in a van one afternoon to get there. In Italy, they liked to practice twice a day ahead of the season. The mornings were for conditioning—jump ropes, jumping over benches. In the afternoons, it was game work. It didn't make a ton of sense to me at the time, but I was okay to go along with it. Along with the number of practices, we had some exhibition games in those mountains. When we got there, every person in the crowd seemed to be looking at us, especially me and Terry. At first, I wondered, *Why are they looking at us?* I asked one of my teammates for an explanation, an American named Mike Sylvester who'd played at Dayton before making his way across the Atlantic to Italy. Mike was an Italian-American and nationalized Italian, so he didn't officially count as an American, for which they were only allowed two spots. (Me and Duerod were the team's two Americans.) I asked Mike what was going on. He responded, "They've never seen Black people before!"

Oh. In the first exhibition game, our Yugoslavian coach, Peter Skansi, ran a standard game. I got the sense he didn't like me much and that he'd have preferred to be coaching his own Yugoslavian players with the Pesaro team. He didn't want Americans, wasn't happy about the choices the Pesaro owners made for the roster. But here I was. Skill-wise, the Italian opposition had nothing on me. But my whole thing at the time was fitting in. I wanted to go overseas and play with the team, as a team. Get in, get out, and get back to the NBA. So, that first game, I scored about 15 points, grabbed about a dozen rebounds, and dished a few assists. I just kept the ball moving and shot when I knew I could make it. Just fit in. That was the gameplan.

But after that first contest, there was tumult. Italian leadership, at least in basketball, loves meetings. And everyone who ran Pesaro seemingly was in a meeting after that first game. I was on the outside looking in, but I could see them all there in a room, talking about me. I could hear my name over and over. I couldn't understand what they were saying, but I kept hearing "Cureton, Cureton, Cureton." Finally, I had to know what was going on. I found my translator and I sat down with leadership. I asked, "What's wrong?" Their reply to me was that I needed to be more aggressive on the court. Leadership said, through the translator, that they needed me to "take over." They wanted me to "carry" the Pesaro team. I'd been trying to play team ball and fit in, but if this is what they wanted, so be it. Right? I could do that. I had the talent.

After that meeting, I changed my whole attitude on the court, my whole approach. During our next exhibition game, I came out shooting. I mean it, I came out firing. I came out hot! I must have taken the first seven or eight shots in the game for our team. By the time the game was done, I'd scored nearly 40 points and wrangled in 20-plus rebounds. But our coach was fuming. Dude apparently couldn't make up his mind. He'd been in that big meeting, had heard the ownership tell me to take over, but when I did, he couldn't take it. He yelled at me, "You need to play as a team!" I'm looking at him, like, "Huh? What?" We got into a confrontation. I'm a bit ashamed to say it now, but I went a little crazy on him. Nothing physical at all, I just yelled and screamed at him. Here I was, killing it for him. After being told to do so. And he berated me for it. Were they trying to make me go crazy?

The American basketball player Jim Brewer was there, and he pulled me aside at some point during my heated exchange with Coach and said, "You're not in the U.S., brother. You'd better be careful!" But I wasn't hearing it. I was angry, fuming. Frustrated first to even be in that situation. I'd come to Italy just weeks prior, to fit in, to get around the NBA's right of first refusal, get a paycheck and play well. I was far from home. And already, I was in a bad place, fighting with my coach over some bullshit that he and the team's leadership had started. After my confrontation with Coach, he made another bad choice, in my eyes anyway, and went to the president of the team and told leadership that he was "afraid" to coach me. Mind you, Coach Skansi was *seven-feet tall*. He was no wallflower, no shrinking violet. But that's what he said. He said he *feared* me. More bullshit.

The president of Pesaro, however, liked me. He wanted me to stay. After my confrontation with Skansi, the team president wasn't ready to get rid of me. He wanted to keep me on and see how I responded. Maybe it was all a game to everyone. But it wasn't to me. The bad blood was unfortunately already in the air. After that tournament, we left the mountains and played a few more games. Skansi continued to dislike me and eventually he convinced the higher-ups that they had to get rid of me for good. They were set now on terminating my contract, voiding it. So, in need of help, I called my de facto agent for guidance back in the U.S. I told him what had happened. He reminded me that I had a guaranteed contract. He also, somehow, was able to help me track down a lawyer in Rome to help straighten things out.

When I went to play for Pesaro after leaving the 76ers, the press began to write about me often. I was on the cover of magazines and newspaper sports pages all over Italy. *Super Basket* had a picture of me, sweaty, shooting a ball, wearing my number-11 Scavolini jersey with the headline, "Incredible, the Strongest of All!" On another, the magazine had me, arms out, holding a basketball, big smile on my face. But now the papers and magazines were writing about me for the wrong reasons. My issues with Skansi were hitting the headlines and my life was that much more uncomfortable. I needed help from my new Roman lawyer. I knew no Italian; I was a foreigner in a foreign land with only Duerod and Diana (and her poodle) in my corner. But I managed to catch a train all the way from Pesaro to Rome to meet my lawyer, Enrique. He helped me fight for my contract. We had a plan for me to keep my head above water, and, with that, I went back to Pesaro, feeling a bit better.

But when I got back to town and to the team, they wanted me gone. Permanently. It was over. Yet, with every closed door, as they say, there is an open window. A bit of luck and serendipity found me in that moment. Thanks to all the magazine and newspaper headlines, both good and bad, my story had traveled through the Italian basketball channels in the country. With news that I was on the outs in Pesaro, another Italian team was ready to reach out and ask for my services. A new journey was set to begin. I got a call from a team in Milan. Olimpia Milano (later known as Simac and Philips, depending on the year's sponsor). They said that if my contract with Pesaro was actually terminated, I could come play for them. With my contract now officially *en route* to being voided, it meant I would need a new squad. I'd only been in Italy a month, or so, and already there were loop-di-loops. I told Milan I'd be open to meet and if that went well then, I'd be open to play for them.

Milan was night and day from Pesaro. Milan is a huge city, full of fashion, models and business. It wasn't a small town that closed nine months out of the year. The Milan team officials called me once my time with Pesaro was officially over, and they came to get me. Once the Milan officials and I met, we stayed up that whole night hammering out a contract and game details. Then I packed my clothes, Diana packed hers, and we were off (with her poodle). Duerod stayed with Pesaro. Diana, the dog and I took a train to Milan in the middle of the night. We headed for the big city. Good riddance, Pesaro! With Milan, I agreed to a one-year deal for about $225,000. It's all I'd wanted. Stability and kindness. I was back on track. If I'd found the Milan team from the beginning, I'd have been fine from the start. But that's how things go sometimes. Rollercoasters.

The best thing about Milan was that's where I first met Mike D'Antoni. Mike was a player on the team, one of its best. And Milan was also coached by American, Dan Peterson. It was helpful to work under an American who knew the way U.S. players worked. The team also boasted the future Hall of Famer Dino Meneghin, a 6'8" standout player from Italy. Today, he's in the Naismith Hall of Fame in the United States. I wasn't there, but when he was inducted, people said he mentioned my name in his speech. Dino was a tough guy. We went at it in practice. Some say he might have been a dirty player, but I thought he was just hard-nosed. On top of that, D'Antoni was a godsend. He helped me every time I needed it. By now, a month or two had passed and I had some stronger footing in Milan. I'd scrapped Pesaro for a better situation. *Maybe things here would turn out okay?* I had hope again.

D'Antoni was playing for Milan as an American. I filled out the second of two American roster slots. After my arrival, I was content. Things seemed to be going smoothly, especially when compared to my prior situation. Out of the gate, the Milan team went 6–0. I fit in like a hand in a glove. We played two games per week, and we were running through the league quickly. I was starting, playing well. I was again gracing the cover of basketball magazines in the country—for good reasons only this time. My name was all over Italy. And players like Dino were learning from me, which felt good. With my success in Milan, the guys over at Pesaro weren't looking so hot for getting rid of me. On top of it all, Mike was taking good care of me, translating when I needed it, introducing me to the best restaurants. I had to thank my lucky stars for him. But that's when another big change happened. One day, after practice, I went back to my apartment, and the phone rang.

I didn't know hardly anyone in Italy, and I'd just left Mike, so, I wondered, who the heck could this be? Who was calling? I picked up the phone and it was "Trader" Jack McCloskey, general manager for the Detroit Pistons. To this day, I have no idea how Jack got my phone number, but I'm glad he did. Over the phone he told me, "Earl, we've worked out a deal with

Philly. We want you to come home." Jack told me the Detroit Pistons were ready and willing to sign me to a four-year contract with the first three years guaranteed. The numbers equated to about $145,000 in the first year, $200,000 in the second, $210,000 in the third and about $225,000 in the final, nonguaranteed year. It was the NBA contract I'd wanted after leaving Philly. Trouble was, I was in Italy, doing well, playing, enjoying my life, meshing with Mike, Coach Peterson and the team. Yet, at the same time, I couldn't help but think: my plan had worked! I could get back to the NBA. That's when Jack added, "Here's the thing, we need you to leave Italy *right away.*"

The issue with Detroit was their first-round pick (No. 8 overall), Antoine Carr, the big man from Wichita State. He hadn't signed. Carr and the Pistons couldn't land an agreement. So, they needed me in a big way to fill the void. Carr and I are about the same height, similar build. He went on to have a great career in the NBA, even averaging 20 points one year with Sacramento. But his rookie season, he was at an impasse with the Pistons. Thankfully, I'd already purchased a round-trip ticket for me and Diana (and her poodle). So, I knew if I decided to head back to the NBA, we had quick transportation. The first thing I did after I hung up with Jack was call Mike. He'd played in the NBA for a few years before finding himself in Italy. Mike had played for the Kansas City Kings and the San Antonio Spurs, along with the St. Louis Spirits in the ABA. He was a good player, cerebral. A good guy, too. Happy to be in Europe.

I told him about the call, that they wanted me in Detroit. That the city was my home. I told him the contract figure, too. Mike responded, "You got to take the deal. You can't turn that deal down." He said he was surprised I was even in Italy, to begin with. He figured I shouldn't have even been there; that the NBA was my spot. When he told me that, I felt better about my instincts to leave Milan for Detroit and the NBA. I had no ill will toward them, but Detroit was where I'd always wanted to be. I had the chance to play for my hometown team! How many people can say that? What's funny is that after I made my decision to depart Milan, the open roster spot was soon filled by…. Antoine Carr. The basketball world can be small. A few years earlier, the Piston's Bill Laimbeer had also played in Italy, the year he was drafted, like Antoine, unable to land a deal with Cleveland. Maybe it *was* becoming a trend!

If I'd stayed in Italy, maybe I'd still be there today, some legendary player in the league like Kobe Bryant's dad, Jellybean, who was playing in the country with a young Kobe following him around, taking it all in. That's what Coach Peterson later said to me. He told me I'd missed my calling as an Italian star. But at the time, that wasn't what my heart wanted. I wanted to be back home in the U.S. and to play for my beloved

Pistons. Jack had told me the Pistons had worked out a deal with Philly to trade me for a couple of second round picks, which would later turn into Toney Mack and Stefano Rusconi. And they were aligned with the contract numbers I wanted. Though I had nothing against Milan, I had a feeling they wouldn't let me go easily. We were winning and I was a major reason why. Plus, they'd stuck their necks out to get me from Pesaro. But the NBA season had just started, and the Pistons were in dire need of a big man like me who could be a glue guy and defend all three frontcourt positions. If my career had come along in today's game, I would have been a standout stretch center, even more valuable now than I was then. But the Pistons didn't have to ask me twice!

I was ready to come back to the United States. I'd made up my mind. So, in the middle of the night, Diana and I loaded all our stuff (dog and all) and we left for the airport early in the morning. Milan, though, had gotten wind of my impending departure. And as we loaded the taxis with bags to head to the airport, the team followed us the whole way there, trying to stop me from leaving the country! Diana and I eventually made it to the airport, boarded the plane safely and flew back to Philly. When I got off the plane, I kissed the terminal floor.

I was in my mid–20s, negotiating an unsure future. I'd been scared my career wouldn't start back up in the NBA. I'd taken a major gamble. But it had all worked out. It was a miracle, really. I felt blessed. I kissed the floor, as if in a prayer. I was home. Little did I know, a couple of years later, Milan would sue me for breach of contract, and I'd have to see about paying them some tens of thousands of dollars for just getting out of Dodge! But that didn't matter now. Everything had been worth it.

Memory Lane: Dave Bing

"I met Earl when I came to the University of Detroit when the program was under Dick Vitale. I didn't know him when he was in high school but when he came to the university, my first impression of him was that he was a very athletic guy. He was six-foot-nine, and he added a dimension to the team that they didn't really have. The school had good players, but they didn't have big men like him.

"Earl could run, he could jump, and his focus was not so much as an offensive player but as a rebounder and a defensive player. That molded him into the kind of player that allowed him to have a long career in the NBA. Back then, the University of Detroit was an up-and-coming program because of the personality of Dick Vitale, who just had an unbelievable amount of energy. He was a little different. He was outgoing, outspoken and quite frankly he was loud! His focus was getting as many local players as he possibly could to play at the university.

"But Earl's impact, just his presence, is outstanding. His commitment later to the Pistons, his commitment to the city of Detroit, a lot of kids won't remember him because he wasn't a superstar but he's the kind of guy—you need guys like him. He's the glue. He makes everybody a little better around him. He does the dirty work. As far as the Pistons and the city, I don't know that anybody does a better job. He's all over the place these days! Everyone knows who Earl is. He's dependable. And he represents the Pistons and the city at a very high level.

"I'm not sure there's anybody in the organization who does better a lot of the things he does. I think Earl understands what he's been able to accomplish. I think he's the kind of guy, the kind of player that you can look at and appreciate because of all the hard work he does. So, I enjoy him as a person. I respected him as a player. There's not a whole bunch of people who can say they played on two championship teams. He's one of the very few who have done that."

Building the Bad Boys

Once I'd gotten to Detroit, I signed my veteran free agent deal with the Pistons as fast as I could. Officially, that was on November 12, 1983. Four years, three guaranteed. It was a dream come true. The deal marked my third contract in two months, counting Pesaro and Milan. But I'd made it back to the NBA. The season had already started for the Pistons. The team was about ten games in. I found out that the reason I was even in Detroit was due to the former assistant coach Chuck Daly. He'd saved me. He'd now taken over the head coaching job of the Pistons in '83–'84. A few years earlier, when Dick Vitale took over the team, the Pistons finished just 30–52 in his first season. The team followed that up 16–66 the next year, letting Vitale go after 12 games and bringing in Richie Adubato to coach. The next season, 1980–'81, Scotty Robertson took over, but the Pistons still finished 21–61. The team improved to 39–43 in '81–'82, then 37–45 the following year, also under Robertson. Daly took over in '83–'84 (after a half-season as the head coach in Cleveland in '81–'82) and that's when things really got going for Detroit. He was the right man for the job.

Isiah Thomas was the starting point guard for the Pistons. His rookie year had been the '81–'82 campaign, and he was immediately an all-star that year and would be one each season until 1993–'94, just before he retired. That's 12 years in a row as one of the best in the entire league. My first year on the Pistons, we had a strong lineup. Kent Benson, Lionel Hollins, Vinnie Johnson (who was in my draft class), Bill Laimbeer (who was also in my draft class), my old University of Detroit teammates (during my redshirt year) John Long and Terry Tyler, Kelly Tripucka and, of course, Isiah. Even with those players in tow, we overachieved. With Coach Daly leading the way, the team, which needed another big man, found me in Milan, and was now set.

Coach knew me from my Philly days. He'd seen what I could do off the bench as a nimble 230 pounder, knew I could run and that I could be trusted in the playoffs (and even in the Finals). I was young and he thought I still had room to grow on the court, both offensively and defensively. He was the one who'd driven me to the Phillies game to meet Fitz Dixon when I found out I'd first made the 76ers roster and now he'd brought me back in the NBA. If I'd have had a son born that year, I probably would have named him Chuck Daly Cureton.

John Long was the starting shooting guard for Detroit before stars like Joe Dumars came in and before Vinnie made a real name for himself. John had been with the team since 1978. As Detroit built itself into a stronger squad, the Pistons were known for a knock-down backcourt. They had a three-headed monster with Isiah, Vinnie and John (and later a four-headed one with Joe when he arrived in 1985). It was an embarrassment of riches to have such talent. John started for the team that season, too, but after he missed a game for the birth of a child, he lost his spot to Joe, not unlike the famous baseball situation with Wally Pipp and Lou Gehrig. But John's last year in his initial eight-year run with the team was also mine (he left for Indiana in '86). In the meantime, together, we helped build the backbone of the Bad Boys.

Later, though, because he was so valuable, Detroit brought him back in the middle of the '88–'89 season, and John was there to help win Detroit its first ring. Vinnie, Detroit's sixth man, would end up hitting a crazy last-second shot with 00.7 seconds left against Portland in the 1990 NBA Finals to cement the second of the Pistons' two championships. That's how good the team's guards were. But John, like all the others, was integral the whole way. He could have started for just about any other team in the NBA and shouldn't be forgotten to history.

Terry Tyler played for the Pistons for seven seasons, from 1978 to 1985. An undersized power forward, Terry would be a standout in today's game (he later participated in one of the first-ever dunk contests in 1986 when he was with Sacramento—something I always wished I could do). Terry was 6'7" and could play both forward positions. He averaged 11.6 points per game in his years with Detroit. But more than that, his presence, along with me, Duerod, John Long and Joe Kopicki, marked the coming together of many University of Detroit standouts. Most of the guys had been brought in by Vitale, which goes to show just how loyal a guy he's always been. He drafted so many of us, giving us our chance in the league—or, as in my case, at least making us believe we could make it. Later, Terry even played for Coach Bill Russell with the '87–'88 Sacramento Kings. Tyler was an iron man. He didn't miss games. He was what I call a "cookies and milk" guy. He did everything by the book. One of the nicest guys off the court, he was *fierce* on it. He made me better every day we played against one another.

I could see that the Pistons were building something—and the fans were loving it. The Pistons were first in attendance in the '83–'84 season. Laimbeer had been an all-star the year before in '82–'83, averaging

13.6 points and 12.1 rebounds per game. And the team had Isiah, who was already one of the best in the NBA. In Philly, I'd averaged about 13 minutes a game to go along with 4.3 points and 3.6 rebounds. In my first year with Detroit during that '83–'84 season, I played about the same, averaging 12.4 minutes in my 73 games to go along with just under four rebounds and just over two points a contest. These weren't stunning numbers, of course, but I was a dependable contributor, and a strong defender.

In the beginning of the season, I had to get back into NBA shape. That was my top priority, coming from Italy. The Italian league had been good, but nothing can prepare you for the NBA's pace and the strength it requires. I had to get back in NBA shape to solidify my spot in Detroit's rotation. I'd already missed games and camp. There was a pretty big learning curve. But when I arrived in the Motor City, I was surprised to hear Isiah already talking championships. With so many poor seasons in the team's recent past, I wasn't sure he knew what he was talking about. I'd seen what a championship required in Philly and Detroit wasn't there yet. No Dr. J, no Moses. Yet, the Pistons were working toward it. Isiah had won a college championship as a sophomore at Indiana University under Coach Bobby Knight during the 1980–'81 season. In fact, he had won just about every individual award that season, too. Now, with Detroit, he was bringing that same championship mettle and confidence to the squad.

Isiah was tough-minded and an all-universe talent. While Laimbeer wasn't a perennial all-star yet and Vinnie Johnson wasn't the prolific scorer known as "The Microwave" yet, the team was working toward something. In a few years, the Bad Boys would rule the NBA. But the team wasn't there (yet). The team did, however, have a winning attitude when I arrived. It began with Bill and Isiah. Both guys were very different, as people. But both had the same goal in mind. They were perfect for each other. Complementary. Laimbeer had been drafted the same year I was. Also like me, he'd already been through Italy (in his first pro season, '79–'80). He'd played in Cleveland in the '80–'81 season, and the following year was traded to the Pistons, where he blossomed into an all-star. He was a fierce competitor.

While the team didn't have high-flying talent (other than Isiah), we did have more drive than a NASCAR track. Looking back on it all today, I can see where the Bad Boy DNA came into focus. In a way, though, it cemented with Rick Mahorn. After Rick got to the team in '85–'86, he taught Bill how to really fight. Prior, Bill wouldn't retaliate when people got in his face. He was a hard-nose guy, but he didn't welcome mixing it up and didn't much know how to return the favor when he got it. But that all changed with Big Rick. But Mahorn didn't get to the Pistons from Washington, D.C., until my final year with the team. In between, we still had a long way to go.

What Bill was best at early on was baiting his opponents into dumb mistakes. He was a smart player. He'd always try to get his man to be ejected. He'd get under his skin. He'd trip you, pull you out of the air, knock you on your butt with a hard foul. And those tendencies only got stronger as Detroit evolved into the Bad Boys. Bill liked to push people's buttons (even those of some of his teammates). If he got in your head, it was over. He was an asshole that way. Bill wasn't a jumper, wasn't a runner. But he understood the game. Whatever advantage he could find, he'd take it. He and Isiah wanted to win by any means necessary. They were linked. At first, Bill wouldn't fight back if you got in his face. But after Rick got there later, he told him, "If you're not going to take care of yourself, then I'm not either. But if you take care of yourself, I got your back." Bill was 6'11" and 300 pounds. And with each passing day he became more and more of a Bad Boy, especially so thanks to Mahorn.

When I was there, Laimbeer and I had our run-ins in practice, but today I call him a pal. In my first year with the Pistons, we played in the highest-scoring game in NBA history, against the Denver Nuggets. It was December 13, 1983, and the final tally was 186–184. We won! The game went into triple overtime. The score was 38–34 after the first period, 74–74 at the half. It was 108–113 after three quarters, 145–145 after regulation. We each scored 14 in the first overtime, 12 in the second, and we eked out 15 points to Denver's 13 in the third OT. The box score was staggering. Isiah had 47 points, 17 assists and five rebounds. Bill had 17, 6 and 12. John Long had 41, 8 and 6. Kelly Tripucka had 35, 2 and 4. I scored 9 with 2 assists and 7 rebounds. Terry Tyler scored 18 points and Vinnie added 12 more. On the Denver side, star Kiki Vandeweghe notched 51 points, Alex English had 47 and Dan Issel had 28. It was good to come out on top.

In the locker room ahead of the games, there was always music. Often supplied by me. Albums like Prince's *Purple Rain* could be heard filling the catacombs of our arena. I used to put mixtapes together for a lot of the guys on the squad. Isiah liked to listen to music ahead of the games. Sometimes he'd lie down on the floor, just dribbling the basketball and listening. He'd go behind his head, around his back. He'd lock in with the songs, lifting his legs up and dribbling underneath them to warm up his fingers. The music could even let you know what kind of mood everyone was in, depending on what was playing on the speakers. Vinnie Johnson liked to sit in the locker room with his ginseng tea. That's what helped him come out ready to play.

Back then, cassettes were the preferred musical format. Everyone had a Walkman. I made mixes with all the latest stuff. One day, Chuck Daly found out that I was the team's de facto DJ and he brought that up in the huddle during a game. We were getting beat that day by Denver pretty bad and Chuck called a timeout. We were getting our asses kicked and Chuck looked at me. "Earl," he said. "What happened? You forget the music today?"

Isiah kept saying the team would win it all, and soon. In this way, Isiah was THE Bad Boy, the one that revved the team's engine. He was the spark to the whole bonfire. That positive, tough-minded encouragement from our leader and best player began to pay off. He could take over any game, but he also knew basketball is a team sport and he was better served getting his teammates involved as often as he could. With that, heading into our final game of the season, we were 49–32. Sadly, we lost in the final game of the season to the Atlanta Hawks 107–115, but had we won, it would have been the team's first 50-win season in something like forever. As it was, my first year with the team was the Pistons' first winning season in almost as long.

We finished second in the Central Division that season, a game back of the Milwaukee Bucks at 50–32. We'd made the playoffs, a first for the Pistons in years, matching up against the New York Knicks in the Eastern Conference round-one playoffs. That ended up being a hard-fought series. But sadly, we lost to the Knickerbockers 3–2 in five games. The Knicks' Bernard King torched us, scoring what seemed like 50 points per game—he even hit the series' ending shot on me in game-five at Detroit at Joe Louis Arena where we were playing because our home arena had been booked for a motocross event (officials obviously not thinking the Pistons would make the playoffs that year). That series loss was a blow. We'd lost game one by a single point. Had we taken that, there would never have been a game five. Isiah played well, notching 21 points and 11 assists. Laimbeer, too, grabbing rebound after rebound. But it wasn't enough.

It turns out the '83–'84 season was a notable one for the league, on the whole, too. During the all-star break, Isiah had won the MVP and Larry Nance, Sr., of the Phoenix Suns won the first-ever Slam Dunk contest. That year, David Stern also became the league's commissioner, replacing Larry O'Brien. By the time the season was over, Larry Bird had earned MVP for the regular season (his first of three in a row) as his Boston Celtics took home the Championship. Personally, though, I was just happy to be back in the league. And I knew the Pistons would be even stronger the following season, my second with the team. I knew, too, I'd be better with a full training camp with Detroit. I wouldn't be flying anywhere that summer, least of all to Italy. I'd been part of a valuable bench unit, along with players like David Thirdkill, Vinnie Johnson, Lionel Hollins. We called ourselves "The A-Team."

Let's take a second here to talk about David Stern. The man, along with Bird and Magic and, later, Michael Jordan, saved the NBA. It was his genius creating a revenue sharing system between the teams and players that began it. Lakers owner Jerry Buss said that without that move, the league would have folded. Stern also instituted a salary cap. He increased revenue and maintained players' free agent rights. He was a little like the NBA's Alexander Hamilton, making important decisions that solidified the undertaking on the fly but not haphazardly. He threaded a tight needle. Stern brought in the dunk contest to the NBA all-star game, borrowing it from the ABA. And he brought companies like Gatorade and American Airlines in to sponsor it. He also helped eradicate the NBA's drug problem, going so far as to reach out to law enforcement organizations in each NBA city to snuff out dealers selling their wares to players. He turned the league from a multi-million-dollar operation into a multi-*billion*-dollar one.

The following season, we finished the regular season with a 46–36 record, which was about as good as the season prior. What killed us was a 5–16 stretch in the middle of the year, spanning November 27 to January 11. Again, though, we were second in the Central Division, behind the Bucks, which had increased their win total to 59 with only 23 losses. Bird again won the league's MVP (his second). The season marked the first for Michael Jordan, who won Rookie of the Year. Isiah was the season's assist king. Bernard King won the scoring title and Moses Malone won the rebounding title. The Lakers won the league championship, defeating Boston in the '85 Finals. It seemed like the two were always in the championship round together. But the Pistons were getting closer, it felt. Isiah wouldn't let us take our eyes off the prize. The problem, though, for me, was that with each season, it felt like my

Earl doing the dirty work downlow, posting up Jay Vincent of the Dallas Mavericks

situation with Detroit was getting more precarious, more tenuous. I wore the number-23 jersey but wondered if I'd be turning in my jock sooner than later.

Our biggest rivals in the Eastern Conference were the Celtics. They had Kevin McHale and Robert Parish in the front court, along with Bird. The Bucks, another rival, had Terry Cummings. In my second year with Detroit, I played 81 games and started in one. I averaged more than 6 points and 5 rebounds to go along with 1 assist. I was also 19th in the league in offensive rebound rate. It's clear I wasn't a star, but I didn't belong at the end of anyone's bench, either. And though I'd played for four professional teams in my journey as a pro since leaving the University of Detroit, I was solidifying my place in the league. In my second year with the Pistons, the '84–'85 campaign, we matched up with the upstart New Jersey Nets in the first round of the playoffs. We swept those guys and then faced Boston in the Eastern Conference Semifinals. Boston, which beat us 4–2 then, went on to beat Philly 4–1 in the Eastern Conference Finals. The Celtics went on to lose to L.A. in the '85 Finals.

What was amazing about that Boston series loss, though, was one of our players, Dan Roundfield, at halftime during one of the games, took off his jersey and retired, leaving me to guard McHale. That was the end of Danny Roundfield. McHale was a tough guard for anyone, though. One game in March during the regular season he had 56 against us. I saw that game years later on a TV at Majerle's Sports Grill in Phoenix when Sari was about 11 years old. She said, "Dad, he's killing you!" We had to switch tables.

Speaking of my second year with Detroit, I remember an odd story. Odd stories can happen when you're on the road, and this was certainly one of them. We were out playing Utah in Salt Lake City during the regular season. Ahead of the game, after we got to the hotel, we all went to check into our respective rooms. I lugged by bags upstairs, I put my key in the door and opened it. That's when I saw a white girl in the bed. Naked as the day she was born. I could see that much, even though she hid under the sheets. So, what did I do? I turned my ass around and walked right out! I'd seen the room. It was clean, everything was made-up. Yet, here was this strange girl in bed.

When I told my teammates about it later, they joked, saying, "Why'd you leave, Earl?" "Go back in there!" But trust me, I was too scared to do anything other than dart out. I wondered if someone was setting me up? To this day, I don't know how she got in there, I don't know how the maids didn't notice her or shoo her from the room? Back then, NBA games were scheduled close together. She probably had been there the night before with another player from another team, and just decided to sleep-in past breakfast. But all I could muster when I saw her was, "What the hell?" So, I went back downstairs and told the people in the lobby, "There's someone in my room. I need another one."

Back at home, Diana and I were still together, even though that relationship was getting rocky. Mixing professional goals with personal ones can be tough. Every NBA player learns that along the way. On top of that, it's odd to play for your hometown team. It can be a big responsibility, along with a big honor. But the biggest thing to deal with was the ticket requests. I was thrilled to be home. To be playing with the durable Terry Tyler and high scoring guard John Long, along with Isiah, Bill and everyone else. It was unbelievable. And I tried to pay it back every home game by supplying friends and family with tickets. The requests were crazy, though. I had to get some 14 or 15 for people every night, folks who just assumed the tickets would be there for them. I had to scrape, at times. We were playing in the cavernous Silverdome and luckily there were tens of thousands of seats to fill—40,000, to be exact. So, I was almost always able to get enough. But it was a daily task. We had huge crowds there.

My third year in Detroit was my best season in the NBA to that point. I played in 80 games, starting 19. I averaged 8.6 points and 6.3 rebounds to go along with just under two assists per game and just under one block and one steal. I was top-20 in offensive rebounds for the '85–'86 year, hauling in 198 (about 2.5 per). I even notched my career high, scoring 25 points with 14 rebounds off the bench in a 129–113 win over the Denver Nuggets on January 17. That was a special year—Spencer Haywood had come to camp prior to the season and though he was at the end of his career and didn't make the final roster, it was fun to dream about having so many University of Detroit alums under one basketball roof. But that year, by the all-star game that season, I'd began to get a funny feeling. The Pistons were playing well—the team finished 46–36 that season—but it wasn't well enough for Coach Daly and Isiah, who was again the all-star game MVP.

We finished the year third in the Central Division that season, behind the Bucks and up-and-coming Atlanta Hawks, who had the high-flyer Dominique Wilkins and steady point guard, Doc Rivers. That '86 season, the Celtics finished as champions, winning with one of the best teams of all time, beating Houston and Twin Towers Hakeem Olajuwon and Ralph Sampson. The Pistons roster was solid and getting better. Vinnie Johnson was taking off, averaging about 14 points per game. The team had drafted future all-star (and, later, team general manager) Joe Dumars. Laimbeer led the league in rebounds at 13.1 and had just come off three straight all-star games. Isiah averaged about 21 points, becoming a league MVP candidate.

But the writing was on the wall for me when the Pistons acquired

Mahorn. I was feeling the pressure suddenly. An NBA roster can only include room for so many, especially so many at one position. The Pistons already had small forward Kelly Tripuka, who'd been a two-time all-star and who averaged 20 points per game in '85–'86. So, looking around, the team seemed to have a standout at every position but *mine* at power forward. If they were going to upgrade, it would likely be at my spot. I was now in my third year with the team, and in my last guaranteed one. In the playoffs that season, we matched up with our division rivals, the Hawks and lost 3–1. I'd averaged 9 points and 7.5 rebounds in 31.5 minutes per game. But for us, changes were unavoidable now. I just knew it. Even though I'd averaged the most minutes in my career in the playoffs that year, I was the odd man out.

In the off season, the Pistons drafted rookie Dennis Rodman, a small forward from a small school who could rebound and defend anyone, and John Salley, a big man nicknamed "The Spider" from Georgia Tech. Plus, they already had Mahorn. Time to call my travel agent.

The Pistons' scouts were some of the best in the league. Looking back at their championship rosters, they're comprised of guys you wouldn't expect to stand out and win multiple rings. Sure, there was Isiah from Indiana University. But Rodman had gone to Southeastern Oklahoma State University. Dumars was from McNeese State University. Vinnie Johnson was from Baylor—even getting Vinnie from Seattle for my old pal Greg Kelser was a coup. Mahorn was from Hampton. I was from the University of Detroit. The same could have been said for my 76ers squad, too. Back in Philly, Jack McMahon was tremendous. Dr. J had gone to UMass. Darryl Dawkins had been drafted out of high school. Andrew Toney had gone to Louisiana. Maurice Cheeks was from West Texas A&M University. McMahon said he'd seen me in college play against Sly Williams. That's how I got on his radar. This is the stuff that builds contenders.

The next year, ahead of the '86–'87 season, the Pistons also picked up high-scoring forward Adrian Dantley from Utah. And, well, they got rid of me in the process. Coach Daly had talked about the team needing a change after we'd lost again in the playoffs to the Hawks. After the draft that summer, the Pistons dealt me to Chicago for Sidney Green, a backup big man who'd had a good year with a bad Bulls team, averaging over 13 points and about 8 rebounds, but who seemed to have run his course with Chicago. I had mixed emotions about getting sent packing again. Here I was, leaving my hometown, a place I loved. But I was ready for new challenges, too. I was headed to play with maybe the best talent in the league in a young Michael Jordan and I'd be playing for Doug Collins, my old teammate with the 76ers. The Bulls wanted me, so that was a positive thing. But the problem was, in many ways, I was back where I'd started after leaving

Philly. My fourth year of my contract wasn't guaranteed. And if I played out the year without a new deal, I'd be staring straight at my old foe: the right of first refusal.

Memory Lane: Lionel Hollins

"My first impression of Earl when I was on the 76ers was that he was very athletic. My second impression was how hard he worked. Every day in practice, he would come in and I don't care if he was stretched or fresh, he was dunking everything in the layup line. Like, *Dang, this dude is getting after it!* When we played in Detroit, he was older, but he was still coming out and making an impression from the time he walked on the court.

"He wasn't much of a scorer except around the rim, though he had a little post-up game. Opponents had to keep him off the offensive glass and run with him. And he was a great weakside shot blocker. He could make the free-throw line jump-shot and he had a jump-hook in the paint. There's a lot of value to a guy who will embrace his role. Earl could sit for three quarters but if you needed him in the fourth, he would play as hard as if he'd started.

"It's not easy to get players to embrace their roles and stay ready to play. But Earl was that kind of a guy. Some guys become stars by playing roles, like Michael Cooper or A.C. Green. And as I got along in my career, Earl was still going out on the track and running. We'd play pickup games and we'd run. He would always get on me about staying after it. I think that's what I remember the most: that work ethic and drive."

8

Running from the Bulls

In the offseason, I worked out at the St. Cecilia gym. I got ready to go to Chicago. I wanted to put my best foot forward. To be frank, I was crushed to be leaving my hometown team in Detroit. But that was my career, that of a journeyman. I had to be able to move at a moment's notice, integrate into a new team and play my role well. While I didn't want the day to come, I could see it approaching. There were all-stars at every other position in Detroit, between Bill, Kelly, Joe and Isiah. Vinnie off the bench was a star, too. After they dealt me, the Pistons weren't done. They made more moves to solidify the power forward spot, from Dantley to Mark Aguirre (both big scorers, both former all-stars). The team was stocked at guard. They had maybe the best backcourt in basketball. So, the Pistons had to find the right front court to match. They tried Dan Roundfield. They tried Mahorn. They eventually landed on Rodman and Salley. They'd also tried Kent Benson, a former No. 1 pick. Veteran center James "Buddha" Edwards played an important role. In hindsight, the team made the right moves. They won rings in '89 and '90. Roster building is tough, and it was just hard to be on the outs.

But that's life and why you've always got to have a backup plan. I knew I'd helped Detroit get to their winning ways. Helped build the Bad Boys. Now, I had to do that in new surroundings. The '86–'87 Bulls were not the '90s Bulls. Along with Jordan, the best players included power forward Charles Oakley, who averaged 13.1 rebounds a game that year, and scoring guard John Paxson, to go along with several solid role guys. Coached by the emotional Doug Collins and run by the pressing Jerry Krause, the team finished 40–42 the year I played for them. That season, Jordan, gold chains, namesake sneakers and all, led the league in scoring at 37.1 points per game, his first of seven such seasons in a row and 10 total for his career. He also averaged nearly 3 steals, nearly 5 assists and more than 5 rebounds. If you wanted big numbers, he was your guy.

In our first game that year, which was against the New York Knicks in Madison Square Garden, Michael had 50 points, earning Coach Collins his first-ever coaching victory. Coach had been brought in to steward the team after the Bulls had let the curly-haired Stan Albeck go. In that first game, I was Chicago's second-leading scorer behind MJ, notching 17 points and grabbing 13 rebounds (including 9 offensive) to go along with one assist. I could get used to that!

I started the first game, wearing my number-25 jersey, along with Jordan and Oakley, who also had 17 points to go along with 8 rebounds. In fact, we needed every point that night. Our first game of the season— and Doug's first as coach—was closer than any of us would have liked. We would have lost it without some late game heroics from Michael. By the end of the game, with two minutes left, it was tied. Coach was soaking with sweat. He'd chewed his gum to a powder, staining his lips. Michael must have noticed how nervous he was and he reached out and handed Doug a cup of water. He told him, "Coach, take a drink of that water. Clean that stuff off your mouth. I'm not going to let you lose your first game." And Michael, as usual, was correct. That night, Jordan shot 15-for-31 and 20-for-22 from the free-throw line. He also had 6 rebounds, 4 steals, 3 assists and 3 blocks in his 41 minutes.

We ended up winning the game 108–103. Michael's 50 marked the single-game scoring record at MSG by an opponent. That was MJ. My new season with the Bulls was Michael's third with the team. He'd been an all-star in the prior two (despite injuring himself in his second campaign). The Bulls, after Jordan returned from his foot injury, had played the Celtics in the opening round of the '85–'86 playoffs. While the Celtics won the series, Mike made a major name for himself, scoring 63 points (then a record) on the parquet floor of the Boston Garden against Larry Bird. That's the night Larry said Mike played like "God disguised as Michael Jordan." Going into my time with Chicago, I'd heard all about Mike. There were grumblings in the league about him, how his star was shooting upwards at an all-time quick rate. It wasn't his fault. He was in the right place at the right time with the right big-time agent, David Falk.

Michael was in commercials, selling his "Air" Jordan shoes. Everything was jumping off for him. He was taking the league by storm. I was looking forward to playing with him. But I especially got along well with Oakley. He and I are friends to this day. I love Charles. He's a hard-nosed player, like me. And one thing I'll say about him, he hasn't changed since the day we met. He was no-nonsense then and he's no-nonsense now.

Oak and Doug would go at it in practice. Oak was a strong competitor. He worked his butt off. Michael was a strong competitor, too. Maybe the fiercest I've ever seen. In Chicago, during preseason, Coach Collins had us do the preseason mile run. He'd brought that over from Philly. It seemed wherever I went, thanks to my ties there, we started the year with the mile, which was fine by me since I was fast around a track. It wasn't nepotism that my older relationships gave me new opportunities, so much as trust that kept me in touch with guys from Philly. Trust is important in the NBA.

With the Bulls, Doug split up the team between bigs (Oak, Gene Banks, Dave Corzine, Brad Sellers) and guards (Paxson, Sedale Threatt, Steve Colter) for the mile run. The bigs had six minutes to make the mile and the guards five minutes and forty seconds. No one, not even Doug, knew how well I could speed around the track. I was ready. Jordan decided to run with the bigs. He said he wanted to "pace" us. I said, "Okay," to myself. I looked at Mike like he didn't know what he was in store for. When the whistle blew, we took off. Me and MJ were neck-and-neck for the first 12 laps, with four more to go. Mike said, "You better slow down." I said, "You better pick it up!" And then I put on the jets. I left him behind. After I won, Mike dropped his head and walked out of the practice facility that day. I knew I had him before we even began.

Michael is obviously one of the greatest players in history. But on that day, he knew I was pretty good, too. If nothing else, I showed him I could run. And that laid the groundwork for a solid relationship. In practice, Mike was great every day. Doug gave him the reigns. Doug was a great X's and O's coach. But he was also sensitive, as a person. We all have our blind spots, as people, and Doug's was sometimes interpersonal skills. He may have hidden behind Michael somewhat that year, using him as armor. Yet, we were happy to have Jordan as our team leader. He was *that* good. But as the season started, the local papers began writing how MJ didn't have any support on the team. They famously called us "Jordan and his Jordanaires." Once I saw that, I said, "Oh shit!" I knew I played too hard to be called that. Oak and Paxson, too. Seeing those headlines made me think the team was in store for a lot of change.

On November 17, 1986, *Sports Illustrated* wrote that Michael didn't "have another blue-chip player. The four players who start with Jordan— Oakley, Earl Cureton, Steve Colter and Granville Waiters—have a combined average of 33 points per game." The headlines and sports stories set off alarm bells when it came to my worries over the right of first refusal. But I knew I'd just put my head down and do my best.

At the time, I got myself a place in Highland Park. The team practiced in nearby Deerfield, Illinois. Over the early part of the season, I started most of the games. I was getting major minutes, which I loved, of course, playing multiple positions. In our first 10 games, we were 7–3. But after that, we dropped some. We lost six of our next seven. It was an up and down year, for the most part. One step forward, one step back. One of my most memorable highlights from that season was a dunk I had on New York Knicks center, Patrick Ewing. If you're a shot blocker, you're bound to get your fair share of blocks and your fair share of times getting dunked on. Patrick knows that as well as anyone. But in one game in Chicago against the Knicks, I stole an outlet pass from Ewing after he'd got the rebound.

Suddenly, there was a clear lane for me, just me and Patrick, with MJ trailing to my left. I decided to take it home. I drove hard, rose up and got Ewing. *Boom!* The big fella, in his blue Knicks uniform, could only fall back to the hardwood. You can find that baby on YouTube.

At first, Jordan led us that year by example. But as the season went on, he became more vocal in practices. Many might call him cutthroat. He was a businessman as much as a ball player, expanding on the mold Dr. J created as a high-flying pitch man. He held grudges—like against Magic and Isiah for freezing him out at the NBA all-star game in '85— as if his life depended on it. He didn't care much for peer acceptance. He was even commenting on personnel decisions the team made. The year I was on the Bulls, Brad Sellers was one of the new, big rookies. But MJ had wanted the team to pick Johnny Dawkins out of the college ranks. Jordan was unhappy with Sellers. Dawkins went 10th, Sellers 9th. And Dawkins did have the better career.

If Jordan was in a bad mood, everyone on the Bulls would know. In practice, he wanted to win everything. Mike would throw a tantrum if his team didn't win in the scrimmage. Doug sided with him every day. One example of that was on team picture day early on. Photographers came into practice to take photos of the team. It was a customary act. Eventually, Mike got tired of them being around and said, "Okay, that's it, that's enough. No more pictures!" Immediately, Doug shouted, "That's the last picture!" Then Oakley said, "Oh shit, I know whose team this is now!" We all just laughed. But there's truth in jest.

Michael played hard. Practices were brutal. He would go at this one guy, rookie Pete Myers. But Pete wouldn't back down. He was a fourth-round pick, No. 120 overall, a shooting guard like MJ. And Mike would just kill him. But every time Pete went down, he'd get right back up and stay in MJ's face. He was able to endure the whooping MJ put on him. I think it endeared him to Jordan, in the long run, how Pete never backed down. Mike liked those kinds of guys. (Though Pete left town after one year in Chicago.) Mike carried the squad on his back. Doug put the ball in his hands, did what Mike wanted him to do. In years later when Phil Jackson took over the Bulls, that would change. But so would the roster, which helped Mike and everyone else spread out the load of responsibility. When I was there, MJ did whatever it took to win. He scored 40, 50 points in games. After playing with Dr. J, it was a chance to see the future of the league.

Jordan would ask me about The Doctor. He wanted to know how he acted, what he could learn from him. I told him how professional Doc was, how he always came to play, how he worked. Then on January 17, Philly came into Chicago and Jordan could see Doc up close. Julius was getting up in age (in fact, this one was his last season in the NBA). I started that game against Philly. I played 25 minutes and scored 12 points with a couple of rebounds. But the real story was Dr. J vs. MJ. That's what everyone wanted to see. Michael went to work on him in the first half. He ended up with 47 points, 10 rebounds and six assists. But in the second half, Doc went at MJ, scoring on Jordan and doing his best to show the young buck that he still had gas left in the tank. *"Young fella, I ain't done yet!"* We won that night, 105–89. And Doc didn't finish with nearly as many points as MJ. But it was fun to see the proverbial torch passed.

Along with the team playing up and down, I was concerned with playing well, myself. Facing the last year in my nonguaranteed contract, I knew I had to play well enough to earn myself another deal at the end of the year—easier said than done. I was starting games, but then a few guys like Gene Banks got healthy and pushed me out of the rotation. I didn't help my chances when I got into a shouting match with Coach Collins. We bumped heads. To be honest, I don't even remember what it was about. I'm sure it was something stupid, probably would be something we would laugh at now. He started screaming something and, instead of just nodding, I said something smart back to him. I told him I was a veteran, and he couldn't talk to me that way. We got into it. He was likely under a lot of pressure to win since he had the best player in the world on his roster. I should probably have kept my mouth shut, but I was worried, facing the prospect of the right of first refusal. I was on edge.

My life with the Bulls started quickly to turn. I went from playing about 35 minutes a game, to playing much less. I'd landed in Chicago after the team traded Sidney Green to Detroit on August 21, 1986. Sidney had been the fifth player drafted overall in 1983 and the team had soured on him. What did that mean for me? I knew I couldn't afford to sit and slip into obscurity. In hindsight, maybe I should have relaxed, waited it out. Maybe I would have been on the team in the '90s and won all those rings with MJ, Scottie and Phil. But I knew I had to act with my short-term future in mind. I wasn't necessarily someone Michael would fight to keep. I never played cards with him. We were cool but not tight. Hell, the Bulls even traded his best friend, Charles Oakley, when it suited them. So, I knew I had to watch my back. I tried to be calculated with my career, which meant making decisions on the fly.

But one thing I had going for me throughout my career was positional flexibility. I could guard all three frontcourt positions. Most centers couldn't keep up with me, but I was strong enough to stay with them. And I could keep up with smaller guys and muscle them if I needed to. I had my advantages. I knew I could run, and I'd do so off a rebound, trying to beat my man down the floor every chance I could. While I couldn't always stay in front of world-class athletes like Dominique Wilkins, I could hold my own against most. I even blocked one of his shots, a feat that landed me on the front page of the sports section in Chicago. (But in another game that year, he hung 50-some points on me!)

The hardest thing for me to do, though, was hang with Coach Collins. There was one occasion when he put me in the game when the Bulls had the ball. But then Doug pulled me just as quick, before I even had a chance to run back on defense. I held my hands up as I walked back to the bench, like, "What was that all about?" He quickly started yelling and screaming. I sat back down. It made me think about when he was released by the 76ers. We'd played in just 12 games together. And after he was cut, I remember seeing him in the team shower, saying how Coach Cunningham "didn't have a heart." Maybe he was taking that out on me now. Maybe that's why I was here? It didn't seem likely, but the thought crossed my mind.

In the end, I think the issue was that Doug saw me as a young, happy-go-lucky guy, the same kid, the same rookie he'd encountered in Philly my first season. But when the Bulls acquired me, I was older, a veteran, and I didn't take shit from people. I'd grown up. And that maybe rubbed Doug the wrong way. The same thing had probably happened with Sidney Green. That's probably why the team had traded him out of town. Other players in my position might have figured out how to stay with the Bulls. Maybe I could have been the team's Robert Horry, a perennial winner. Perhaps, looking back on it, I might have hardware like Big Shot Bob. But it wasn't meant to be, in the end.

People throughout the NBA have always loved Doug. And I don't mean any real malice against him. I have no vendetta, either. I'm just telling it like it was for me. Doug was an Olympian who notoriously lost to a crooked Russian team in 1972 in one of the most controversial endings in basketball history. Later, he was a No. 1 pick, but his career was cut short by injuries. He was great in many ways, but he lacked the personality of a Chuck Daly, who was amazing with people. Later, Doug went on to coach Grant Hill in Detroit and Michael Jordan again in Washington. He remains an all-time NBA figure and fellow to many.

On January 10 against the Nets, I'd started the game, scoring 15 points in 26 minutes. We won that one 119–109. But compare that outcome to one a few weeks later on February 3, just two games before the all-star break. We played the Washington Bullets and my old friend Moses

Malone. I scored zero points in only 5 minutes. By February 11, 1987, after just 43 games, I was history with the Bulls, traded to the Los Angeles Clippers for a second round pick. Coach Collins, still just in his first year with the team, got his way, and I was gone. He'd been pissed off at me after our spat and must have told Krause to send me away—the worse the team the better. I'd heard I might have been sent to Utah for small forward Carey Scurry, who was at odds with Coach Frank Layden there. But in the end, it was the Clippers. I didn't like the idea of getting traded twice in one year. The optics of that weren't great. But so be it.

In some ways, I was surprised to be let go. Krause, the Bulls' general manger, liked me a lot. He said he wanted me in Chicago. But turnover was the name of the game. The team didn't want to waste a second of its star player, Jordan. So, they were constantly tinkering. And Krause loved to make moves. The more the merrier. I remember telling guys their numbers were probably going to be up soon, too. I told Sedale Threatt he was probably out, I told Oak and Elston Turner, too. Few would outlast the heavy hand of Jerry "Crumbs" Krause. In later years, MJ and Pippen and others would ride the diminutive Jerry hard. They didn't have much respect for him, starting with all the donut crumbs he'd have on his shirt. Jerry was good at his job, though. He found Scottie, Horace Grant and Toni Kukoc in obscure arenas. But now "Crumbs" was in my rearview mirror. I had to brush him off, too.

When I first got with the Bulls, Jerry told me about a college game he'd been at while scouting Norm Nixon. Krause was a scout for the Lakers then and, sure enough, Norm eventually landed in L.A. Jerry had a real eye for talent. But he was also an easy target to mock. I remember hearing stories about his being a ball boy in college, how the team would stuff him into ball bags. Even though he traded Oakley, Oak always had an affinity for him. When Jerry passed away, I was invited to his funeral. Sadly, I couldn't make it. But I wished I could have. I don't hold a grudge with him. I know that as Michael was ascending, he had to do what he had to do to make the team better. Ownership demanded it. That soon even meant getting rid of Doug, too. Live by the trade, die by the trade.

This article from *The Chicago Tribune* on February 11, 1987, talks about how I was dealt:

> *The other shoe finally dropped Wednesday night. In a much expected move, the Bulls traded Earl Cureton to the woeful Los Angeles Clippers for a 1989 draft choice.*
>
> *If Cureton makes the Clippers' roster next season, they will give the Bulls a second-round pick. If Cureton doesn't make it in Los Angeles, the Bulls will get a third-round pick.*
>
> *The trade ended a season of turmoil for Cureton, the 6-foot-9-inch, 215-pound*

forward who came to the Bulls before the season began from the Detroit Pistons in return for Sidney Green.

Jerry Krause, the Bulls' vice president for basketball operations, said: "We hated to part with Earl, but we feel the development of our young players like Charles Oakley, Brad Sellers and Mike Brown along with veterans Gene Banks and Dave Corzine gives us good front-line stability."

Cureton, who had thought he was used too little by the Bulls, started 36 of 43 games this season and had averaged 6.9 points and 5.3 rebounds in 25.7 minutes a game. He was shooting 46.7 percent from the field and 54.3 percent from the free-throw line. He joins the NBA's worst team. Going into Wednesday night's game, the Clippers had won seven and lost 39.

It's funny to read Krause touting the other forwards, all of whom he later got rid of! But thinking about my departure from Chicago to the Clippers, I was of two minds. In one sense, I knew I had to get out of Chicago to secure a new deal the following year. I couldn't end the final year of my contract not playing any meaningful minutes, trapped in Doug's doghouse. If so, I might have no chance to get a new contract with any team. But then again, going to the Clippers was like going to the NBA's version of Siberia. The squad was owned by a widely known jerk (Donald Sterling) and was awful on top of that. But that also meant I'd have a chance to play and, perhaps, a chance at a new deal. I had to take that change.

Memory Lane: Charles Oakley

"I met Earl back when we played for the Bulls. Back in '86. He'd played with Doug Collins in Philly. Earl was a hard-working guy from Detroit. He grew up in the inner-city, same as me. We got along real well. Matter of fact, the summer after we had played together, I came to his house in Detroit. We barbecued. We went to an open mic and were singing Alexander O'Neal's 'Fake.' We did a lot of stuff together. From there, meeting back then, we stayed in touch. We talk on the phone about the game, about Moses Malone, Dr. J, our favorite players from back in the day.

"Earl was just a guy who kept it grinding. He likes to tell a lot of stories. Back in Chicago, we just, you know, we had to get Mike the ball. *Get the ball and give it to Mike.* Being a power forward back then, we didn't bring the ball up. You had to get it to the best player on the team or the point guard. Nowadays Giannis brings it up, Anthony Davis. The game was low-scoring. Now it's a high-scoring game. Turnovers come with the territory. There have been a lot of rule changes in the past 10–15 years. Flagrant fouls, changed the hand-check.

"But I still remember fun times with Earl, acting like we could sing together. Pretending to be some artists that never got our contracts! Now, he's up in Detroit working with the Pistons, doing stuff for the kids. Every time I talk to him, he's like a yo-yo, going this way, going that. We even did a podcast together, *3 OGs*, with Muggsy Bogues. Talking about the new generation, the older generation. Yeah, Earl is a great guy. He'd give you the shirt off his back."

9

Sinking with the Clippers

There were 35 games left in the year for the Clippers when I arrived in L.A. and the team was by far the worst in the league. They'd won just eight games—total—by the time I got there, and, in the end, the Clippers would finish just 12–70 that season, practically the inverse of my time in Philly. Donald Sterling owned the team, and he was both a notorious slumland and an asshole. Why the NBA let him own a team for so long escapes me. Sterling would, a few decades later, be forced out after he was caught saying racist things about Black people on tape. Good riddance. For the 1986–'87 year, though, the team was in full swing as the worst in the league. Maybe Sterling liked it that way. Coached by former Celtic Don Chaney and run by the legendary player Elgin Baylor, the Clippers, which had relocated from San Diego to L.A. ahead of the '84–'85 year, were a laughingstock, I'm sorry to say. People always say professional sports is a business. I knew then, again, that it was. Sometimes a bad one.

While I wasn't enthusiastic to be playing for the Clippers, I knew at least that I'd get minutes on the court, which would help me get a new deal—or so I hoped. So long as I didn't have the stink of the Clippers on me permanently. It was a gamble.

The roster that year included big men Benoit Benjamin, who was injured but who also never seemed very passionate about the game, and Michael Cage, who was one of the league's best rebounders. That season, Cage averaged 15.7 points and 11.5 rebounds per game. I played center and he played power forward for the team. Mike and I were almost college teammates back in the day, too. He was going to come to the University of Detroit to play for Smokey Gaines, but Gaines took a job with San Diego State before that year started and Cage followed him there instead. Mike was a physical specimen, a nice guy with big, broad shoulders. Norm Nixon used to jokingly call him, "Body Beautiful." He had muscles for days. He also had a jerry curl. We would laugh when he went up against the Lakers and A.C. Green, a famously celibate frontcourt player with a legendary jerry curl of his own. Cage got boards every night. He was a star on a team that didn't have much else when I arrived there.

Larry Drew was a solid guard for us that year. And former Milwaukee Buck, Marques Johnson, was on the team, but he was injured and only played 10 games that season. Former Celtic standout Cedrick Maxwell was on the team too, but he was traded to Houston midway through the season. My old friend Norm was around the team. He'd been an all-star with the Clippers in '84–'85 after leaving the Lakers. But he was hurt with knee trouble. Mike Woodson was a solid guard on the roster. But other than him and Cage, who would later be a basketball broadcaster for the Oklahoma City Thunder, the team was thin and hurt. We had a bunch of decent players but no real stars, no one who could carry us night after night. Again, that meant minutes for me and a chance at earning a new deal in the face of the dreaded right of first refusal. For me, it was better to get playing time and stats on the Clippers than be buried on the bench with the Bulls. We didn't have a deep team, and that meant I'd even start some games.

In truth, the Clippers were one of the worst-run franchises in the NBA and they remained so for decades. The whole organization was bad, missing on draft picks and treating its players horribly. In fact, a *Bleacher Report* article from 2020 later summed up our '86–'87 roster: "From 1981–'82 through 1990–'91, the Clippers had 10 consecutive seasons with a winning percentage of 0.390 or worse. This was clearly their lowest point during that stretch, but this wasn't some calculated effort to get bad in order to get better. They were simply an embarrassment for an entire decade."

Oof. The way I tried to look at it was Coach Collins had done me a favor, whether he knew it or not, even if the Clippers situation was a sad one. To me, it didn't matter *where* I played, just as long as I was in the league contributing. Wearing jersey number 25, I knew I'd get minutes in L.A. And I did well, too, finishing 14th in the league offensive rebound rate that year and scoring my season high 23 points in an April 14 game against the Warriors. I also grabbed 18 rebounds in an April 7 game against the Rockets. My old team, the Pistons, finished with a 52–30 record, losing to the Celtics in the playoffs after that famous steal by Bird off Isiah (afterwards, sadly, there was an ugly uproar when Isiah and Rodman said Bird was only thought of as good because he was white). The Bulls got bounced in the first round. And the 76ers were enjoying a strong year with third-year player Charles Barkley. The "Round Mound of Rebound" came to the team ahead of the '84–'85 season, just a year after I'd left the squad, playing alongside Dr. J, defensive stalwart Maurice Cheeks, longtime veteran World B. Free, Andrew Toney and the crew. Chuck was a star in the making.

What made the Clippers situation even worse was that they shared a city with the "Showtime" Lakers. Not only were we horrible, but Magic was the MVP that season and the Lakers were champions in '87, again defeating the Celtics, who were without rookie Len Bias, who'd died after a drug overdose ahead of the season. Magic hit his now-famous "junior sky-hook" over the outstretched arms of the Celtics' frontline in that Finals series. Talk about standing in someone's shadow here in Los Angeles. After my first stint with the Clippers was mercifully finished, however, I was again a free agent. I'd averaged nearly 25 minutes a game along with 7.7 points and 6.4 rebounds in those final 35 contests. But now the four-year contract I'd signed with Detroit after leaving Milan was up. I vowed to stay in the league.

But other than that, I had no real idea what would happen. I didn't know what the Clippers would do. I couldn't guess what Donald Sterling or GM Elgin Baylor would have in store for the squad, let alone me, a new player on the roster. So, I went home to Detroit and sat, waiting for the summer off-season to hopefully bring some good news. The Clippers were now my sixth professional team in my career, following two college teams and five coaches in the NCAA. It had been quite a ride thus far and the rollercoaster showed no signs of slowing down. As my old friend, Dr. J, hung up his sneakers and retired from the 76ers and the NBA that summer, I was planning how I could try and stay in the league with new representation.

In the offseason, I made a switch, myself. I got a new agent. In Italy, after I'd signed with Scavolini, the team was supposed to send me a $25,000 signing bonus. But it had never arrived in my bank account. I'd argued with them, fought with them, asking them where my money was. Rather angrily, truth be told. It turns out, though, my old de facto agent, who was supposed to be representing me and taking care of my contracts and team-related finances, had pocketed the entire sum. Remember how I'd said he'd screwed me? Well, this was it. A thief, he'd also been taking money from Terry Duerod (who would later sue for it). I couldn't believe my rep would hurt me or Terry like that, but it just shows how someone you trust can turn out to be someone whom you should never have in the first place. It was sad, really. I moved on from him to a new agent, Bob Woolf, who was known then as a premiere agent, one who helped usher in the millionaire sports celebrity. He'd gone at it in the early days of the league with the likes of Red Auerbach. I was glad to have him on my side.

Back home in Detroit that summer, I waited and I waited some more. I went back home, as usual, to work out and prepare for the new season. I always trained like a madman in the summers, running mile after mile on the track (today, in my 60s, I walk mile after mile), lifting weights, playing in the terrific Motor City summer leagues. I'd swim, ride the bike. I'd go back and play against the Detroit basketball royalty, from Derrick Coleman to Rick Mahorn and more. Summer was my money-making time. I knew I had to start each year in the best shape possible to give me the best chance of making and staying on an NBA roster. In between seasons with the Clippers, I thought about staying in L.A., but I knew that was more the devil on my shoulder talking. L.A. was fun—glitz and glamour. But I knew I needed to work, which didn't jive with the festivities La-La Land had to offer. I was concerned where my next check was going to come from. That was priority number one through 100.

The summer was going by fast. Then, quickly, it ended. The season was starting any day and I had no contract. The right of first refusal had finally sunk me, I thought. The Clippers hadn't done anything one way or another with my contract. But then, at the last second in the 11th hour, the Clippers called near the end of training camp. Elgin Baylor, who'd once averaged 38.3 point per game in the '61–'62 season and was the league's all-star MVP in '58–'59 with the Minneapolis Lakers, said the Clippers wanted me to come back to the team with a 15 percent raise from my prior year's salary. I'd made it yet again! *By the skin of my teeth.* I was an integral part of the team and they decided to bring me back in just three days before the regular season. While I was hopeful, I knew the team would stink again.

The Clippers had Gene Shue to coach them now after firing the previous coach. Sadly, it would be another horrible campaign. Don Chaney couldn't help that the year before and now Shue and the rest of the team couldn't this new season, either. Yes, we only won 17 games in the 1987–'88 season—we had more losses, it seemed, than the Washington Generals against the Harlem Globetrotters.

The Lakers would go on to win their second ring in a row in '88, putting us to even more shame. They beat the Pistons, who finally broke through to the Finals (beating the Bulls to do it) and looked like they might beat L.A. But Isiah hurt his ankle in the series and the team couldn't keep up with Showtime. Ahead of the '88 Finals, good friends Isiah and Magic famously kissed each other on the cheek (later, Magic gave Isiah a forearm to the chest during a game). But at least I was back in the league, keeping my career headed forward. After I'd gotten the call from Elgin, I flew from Detroit to L.A. to sign my contract. I rented a condo near Cal State University in Dominguez Hills where we practiced, though I kept my permanent place in Detroit because I was moving around often and tried to feel at home.

With the team, Coach Shue gave me the plays, a whole loose-leaf folder of them and I started to study. I'd missed camp and was trying to cram. It can be hard to acclimate to a team without training camp, especially if there's a new head coach. I played 16 minutes in the opening game against Denver, which we lost by 36. And then in the next game, against the Portland Trailblazers, I started and played 39 of a possible 48 minutes, scoring 12 points and grabbing 11 rebounds. We lost by 25. I also started the next two games, one against the Utah Jazz, which we won 100–88, and one against the Lakers, which we lost by 29.

Against the Lakers, I matched up against my old on-court foe Kareem Abdul-Jabbar. When Coach Shue asked if I could start that one, I didn't know what to say to him. *"Sure?"* Our team was bad, and I was still getting my feet wet after missing all of training camp. But I couldn't say no to starting. Kareem destroyed us. We were just no-good. The only bright spot for our team that season was Michael Cage leading the NBA in rebounds at 13 per, beating out Charles Oakley by just a few boards. I helped him out with that one, boxing guys out so Mike could grab all the rebounds. We had a few good rookies too, including Reggie Williams out of Georgetown, a former high school player of the year from Baltimore who'd played in high school with Muggsy Bogues, David Wingate and Reggie Lewis. But we should have known the year would turn out badly in the early part of the season after Norm Nixon popped his achilleas and was out for the year. The funny thing was, despite all the issues, we had so many future standout pro coaches on the roster, from Mike Woodson to Roy White to Larry Drew. The one thing I learned for sure on that team, though, was the value of winning—since we did so little of it. I'd never lost so much on any pro team prior.

Coach Shue, who was no standout, had stopped an early practice to talk to us for about 15 minutes and when we started back up, Norm took two dribbles and collapsed to the floor, injured. I'll never forget that moment. I felt for my guy. I also remember another bad practice with Coach Shue. I'd had a less than desirable NBA breakup when I left Chicago with Doug Collins. Like I said, he'd tried to send me to Utah (an NBA outpost at that time) before landing me with the Clips. We'd gotten into a few shouting matches, unfortunately. Mostly, for me, they were born out of frustration. If Doug wasn't going to put me in games in Chicago, I knew I had to get out of there, because of the right of first refusal. I knew the less I played the smaller the chance I had to sign a new deal and those odds would be even slimmer if a team had to give the Bulls compensation for inking me. I had to survive, first and foremost. So, I was frustrated, and it boiled over at times between me and Coach Collins. Doug seemed to take it personally.

Frankly, Doug had a reputation of burning out with teams and players. During his coaching career, he only stuck with teams for a few years.

Now, when we see each other, it's "Twirl" this and "Twirl" that. It's all hugs. But back then, he was hard on me. I don't know if I represented something triggering for Coach Collins. Maybe because I'd arrived during his last season with Philly, he disliked me. Doug was a four-time all-star from the '75–'76 season (his second year in the league) through the '78–'79 year in Philadelphia. But bad ankles forced him out. He only played eight years, a former No. 1 pick in '73–'74. He was waived by Philly 12 games into my rookie year in '80–'81. That season he was there in training camp with us, but he couldn't get past his bum ankles. They'd hampered him throughout his career. In previous seasons he'd mustered 36 games in '79–'80, 47 the year before. His rookie season, he only played 25 games. After the team drafted Andrew Toney, Doug was out of their plans. After he twisted his ankle in '80, he just vanished from Philly. Lionel Hollins and Toney took his place.

In Chicago, I'd hoped we'd work together. But that wasn't the case. My first year with the Bulls was his first year, too. He lasted two more before Phil Jackson took over in Chicago with Krause's blessing. With the Clippers, I'd had a good relationship with Coach Chaney. But the team fired him after that season and brought in Shue. That's when the problems began again. Coach Shue and Coach Collins were buddies. Shue had coached Doug in Philly. So, when Shue took over in L.A., the two of them must have talked about me. That's the only reason I can think of why the Clippers took so long to offer me a deal before my second season with them. That and if they signed me, they owned a better pick to Chicago for the trade last year. Coach Chaney and I had never had a problem. But Coach Shue and I did. In practice, Shue went off on me. In went like this: during shootaround one morning, he blew the whistle to gather us together to tell us something. Just after the whistle blew, before I gathered with the team, I took one final quick shot. It's something that's happened in an NBA practice 10 billion times. But Shue went off on me for it. He said, "Earl, you don't know nothing! You been around a long time, and you don't know nothing!"

Everybody stopped and just looked at me. All I could say was, "Man, that's cold, coach." He said, "Yeah, it is. Because you don't know nothing!" Thinking about it now, the only thing I can come up with is that Doug had poisoned the well. Doug always seemed insecure, and he'd later bring that temperament to Detroit as a coach with the Pistons in the '90s and later with the Washington Wizards when Jordan hired him. But in that moment with Shue, it felt like he was trying to get me to start something, maybe he wanted an excuse to get me off the team. Was he picking a fight? Did he want me to retaliate? But I wouldn't take his bait. He had no reason otherwise to jump down my throat—not because of one quick shot after his whistle. I was one of the better big men on the team. I was solid for the Clippers, now an eight-year veteran. And he talked to me like a child. But since I never bit on his aggression, the season continued to play out. However, I knew I likely wasn't long for the Clippers. And that after the season, I knew I'd be in the same situation again as I had been so many times.

The Clippers were a bad organization. Some might even call them cursed. Sometimes we didn't even have enough healthy players to scrimmage in practice. Elgin, who is an all-time NBA great player, wasn't the savviest GM. He'd come to just some of the games, sitting with his wife in the stands. But he didn't make a big effort to know many of the players. I didn't see a lot of Sterling either. He'd sit courtside occasionally, but I never had interactions with him. When they say an organization works well from the top-down, then it's easy to understand why the Clippers weren't full sails ahead. Sterling hardly ever seemed to re-sign his veterans. I got a new deal, but it wasn't an especially lucrative one and it came at the 11th hour, probably when the team was desperate. Most of the time, Sterling let his big names walk. If you look at all the team's injuries, from Bill Walton to Blake Griffin, it's clear: the team was under a dark cloud. Ron Harper was injured, Norm Nixon and many more, too. Danny Ferry refused to play for the team and instead played overseas. Danny Manning left when he could.

Sure enough, after game 82, the season was done. No playoffs, of course. I'd signed a one-year contract with the Clippers for $265,000 and now that was over. So, what now? The story of the '87–'88 season for me was getting my contract and managing to keep my journey alive and stay in the NBA. That was like winning a ring for me at this stage in my career. I knew the Clippers weren't going to be the class of the NBA, the team never was. But to get a contract and some more stability was all I could ask for. That season, I played in 69 games, starting 11. I averaged about 4 points and 4 rebounds, along with an assist, half a steal and half a block in just 16 minutes. We were lightyears away from the playoffs or winning a ring. We'd missed the playoffs both years I was there. Now, the team was officially done with me. They were moving on. I was released officially on July 1, 1988. Over the past five seasons, I'd averaged about 20 minutes per game, along with 6 points and 5 rebounds. I was a veteran. I knew I deserved to stay in the league. But I was at yet another crossroads. That's when I got lucky. *Finally!*

That offseason, the NBA decided to mercifully do away with the right of first refusal. Suddenly, it was gone, no longer a factor in my or any other free agency decision. *Hallelujah!* I was now a bona fide free agent with no restrictions on where I could go. I could choose my path and not have to worry about a team offering any sort of compensation to my former squad.

I could decide my own fate now and forever. It was a miracle! That's when I got a solid contract offer from the new expansion team, the Charlotte Hornets. The team in the mid–Atlantic wanted me to come in and provide a veteran presence in the locker-room. But just to cover my bases, I took that offer back to the Clippers to see what they had to say, on the chance they wanted to match it or give me even more money to stay in town.

I brought it to Clippers assistant coach Don Casey. I'd had a good relationship with Don. I decided to be diplomatic with him. I told him about the offer, how the Hornets had offered me two years guaranteed along with an option for a third. I asked Don if the Clippers wanted to match it. Suddenly, Coach Shue jumped onto the phone line with us, talking shit. I thought it was just Don and me on the line. With that, I realized my Clippers tenure had probably been worse than I'd ever even known at the time. Needless to say, the team didn't match. So, I was gone. Good riddance. That summer, the Clippers drafted Manning, the University of Kansas star forward. I could again see the writing on the wall even clearer. It was my time to go. To move across the country again.

Thankfully, the Hornets wanted me and that was enough for me. The team was a new franchise in the NBA, part of the league's expansion that year, along with the Miami Heat. The following season, the NBA would usher in the Orlando Magic and Minnesota Timberwolves, too, increasing the number of teams in the growing league. The Hornets needed veteran players to fill out the roster and I fit the bill perfectly. So, with a new three-year (two of them guaranteed) contract, I was headed back to the East Coast. On July 18, 1988, I signed for $280,000 for the first year and I was set to go and play with the brand-new franchise, which included standouts like the small but mighty Muggsy Bogues, high-flying rookie Rex Chapman, sharpshooting Dell Curry, former Laker Kurt Rambis and more. I was grateful.

Memory Lane: Derrick Coleman

"When I first met Earl, he used to play at a gym that everyone used to go play at, St. Cecilia. You would have all these pro guys come in and play, from him to Isiah Thomas to Rick Mahorn. And the top college guys, also. But I was still in high school. My first impressions were that I was looking at this guy who was actually doing what I wanted to do. I was like, 'Man, I'm really playing against this guy!' So, I thought, 'I got to get where he's at. And how do I do that?'

"In Detroit, we're a very close-knit basketball community. We have a rich heritage here in the city. So, when anyone says 'Earl Cureton,' we all know who you're talking about. We know him from high school, from U. of D. And that's the great thing about playing basketball in the city of Detroit, being able to be around guys like Earl. But it wasn't just about the game of basketball. It was about the conversations afterwards. We'd sit outside the gym—and I'm like a fly on the wall, looking up to these pros, guys like Earl.

"They're giving us information and having real conversations with us. About basketball and about the meaning of life. Earl is like all of our big brother. He's a hard worker, relentless on both ends of the court. He always understood his role in the game. I've seen him go from starting to coming off the bench, but his demeanor, his intensity never changed. I remember one time I was playing against him and Isiah, and Isiah got to trash talking. We were going at it back and forth and I remember Earl telling Isiah, 'Hey man, D.C. is going to whoop your ass for real!' We all laugh about that one today.

"But Earl has always been this constant in all of our lives growing up, no matter what we were doing. We do food giveaways and he's always one of the first guys to be there and give back to his community. He's one of the first ones to do it big from Detroit. Earl is everything. Shit, he's a two-time champion. He's been a coach at all levels. He's a role model when you talk about basketball, one who we all followed growing up. Like, if Earl can do it, I can do it. And he's going to help us all do it, too."

10

The Sting of the Hornets

When I arrived in Charlotte, I got my customary jersey, number 25, and I was ready to go. As it would turn out, I'd tie for the league lead in games played that season, playing a full slate of 82. These days in the NBA, there is so much talk about "load management," and hardly anyone, from star to role player, ever competes in all 82. But I did it in 1988–'89 with the upstart Hornets. I scored 17 points and grabbed 12 rebounds, starting the contest against the San Antonio Spurs on February 25, 1989. A month prior, I'd hauled in a season high 17 rebounds against my old team the 76ers on January 16. I knew my role wasn't that of a star, but even in my limited time, I played well. I wanted to play well. The NBA keeps game stats, as well as stats tallied at "per 36 minutes." Had I been able to play that many minutes, there would have been several seasons in which I'd have averaged double-digit points and rebounds. But I knew my role and I was happy for it. I was happy to be in Charlotte, doing what the team needed.

One of the reasons I liked playing with the Hornets was my teammates. The squad felt like a family. We'd often go out to eat together, both at home and on the road. There were some legendary restaurants that players liked to go to back then around the NBA map, including the St. Elmo Steak House in Indianapolis and Ms. Perkins' Family Restaurant in Milwaukee. We often liked to eat at hole-in-the-wall places, not only because they had the best food, but because they treated us well, like human beings, not basketball machines. In Charlotte, I got a place for myself. But a lot of my teammates, including Muggsy, Rex and others, lived in the Strawberry Hill Apartments. In fact, they began to call themselves the Strawberry Hill Gang! They were tight, laughing together as much as they strategized and worried about NBA players like Bird, Magic, Isiah and Jordan.

Dell Curry was the first official Charlotte Hornet. He was taken with the team's first selection in the 1988 NBA expansion draft. That was the same draft Muggsy was taken, too. The two would become the backbone of the franchise for years. That same season, in March, Dell and his wife welcomed their firstborn into the world, Wardell Stephen Curry. If you're reading this book, chances are you know who he is by now. Only the greatest shooter of all time. But when I got to the Hornets some months later, Steph was just a baby. Rex Chapman, whom the team had taken with its first-ever collegiate draft pick, used to babysit little Steph, as well as Muggsy's daughter Brittney. Rex looked up to us veterans. Muggs and Dell and their families took care of him. He was still in his teens when he got to the team. They'd help Rex do his laundry, cook for him. I remembered Rex from a tournament in Detroit. He could really jump. He won a dunk contest in that tournament. I went hard at him in practice. I still have a photo of Rex coming off a screen and me laying my shoulder to his chest.

Muggsy and I became close friends, too. And we remain so to this day. For as long as I've known him, Muggsy has been there for me. I was at his wedding to his wife, Kim, too. We talked all the time. He's a generous guy; anything you need, within reason, Muggsy will help. He's truly one of the best friends a person can have. These days, we still talk several times a week. We love to argue. He's a detail-oriented guy and he remembers everything. And he hates to be wrong. Muggsy is also the most impressive player I've ever known. And as you know I've played with Doc and Jordan, Moses and Isiah. At 5'3" Muggsy is a marvel. He's the best athlete I ever played with—no lie. On top of that, he's a people person. I told him years ago he should go into community relations. He'll stop and talk with anyone and take a picture with them. When you go out to dinner with Muggs, it takes an hour to get from the car to the restaurant door because everyone wants to say hello. And he never declines a chat.

Today, anytime I talk to kids at a camp, I mention Muggsy. He's proof anyone can make the NBA. Not only that, he's proof anyone can thrive in the league. Truly, Muggsy Bogues should be in the Hall of Fame. Today. Make it happen, NBA! Not only was he a star as a professional, but he was also a standout in the ACC at Wake Forest and in high school at Dunbar in Baltimore. His team went undefeated for two years in a row! Comprised of Muggs, Reggie Williams, David Wingate and the late Reggie Lewis, the team was the best high school squad in history. That's a Hall of Fame resume. He's a one of one, too. What else could the Hall of Fame want?

The 1988 expansion Hornets were a tight knit unit that played in front of a fervent fan base. The Hornets, from their teal uniforms to their marketing plans, knew how to sell out an arena, even opening the inaugural season on November 4, 1988, with a black-tie affair and symphony orchestra. For years, even after I'd left Charlotte, the team sold out its nearly 24,000-seat arena, the Coliseum. Each year the Hornets drew close to a million ticket holders (tallying 949,858 in our inaugural season, to be exact). When I got there, the team was new, shiny and beloved. And all the players on it, including me, embraced that. The team had brought me in largely because the Hornets' head coach Dick Harter knew me from my Detroit days. Coach Harter, who was the head man for Charlotte in the team's first season, had been an assistant for the Pistons during my three seasons with the franchise. He knew I was a solid veteran and could bring stability to the expansion process. I was more than grateful. And it just goes to show you—be nice to those you encounter; you never know if they'll be able to help later in life.

My old team, the Pistons, finally won the title later that year in '89, sweeping the Los Angeles Lakers, who had beaten Detroit the season prior after Isiah hurt his ankle. I was happy for my friends, though a part of me wished I could have been there celebrating with the team in my former hometown. That year, the NBA also adopted the three-referee system to official games. No more pulled-thin, two-man teams. Bird missed all but six games that year with injuries. And 1988–'89 marked Kareem's last year in the NBA, too. With Doc gone after '87 and now Kareem hanging 'em up, the NBA was embarking on a new phase, marked also by the new clubs like the Hornets. But during the season itself, we were focused on trying to get the franchise off the ground. People often wonder where Charlotte got its name. For example, the 76ers moniker references American independence in 1776. The Pistons were named after the part of the engine that makes a car *go*. And the Clippers, formerly the Buffalo Braves, were named after boats in the San Diego harbors.

And the Hornets, owned by George Shinn, were named after something British General Cornwallis had said of the city. During the Revolutionary War, General Cornwallis had reported that Charlotte was "a hornet's nest of rebellion" after the Battle of Charlotte in 1780. It was a major reason the Good Guys won the war and secured the country's independence. The name stuck for its basketball team, some 200 years later. Previously, during the ABA days, Charlotte had the Carolina Cougars from 1969 to 1974. But they'd long gone defunct. Now, here *we* were, a Hornets nest of rebellion, wearing teal pinstripe jerseys, which quickly became some of the most popular in the league, along with team jackets.

Personally, I also had a Charlotte team scout Joe Ash to thank for landing with the Hornets and their fresh uniforms. Joe knew me from my Philadelphia days. He helped remove the dark cloud of the Bulls and Clippers from above my head by getting Charlotte to sign me. It's funny how these relationships can keep a career going. Someone you impress in one place gets a job in another and keeps in touch and later brings you in there. It's the lifeblood of a career, just as bad relationships can hurt one. Like I said, it's not nepotism; it's trust. Joe knew what kind of guy I was, what kind of talent I had. And nearly a decade later, Joe would be integral in bringing me to another team in Houston where I helped earn a second championship ring. (More on that later in the book.)

Coach Harter and Joe brought me to Charlotte. But just because Coach and I had a good relationship, doesn't mean everything went perfectly between us in the season. When the year started, I was a bit hobbled. In our opening game, I played only seven minutes. In that one, we lost by 40! Even though the fans cheered us on the whole time. The black-tie affair, which began with people taking limos to the game, didn't end how everyone had hoped. But it was a start. And the fans cheered us with a standing ovation when the game was over. Classy stuff. The team had some good players, too, including my former Pistons teammate Kelly Tripucka. We also had Muggsy, Dell, Kurt Rambis, Dave Hoppen, Tim Kempton and rookies Rex and Tom Tolbert. It was a fine roster, especially for an expansion team. Playing the entire season, I averaged 6.5 points, 6 rebounds, 1.6 assists and over half a steal and half a block. I was the second-leading rebounder on the team behind Rambis, same with blocked shots. And eighth in points per game.

Overall, I had a good year with Charlotte. I'd started it a bit injured, which brought my stats down. I probably should have not played in the first few weeks, but I had it in my head that I wanted to play all 82 games and show people I was both talented and durable. I had a pulled hamstring going into the regular season. But, later, I rattled off a number of games with double-doubles, maybe a dozen or more that season. Harter tried to get me to sit out the early games, to go on the injured list, but I declined. Looking back, I'm glad I did. It gave me the chance to play in the Coliseum's first game. In my career, I've helped to open several big-time arenas, from Detroit's Joe Louis Arena in 1979, to the Palace at Auburn Hills and Charlotte Coliseum. At the Palace, which is where the Pistons played after leaving the Silverdome, I'd played with the practice team that was put together to go against the Olympic team that season.

That was the last year the U.S.A. Olympic basketball team was comprised of non-professionals. Four years later the '92 Dream Team, made up of pros, not college players, would turn basketball into a global game. Coach Daly, who coached our practice team, had gotten me on the squad that summer and we played against college standouts like Dan Majerle, Danny Manning, J.R. Reid, Mitch Richmond, David Robinson, Hersey Hawkins and Charles Smith. They were coached by the stalwart John Thompson, but sadly that group didn't take home the gold, losing to the Soviet Union with Arvydas Sabonis and Sarunas Marciulionis.

After the year with Charlotte, the rollercoaster ride continued. Despite my good numbers, despite my three-year contract with two years guaranteed, despite my solid relationships, the team decided I wasn't a fit long-term. The Hornets' brass decided to get rid of me after just one season. I didn't understand why. I was still just 31 years old. I'd played well. Facing that fate, however, I could only joke about it. Muggsy and I laughed that the Hornets were talking the Boston Celtics path: going for mostly white guys. The team kept players like Richard Anderson, Stuart Gray (remember that name), Kelly Tripucka, Rex Chapman, Dave Hoppen, Kurt Rambis, Jerry Sichting to go along with Muggsy and Dell. It was a white out! Muggs and Dell didn't have it that much easier. In the Hornets' first year, Coach Harter was hard on everyone. He only lasted that first season before being replaced by Gene Littles. When I ran into Coach Harter some years later, when I was with Houston, he saw me before a game and apologized to me for how my quick Charlotte tenure tuned out, what the team did to me.

In truth, Harter was a legend with that team—often for all the wrong reasons. Muggs, Dell and I still laugh about it. Harter especially detested Muggsy. He just didn't understand how a 5'3" guard could be effective, which Muggsy was throughout his career. Harter famously walked into the team owner's office one day and got down on his knees, pretending to be Muggsy, making fun of him, trying to tell the owner, "This is Muggsy trying to guard Patrick Ewing!" He hated Muggs, thought he was too small to succeed. He wanted to trade him and Dell, which, in hindsight, would have been a huge mistake. Harter wasn't a bad guy. He just made mistakes. We're all guilty of that. It's just that his mistakes were *loud*.

Harter tried to trade Dell halfway through the year, too. Dell later became the longest tenured Hornet and one of the best shooters in NBA history. Now he's a team television broadcaster. But there was one game Harter took on nearly every player in the locker room at halftime, going down the line, telling us all how we all weren't shit. "Muggsy," he said, "let's face it. You're too little." Then he turned to Dell, who had already played for Utah and Cleveland. "Dell, you've been in the league for three years on three teams. What does that tell you? Who wants you?" He got to Tim Kempton. "Tim," Harter said. "Ah, *fuck* you!" He said to Dave Hoppen, "I want to hire a guy with a baseball bat to chase you around the arena to make you tougher!"

Then he got to Kurt Rambis. Kurt had gotten hurt earlier in the season, busted up his ankle. Mind you, Kurt was a warrior, a real competitor, almost always bloody from something game-related. And before that particular road trip, Kurt stayed back in Charlotte to get some extra treatment. He flew out and met us at the game to play. But even in that one, he wasn't faring well. So, Dick laid into him during the halftime. "Kurt!" he said. "Why the fuck you come, Kurt? You should have stayed home!" I was actually one of the few Harter didn't lay into then, for whatever reason. I guess Dick liked me for at least part of the year. He was a hard-nose guy, a drill sergeant, and maybe he liked the way I played here and there. If you were soft or weak in his mind, he attacked you. So, I narrowly avoided his ire. But to this day, we laugh about Harter's rant every time guys from that year get together. Whenever we see Kurt, we say, "Kurt! Why the fuck you come, Kurt?"

That was the first ever Hornets team, 1988. Needless to say, we didn't finish with a particularly outstanding record that season, ending it at just 20–62. But 20 wins isn't awful for year-one of a new team. It was respectable, about the same number I'd won with the Clippers in *two* years. We didn't win, but the city opened their arms for us. Everyone on that team got along. Many of us are close to this day. And the fans were unbelievable. They had a parade for us once the year was over and we'd only won those 20 games! Our photos were all over town and everyone wore our pinstripe teal jerseys. It was some of the hottest merchandise in the entire NBA. It was a wonderful year. But sadly, I wouldn't be there for a follow-up. I'd have preferred to stay with the team—in a way, it felt like a second home. It was an unusual expansion team. Aside from Harter's locker-room tirades, the team was happy. I could have ended my career there if I'd had my druthers. Muggsy, Rex, Dell and the guys were people I not only got along with on the court and in practice, but they were also people I could spend Thanksgiving with.

But the hand of fate moved again, and I wasn't in the team's long-term plans. When Harter called me into his office to tell me the news, or to at least to try to, I was prepared. I was a nine-year veteran by now. Harter was sitting down, along with executive Carl Scheer. They told me they'd decided they were going to let me go, but that they'd found a team in Italy for me. This surprised me because I still had a guaranteed contract for the next season with Charlotte. But, a veteran, I was used to this sort of thing. I sat there and listened to them. I knew if I left the NBA and went to the team in Italy that they'd arranged, I couldn't make any more money, that my contract would transfer over dollar-for-dollar. So, I had no incentive to go with the plan they'd laid out. And I took their suggestion as nothing but an insult.

When they were finished trying to get me to go overseas with the team they'd lined up, I stood up and said, "Look, you have my address. On the first and fifteenth of the month, send me my fucking check. I don't need an agent, I already got one. And by the way, Dick, you're going to be fired by the all-star break next season." I was right, too. The next year, '89–'90, Harter was gone after 40 games, replaced by Gene Littles, who liked a more up-tempo game, which suited Muggsy and Dell. Harter and Scheer were frozen when I stood up and declined their proposal. I walked out, cursing them under my breath.

Then, a few steps down the hallway, I turned back. Harter called to me, "We don't know what we're going to do. We'll let you know." The next morning, the team released me.

Memory Lane: Muggsy Bogues

"I met Earl in 1988 when we first came to Charlotte. Of course, I'd played against him in '87 but '88 was when I got to know him. We were a mixed team, young guys mixed in with veterans. I gravitated to Earl because of the way he worked, his work ethic. The way he applied himself. He wasn't known as a big-name player but Earl, just his knowledge and his understanding of the game, he brought a lot to the table. He gave us that big man inside presence that we needed, especially in terms of athleticism.

"He rebounded well. He blocked shots. And I always told him, 'You better not let me beat you down the court!' Because of his athleticism, he could beat his man up and down the court easily, knowing that could put such pressure on their defense. He caught a lot of my passes for scores. Earl played a big role, especially having already had the experience of winning a championship with Philly. He came in and mentored guys, especially the young guys we had.

"Earl and I pretty much talk every day now. He's always been supportive of me—he came to my wedding back in 1989! He's a funny guy with a lot of stories to tell. Just seeing a guy like that who never quits regardless of what he's going through, I love how he always finds his way to continue to work to get back on top. We all have ups and downs but when he went through his, he worked his way through and kept his sanity. Everybody respects Earl—or should I say, 'Big Twirl!'"

11

Back to Italy?

Before signing with Charlotte, I told myself I'd never leave the country again to play overseas. Well, never say never, right? It's possible that, upon getting my release from the Hornets after just one year, if I had been patient or stuck around the States, I could have landed back with the Pistons or another team. Hey, they'd brought John Long back after a hiatus, so why not me? And I knew I could still play in the NBA and perform well. I'd just proven that with Charlotte in 82 games not long ago. I was a veteran, about to enter my 10th year, a solid rebounder and defender. I could score a little bit, too. There was word maybe the expansion Orlando Magic would want me for their own inaugural season. They were set to enter the league with the Minnesota Timberwolves. But I wasn't sure of my best path forward.

Not wanting to be left behind, however, I decided to be proactive and examine my options, which included crossing the Atlantic Ocean again. I contemplated it as much as I could, but I also knew that I needed to act quickly. The professional basketball clock ticks fast. As if in the waning seconds of a possession, I knew I had to make a move with the ball. So, that led my mind back to Milan. While the Hornets were happy to get rid of me, teams in Italy were knocking down my door to sign me again. My name still rung out there like the chiming Liberty Bell. So, at the end of the day, I thought, maybe it was a good time for me to just get away and play where I knew I could succeed on the court.

At that time, however, I had even more on my mind than basket-ball. Diana and I were officially splitting up. When it rains, it pours, right? Unfortunately, the relationship didn't remain strong through the seasons. We'd stayed together for a handful of years, even getting married for a couple of them. But with my role, scratching and clawing to stay in the NBA, I didn't have all the time or attention a partner truly deserved. Diana was supportive, it wasn't her fault. She'd quit her job to fly with me to Italy (poodle in tow). We stayed together for five years, or so, through Detroit, Chicago and the Clippers. But life isn't a storybook. Sadly, we chose to part ways. Our failure together was just that: ours. It takes two to tango.

I take a lot of blame and responsibility for it not working out. My world didn't have room for things outside of trying to make the league at the time. When we'd gotten hitched, other friends of mine were getting married, too, including Terry Duerod. I thought marriage would be good for me, but it wasn't right for either of us in the end. So, Diana and I split up. Sometimes these things just don't work the way you plan. No hard feelings. That's life. Thankfully, a few years later, I'd meet another very special woman, Judith Pickop, with whom I'm still together to this day after 25 years. We have a daughter together, who is a star graduate student at Georgetown, getting her masters in conflict resolution. But that's a story for later!

But now, I was leaving the country again. Single and unsure of the future in basically all respects of my life. To be frank, I was feeling a bit messed up in my head. I'd been navigating so much and there was seemingly no relief. The light at the end of the tunnel always stayed at the *end* of the tunnel. I'd been expecting to come back to Charlotte, to stay with my friends on a growing team, but now that lifeline was cut off. On top of that, my personal life was going down the toilet. *Milan*, I thought, *here we come!* Yeesh.

But there was still the matter of the lawsuit with the team for my breach of contract several years ago after I'd left Milan to go to Detroit in '83. The team had sent a lawsuit to me a few years into my tenure with the Pistons. They said I owed them $30,000. So, I did what I had to do, and I'd paid them to free myself from the worry. Now, though, as I was heading back to Italy, I had to address it again (and try to get that money back). As I was figuring out my reentry

Earl and Judith in Los Angeles in 2020, celebrating the holidays together, comfortable and in love.

into Italy, a few teams were after me. Milan, yes, but also a team in Bologna. I had options. Milan was familiar, so they were in the lead. And if I could get the $30,000 back that I'd had to pay, then all the better. Funny how life can come full-circle and then full-circle again.

In the end, Milan offered me a two-year deal to play there, which included getting the $30,000 back. So, I took it. I'd decided against going to Bologna. It's a wonderful place with cured meat hanging in every window and the team was solid, but they were also in a lower division. So, I'd finish out the '80s and ring in the '90s in Milan. In *Italia*. But I wouldn't be the only American there. The legendary former NBA star Bob McAdoo was on the team now, too. He was a two-time NBA champion with the Lakers, a three-time scoring champion in the league. Bob had averaged 34.5 points in '74–'75 with Buffalo Braves, winning the MVP that season. In Italy, we'd play backgammon or go to clubs together. Dino Meneghin was on the team still, too. As was my good buddy, Mike D'Antoni, who was by now nationalized as an Italian player and who I loved as a friend. All these guys were in or around their 40s, though. McAdoo had played on the team for three years already and was set to play a few more. I was only 32, still in my prime.

As I headed back to Italy, I thought how accurate my nickname was. "The Twirl." Seemingly in a never-ending spin cycle. When I signed my contract with Milan, the news made *The New York Times* on November 12, 1989. The newspaper wrote, "EARL CURETON, a veteran of five National Basketball Association teams, signed yesterday with Philips Milan, the champion Italian club he left in 1983. Cureton, who played six games for Philips Milan in 1983 before breaking his contract and returning to the N.B.A., will reportedly be paid $300,000, with an option for another year."

The Milan team was (and is still) in Lega Basket A, which is the premiere basketball league in the country. Today, there are 16 teams in the league (and, as a matter of fact, Milan was the recent 2021–2022 champion). The team boasts the most titles in the league with 29. The league was founded in 1970 and is part of FIBA Europe. It was a good league, though it was no NBA. None of the teams would have come close to the Pistons that year, the team that won the '90 NBA championship against Clyde Drexler, Terry Porter and the Portland Trailblazers, to earn their second ring in as many seasons. Seeing my friends win it again, I thought about how I could have been out there celebrating with them. But life works in mysterious ways.

In Italy, my time with Milan didn't go as swimmingly as it did during my prior stint, short as it was. I played the entire '89–'90 season there, but I was hampered by tendonitis in my knees. For those who don't know what tendonitis is intimately, it's a tricky situation. Like a hampered hamstring, you can still play with tendonitis, can still get on the court, and look okay. You resemble yourself, but you can only play about half as well. Tendonitis will make you look lazy some of the time, too. It was the first time I had a major injury. And I hated having to deal with it, hated not being able to play at top form for my team.

I'd started to feel the tendonitis in my knees the year before when I was with the Hornets. Despite it, I was second on Charlotte in rebounds and blocked shots. In Italy, though, it was significantly worse, and very much still bothering me. It made me feel like an old guy, even though I was still in my prime. The old guys on the team were Bob McAdoo and Mike D'Antoni, both nearing middle age. Dino Meneghin was even older than they. Dino was in his last year with Milan, the team he'd played on for a decade since 1980. And because all of Milan's stars were aging and toward the end of their careers, the franchise looked to me to carry it day to day. But thanks to the tendonitis, that didn't go as planned. On February 6, 1990, *The Orlando Sentinel* even quoted sports agent, Bill Pollak, who had a number of clients overseas, as saying that I hadn't "done the job" in Milan. Even people I didn't know were taking shots at me!

As a result, of course, Milan wasn't happy with what I was doing for them on the court. I wanted to assure them that I wasn't either. But it's not good to blame injuries. Especially back then. No one believed you. And tendonitis isn't noticeable from the outside—not like a broken bone jutting through your skin. There's no obvious visible sign of it. It's just deep soreness. So, Milan pointed the finger at me (they weren't going to blame McAdoo, Mike or Dino). This was irksome, for sure. I couldn't pick up the slack they needed me to. I'd signed a two-year deal, choosing Milan even though rumors were that I could maybe have played for the expansion Magic or for the lower division Bologna team. I had to grit my teeth and take it. To make matters worse, we also had a new coach, a former assistant for Dan Peterson. It was surreal. Even though everything *looked* the same, everything felt much different.

McAdoo was someone who helped me on my journey overseas. It was invaluable spending time with Bob. What a truly great guy and an incredible human being. For me to have the opportunity to chat with him was tremendous. I've played with a lot of star players in my career, but Bob is right up there to this day. He's a Hall of Famer, a former NBA scoring champ and MVP. In Milan, as we rode busses from game to game, we talked about the old 76ers and Lakers rivalries. He'd won with L.A. in '82 and lost to our Philly team the next season. And he'd won again with the Lakers in '85. He even played for Philly in the '85–'86 season after I'd left. He'd averaged some 10 points a game that season and, the next year, he took his talents to Italy, where he played for a whopping seven seasons total, much to the joy of many Italian basketball fans, before hanging up his sneakers finally in 1993.

I remember watching him with the Knicks when I was in college at Robert Morris. He was a beast, regularly notching 20 point and 20 rebound games. He'd go at "Pistol" Pete Maravich in some epic battles. I loved those Knicks teams. I was a big Walt "Clyde" Frazier fan growing up, along with Dr. J and Moses. And to be able to talk with him about these games while riding the bus in Italy was a dream. I'll forever be grateful for spending time with McAdoo. He was there for me as I was injured, he believed I was telling the truth about the tendonitis. He could tell I was hobbled and not myself. We'd watch film and he'd turn to me, offering help, knowing I wasn't the same guy as I had been or could be.

Milan was certainly different the second time around. But maybe, in a way, I should have expected it because it had been years since my first stint there. I'd changed, grown. One of the positives of that, though, was that I could appreciate the country a bit more. I was more aware of my surroundings. Though, I did have friends send me VHS tapes from back home. I was watching the Arsenio Hall show, like, two weeks late! My phone bills were huge, too. But Milan has an atmosphere of models and fashion, food and very fancy things. It was an easy place to travel from, going to cities like Bologna and Monte Carlo. It wasn't far from Paris, either. I could jump on planes and see the world if I wanted. When I'd been here in my mid-twenties, I didn't appreciate it as much. I'd never been out of the United States before and didn't know what to look for. Now I had a much better idea.

Even the food was incredible in Milan. I remember eating dinner there late at night. It often starts at 9 p.m. and can go until midnight with various courses and deep conversations. All the food is fresh, from the pastas to salads, meats to cheeses. In Milan, there was this place everyone liked to party at called Club Hollywood. There, you could see anyone, from locals to celebrities. It was a little spot, but it brought in the big names. I saw Don Johnson with Brigitte Nielsen there on one occasion. In the city, there was no telling what glitz and gossip you might encounter.

Another teammate of mine was a guy named Vittorio Gallinari, father of future NBA star Danillo Gallinari. Vittorio lived around the corner from me in the city. He was a great guy. Maybe not as good as his son would be later, but he could affect a game. He was a bruiser, tough. But he was always there if I needed something. It's been great seeing his son play in the league, too, playing well for teams like Denver and Atlanta. I had another friend in the country, Mike McGee. He played for the Lakers for a number of years and was on their '83 team that we beat when I was in Philly. He'd left the NBA after playing in Phoenix for the '89–'90 season and was now in Italy with me. We always seemed to end up in the same place. In college, Mike had played at Michigan. And I'd later travel with him when we both played for the Magic Johnson Traveling All-Stars. He played for another team here in Italy, one of the worst, sadly for him. During our off days, Mike and I would go shopping together. I bought a lot of Versace stuff before the brand was popular in the U.S. We went to concerts and restaurants, too. We met a few models. It was a fun friendship.

One of the only other highlights for me that year was a day in practice when, doing my best Darryl Dawkins impression, I broke one of the backboards on a big slam dunk. It can be disruptive to break a backboard, but it's something every player wants to do in his or her career. With Milan, we had one of those old, halfmoon backboards. Well, I jumped up one day, slammed the ball home, and split the thing in two. It was a powerful moment in an otherwise tough year. The rest of the time, I tried to keep a smile on my face as best as I could. I didn't want another lawsuit for leaving early!

After our year together, which wasn't very successful, the team decided to buy me out of my second guaranteed season. I was fine with that. We both thought a clean break was best moving forward. I'd managed my goal of extending my career and getting paid well enough. But it wasn't going to be good if we had to extend our now-rocky partnership for another campaign. I knew I had more left in the tank and, I thought, if my tendonitis could heal, I'd have a chance at getting back into the NBA and impacting a roster. More and more players were going overseas and coming back to the league. I thought I could do it again, too. Milan had been unreceptive to me and my injury. So, it was time to head back over the ocean and see where my fortunes took me now.

When I made it back to the United States, I got an offer to play for the Indiana Pacers' summer league team. I didn't think I'd ultimately make the Pacers roster but getting into the summer league would put me on display for the other squads. It was, essentially, a public tryout. And that the summer league took place in Detroit of all places was a big bonus. I could go home, see my family and begin my rehab back into the NBA all at once. *Count me in!* The funny thing about the summer league that off-season were the scouts. The ones particularly that Milan had sent. The Italian league was growing, and they were sending more and more scouts to the U.S. to pick up talented players who might not make an NBA roster but who could thrive in Europe. So, Milan's scouts saw me with the Pacers summer league team, and they must have cursed me out under their breath. Because I killed it in the league!

By now, my tendonitis had finally healed, and I could play like my old self again. Healing from tendonitis can take weeks or months, depending on the physical therapy and amount of rest. Mine took longer since I'd kept playing on it for Milan. But there I was now, suiting up for the Indiana Pacers' summer league at the Palace at Auburn Hills with Milan scouts watching on in disbelief. And what happened? I showed out! I was in shape, comfortable, home. I had my wind thanks to my time in Milan. And now that I was fully healthy, it was my time to shine. Mike D'Antoni was with Milan watching me in the stands. They saw me put up 25 points in one of the games. They came there looking for a player to replace me and saw me at my best, one of the top talents in the whole field. I lit up the league. The Milan officials, including Mike, could only shake their heads.

Truthfully, I felt like a new man beginning with that summer league. I was rejuvenated, not the same guy I was in Italy. That summer, I stayed in the U.S. I went to camp with the Pacers but that didn't last. And then I went to camp with the New York Knicks. With the Knicks, I wanted to prove I wasn't washed up. I was still in my early 30s. The 1990 season was about to begin. It was a new decade. And I was ready for it. In fact, I was so ready for it, I caught the Knicks coaches off guard during camp. In hindsight, the team brought me in almost like a practice player, a dummy for their roster to go up against. I didn't know it at the time. But I certainly didn't think of it that way. To me, it was an honest chance at another roster.

Going into camp, Stu Jackson was the Knicks coach (he'd later be fired just 15 games in, John MacLeod taking over). Legendary NBA lifer and big man Paul Silas was an assistant with the Knicks (he'd later coach LeBron in Cleveland). Oakley was on the team now, too, after Chicago traded him for Bill Cartwright. I was happy to see my old friend when I arrived at camp. Friend or not, though, I knew we would battle. But I was so good in camp, I should have made the Knicks roster. It sadly wasn't meant to be. I later heard, after I'd been cut, that Stu went into the locker-room and said to the guys, "There's someone in here who shouldn't be and someone who isn't here who should be." He was talking about me. I was the one who should have been there on the team in the blue and orange.

The reason, in short, why I didn't make the team is because management had already guaranteed a player a big contract and, thus, couldn't cut him. Familiar story, right? The Knicks that season had good players like Maurice Cheeks, Patrick Ewing, John Starks, Kenny "Sky" Walker, Kiki Vandeweghe, Gerald Wilkins and Oakley. I felt I could help in a solid backup role, able to play multiple spots on the floor and guard any number of opposing players. The team's front office was comprised of Al Bianchi, Dave Checketts and Ernie Grunfeld. They'd brought in the big seven-footer center Stuart Gray. But I knew I was better than him. I'd played against him in practice in Charlotte and no sleight to Stuart, but I was better *and* more versatile.

To be honest, I'd targeted Knicks camp because I saw his name on the roster. Because I'd played with him with the Hornets earlier in my career, I knew I could beat him out. Frankly, he was horrible. But ol' Stuart had close to a million dollars guaranteed heading into that season for that season and the next. When he'd come to the Knicks in the offseason, Al Bianchi had given him *more* money, for whatever reason. That was a big chunk of change in 1990, so he wasn't going anywhere and there was no room left at the Knicks' Inn for me. Those are the breaks, as they say. But in the game right before I was cut, I scored 13 points and grabbed 10 rebounds against Dallas in a single *quarter*. In the end, it wasn't enough.

After that game, team officials came to me and said they weren't going to play me in the team's final preseason contest. They wanted to "look at other guys," they said. They said I was fine though, which gave me hope I'd actually make the roster. So, they didn't play me in that last game against the Pistons in preseason. But then a day before the regular season started, they cut me. Thinking on it, the team probably didn't want to me to play and make both them and Stuart look bad. While I was sullen about New York's decision I would later get my revenge in 1994 in the NBA Finals (more on that later). The basketball gods do look out for you, even when you're not expecting it. As for Gray, '90–'91 would be his last year in the NBA. He only played eight games that season, averaging 1.4 points, 1.3 rebounds and .1 blocks per. At least I'd proven to myself that I wasn't done in the league. Executives could overlook me, underestimate me, but I wouldn't do that to myself.

You know who else thought I belonged on the Knicks that year? The *New York Times*. Sam Goldaper wrote about me on October 17, 1990, publishing an article under the headline "Cureton Taking His Chances with Knicks":

> The Knicks have a major problem…. They have 15 players … [but] by the start of the regular season, Nov. 2, the team must cut down to 12.
>
> The much-traveled Earl Cureton is one of the two players without a guaranteed contract…. It will be up to Coach Stu Jackson to decide how many people he wants to keep…. "I didn't have anything to do with bringing Earl to camp," Jackson said, "but now that he's here, I'm glad to have him. He sets screens well, plays good defense, rebounds, runs the floor well and blocks an occasional shot."

I thought the Knicks could use me at either the forward spot or to backup Ewing. I'd even grown up loving the Knicks. As a kid I was an Earl "The Pearl" Monroe fan. And he won a ring in New York. Maybe it was also because we shared the same first name. Monroe played with Baltimore early in his career, averaging nearly 24 points per game in his first four seasons. Then he was traded to the Knicks, paired with Walt Frazier in the backcourt. He made me want to be a New York Knick. And I always loved Madison Square Garden. Sadly, business got in the way, and I was let go.

The Knicks finished 39–43 that season. The next year, the team brought in Pat Riley, who'd left the Showtime Lakers and had gone into broadcasting for a season. Riley turned the Knicks around and won 51 games in the '91–'92 season. Two years later, they'd be in the Finals. But I wouldn't be there for any of them. My fortunes, however, did land me on an NBA team for at least a few games in the '90–'91 campaign. I reunited with the Charlotte Hornets and my old friends there for a handful of games. It may not have been glitzy New York, but it was a chance to keep my career going. The rollercoaster was still officially on the tracks.

As in the years prior, the '90–'91 Hornets struggled. The team had some good players, but they were a year away from landing standout Larry Johnson in the draft and two years from bringing in center Alonzo Mourning. They did have Muggsy and Dell and a budding star in Kendall Gill to go along with Armen Gilliam, J.R. Reid and a few other solid rotation players. But the team finished just 26–56 in '90–'91, good for 7th in the Central Division and nowhere close to the playoffs. For my part, I only played in nine games for the team, starting in just one. In those games, I averaged two points and four rebounds, playing about 18 minutes. Not bad for not being with the team in camp and trying to fit in where I could on—*get this*—a nonguaranteed contract. I'd been brought in by the team's owner George Shinn and coach Gene Littles, who had replaced Dick Harter. Gene knew how I'd been done dirty by Harter, and he wanted to give me what shot he could. So, he got the team to sign me to a couple of cheap, shorter contracts known as "10-days."

When I'd left the Hornets two years prior, the team had tried, as I mentioned above, to find a place for me to play overseas. If I had taken their offer, that would have removed my contract from their books. But since I didn't go with their plan, the team had to continue to pay me because I'd signed a two-year guaranteed deal and they let me go after just one. This left a bad taste in owner George Shinn's mouth, paying for a backup player who wasn't even on his roster. So, yes, in Milan, I was getting two checks every first and fifteenth! Now that I was back with Charlotte, though, George didn't want to reward me any more than he had to. So, he refused to give me a deal for the entire season. Therefore, after my short couple of 10-day contracts expired, I was gone from Charlotte.

I understood his general frustration, but I had my own agent, I didn't need Charlotte to find me a landing spot after they'd kicked me to the curb. They could have just kept me on the roster, like they'd agreed. So, as usual, I was between a rock and a hard place again and I had to make the best of it. While none of it was my fault, the solution had to be all mine. It was the path I had to walk as a career journeyman. I'd played 82 games for the Hornets just a season prior, a solid performer on the squad, but that didn't help me.

After I left the Hornets in 1991, I connected with the New Haven Sky-hawks in the United States Basketball League. In the history of pro basket-ball, there have been many developmental leagues, including the USBL, CBA and ABA. Today, some of them are defunct or have been renamed. But back in the '80s and '90s, the USBL was a place where players could keep their skills sharp, make a paycheck and try to keep their careers going. The idea was to get noticed there and link up with an NBA team. Many upstart players and veterans have played in the USBL, from Muggsy Bogues to Spud Webb, "Hot Rod" Williams and Manute Bol.

When I got there in spring of 1991, I became one of those standout vets, fourth in the entire league in rebounding. I hauled in 180 rebounds during the short season, nine behind the leader, Willie McDuffie, and one more than future NBA standout Anthony Mason, playing for the Long Island Surf. Sharpshooter Tim Legler was also in the league that year with the Philadelphia Spirit. He was one of the league leaders in assists, along with Wes Matthews, Sr., of the Atlanta Eagles and New York City stand-out (and troubled player) Lloyd Daniels. Mason also was a top assist leader. In 1991 with New Haven, I earned USBL First Team honors, along with Mason and Matthews. *Still got it!*

As the NBA season unfolded, the league saw a new champion. Michael Jordan finally broke through, beating the Detroit Pistons in the east playoffs and overtaking the Lakers in five games in the Finals to win his first ring. That marquee matchup was also Magic Johnson's ninth appearance in the championship since he broke into the league. The Bulls won. Phil Jackson was the coach. Scottie Pippen was Jordan's wing man. Horace Grant did the dirty work, and the Bulls were kings of the court. But their big win, and Jordan's tearful celebration in the locker-room holding the trophy, wouldn't be the only major moment of change for the NBA. Later that year, as the following season was just underway, a shockwave went through the world of professional basketball and, really, the world at large. Magic Johnson announced that he was HIV positive.

At the time, it seemed like a death sentence for the legendary player with the big smile. Back then, the news floored everyone, from me to Larry Bird to Michael, Isiah and many more. Bird also retired a few months later, his sore back, which he reportedly hurt shoveling his driveway, forced him out. Father Time takes no prisoners. What the future held for any of us was always uncertain. Especially in the NBA.

Memory Lane: Mike D'Antoni

"My first impression from when I met Earl was that he was a good guy and a great player. He was exactly what we needed in Milan. That first time, he was in Scavolini and there was some turmoil going on. It was a little problematic. But our coach in Milan, Dan Peterson, came to me and said we were looking for our second American—I was the first American. He comes to me and Dino and says we have a chance to get this guy Earl Cureton. So, when I met him, it just worked out perfectly.

"He was great, it was fun playing with Earl and he's just a super guy. That first year, we were 6–0 in league play and we'd won three games in the European Cup that we were in. But then he comes to me and goes, 'Mike, I've got a problem.' It was, like, a Monday after a game. I go, 'What's the problem?' He says, 'Well, Detroit called me, and they want me to sign with them—right now. And I'm from Detroit and my mom is there.' I say, 'Okay, Earl, do it! What's the problem?' He says, 'I got to go to Detroit now!' I said, 'That's not a problem. You go to the NBA. I know that's what you want to do. You'll feel better for it. We'll miss you; we hate to see you go. But it's okay.'

"They were giving him a three-year guaranteed deal, so I said, 'Just go.' It was a once in a lifetime chance. I was really happy for him. It was weird circumstances; it was too bad it happened right then. But I knew we'd be okay. Maybe not as good without Earl, but we'd be okay. And we got Antoine Carr, who took his place. It worked out, but we missed Earl. Then later in '89, his second time in Milan, I was old. McAdoo was still going but I was old as hell! We just didn't have the juice we had before. It was too bad. Earl was still good, it was a great experience, but we didn't have the result we wanted, win-wise.

"Just generally, though, the reception was great. We had unbelievably great fans. And an American coach Dan Peterson who understood our mentality. He could blend the two cultures together. I remember we would have team dinners after every game. We'd sit there for three or four hours and eat Italian food, which was incredible. But Earl was so American at that point that after he'd be there for three or four hours—I always took him home. Earl didn't drive at that time. So, I'd always take him home and we'd stop by Wendy's on the way to his apartment. It was kind of hilarious."

12

Playing Everywhere

With his announcement, it looked like Magic's career was over. But everyone who knew him hoped his life wouldn't be. (Thankfully he's alive and thriving to this day.) And though I wasn't sick, my career was maybe running out of time, too. Never one to let things end on anyone's terms but my own, I decided to keep working. After my most recent stint with the Hornets didn't bear much fruit, I had some choices to make. Number one, I knew I needed to stay in shape. The best ability in basketball, as they say, is *avail*ability. And I wouldn't be any help to anyone, especially myself, if I wasn't ready to hit the court and contribute physically at a moment's notice. So, with no urgent calls for participation on teams coming my way, I knew the best chance I had was to find a place in a league outside the NBA. I was leery of going to Italy as the last venture out there didn't pan out like I liked. Milan was still sore from my tendonitis bouts, so they weren't an option. I looked elsewhere.

The first place I decided to go was France. And I wasn't alone. My old friend John Long and I went over there together. This was the 1991–'92 season. International basketball was popular but nowhere near as big as it became just a few years later. In 1992 with the advent of the U.S.A. Dream Team with Michael Jordan, Magic, Bird and the fellas, the game suddenly became a global enterprise beyond imagination. But we were still 12 months from that happening here. So, when John Long and I went over, the French league was solid, fine. We were standouts in it. France was still learning about the intricacies of the game and its own potential. Much later, players like Tony Parker, Rudy Gobert, Nicolas Batum and Victor Wembanyama—not to mention other international stars like Dirk and Luka, Embiid and Jokic—would star in the United States. But we were some time away from that when John and I headed over there.

John wasn't the only person I knew in France. Around this time, I'd started seeing someone new. My time with Diana was long over and I'd later met a new woman. Judith. I'd end up spending the rest of my life with her, I'm lucky to say. Judith and I got together before I went back over to

Europe. We'd met the summer before France, and we dated ahead of my flying out. When I met her, she asked what I did. At the time I was taking classes at the University of Detroit so, even though I was a 34-year-old professional basketball player, I told her, "I'm in college." She didn't have a clue who I was, which was great. I told her I was getting ready to go to France and later I told her why. She was intrigued and supportive.

Not long after I went abroad, she came to visit. I was playing for a team a little over an hour outside Paris, in Tours, which was also home to an American University. It was a fine team, filled with mostly young players. John and I were there to help the young guys grow and learn the game, each of us in our mid–30s and all of them in their 20s. The basketball situation, if I'm being honest, wasn't all that special. We won some games, it was nice. I notched several 20 point and 20 rebound games. But it wasn't much to write home about. To be in France, though, was always a delight.

We played in the LNB Pro A in France (the same league French prospect Wembanyama played in) for the Tours Joué Basket team. The highlight was having Judith come visit. I'd only met her a short time prior, so we were taking a risk in seeing if we could handle a new relationship abroad together. It had only been a few months to this point, but it felt *right*. She arrived during a break in the season, and I planned a trip for us. We took the train to several places. And I got to know her. It turned out great. We went into Paris and hung out in the City of Lights, at Notre Dame, the Eiffel Tower. We flew into Milan and met Mike D'Antoni. We took a train to Bologna and met up with McAdoo, who was playing there now. We convinced Bob to drive to Monte Carlo with us. We all stayed there for a handful of days and then we made the trip back to Paris. I told Judith, "I feel sorry for the next guy to take you on a date! He's going to have to live up to this!" But there was no next guy!

In total, Judith visited me twice in France. That second time, closer to the end of the season, we took helicopters from Nice to Monte Carlo. And when the season was done, we flew back to America together. We've had an amazing time ever since, from dates to years grinding professionally, to her giving birth to our daughter, who would grow up to be a Georgetown University graduate, four-year college basketball player and someone who now works in the U.S. Senate. I'm so freaking proud of our daughter, Sari! But I'm getting ahead of myself. In France, my old friend Kelly Tripucka was in the country, too, playing for one of the better teams in the league. He was having a hard time adjusting, though. Kelly was a former two-time NBA all-star. They'd paid him good money to play abroad, but now he didn't like it. He was on one of the top teams, but he was struggling.

Kelly and I talked on the phone, and he told me he wanted to leave and, thus, leave a bunch of money still on the table. I told him not to, I practically begged him not to. I told him I'd come visit him, for him not to leave. In the end, he gutted it out as long as he could. Some just can't adjust to life outside the United States. It's not for everyone. Even I had my issues.

Tours, though, was good to me. The place was welcoming, accepting. Paris can be tough with its big city mentality. But the smaller town of Tours was lovely. I played in France for about six months, through the league's '91–'92 season. They'd signed me for about $150,000 and I made sure they got value for

Sari graduating from Georgetown University, cool as they come, wearing her Adidas shell-toes.

every cent. It was also a way to see the world, another part of Europe and to keep my game as fresh as a morning bakery baguette if I'd ever have another chance at the NBA. But the competition didn't make me better. Thankfully, there wasn't anything as acrimonious that season in France as there had been in my prior two in Milan. But that didn't mean the roller-coaster ride of my career was over by any means.

Later in '92, after my stint in France, I went back to the United States and began to try to get back into the NBA. That summer the U.S.A. Dream Team became legends in Barcelona, Spain. Collectively, they took the game to new levels. Comprised of Jordan, Scottie Pippen, Bird, Magic, John Stockton, Karl Malone, Charles Barkley, Clyde Drexler, Christian Laettner, Patrick Ewing, David Robinson and Chris Mullin, the team blew out every international team to such a degree during the '92 Olympics that their opponents could only ask for their autographs during time outs and after the games. Prior to the Dream Team, Michael had won his second

Earl, Dr. J, Moses Malone and Sari during a 76ers reunion, just four people changing the world for the better.

championship, the Bulls thwarting Drexler's Portland Trailblazers. Jordan was relentless, even ridiculing his Dream Team teammates in the practices leading up to the international competition, talking about how he was king now. Later, though, they all grew close.

Perhaps the most important development of that team was the inclusion of Magic Johnson, who just a few months prior on November 7, 1991, had retired from basketball after his HIV diagnosis (Charles Barkley would switch from No. 34 to No. 32 for the 1992 season to honor him). Later, Magic said the Olympic team saved him from a consuming depression. The team was also famous for who wasn't on it. The dominant Shaquille O'Neal didn't make it, instead the more accomplished Laettner did out of college. But Isiah Thomas wasn't on the team, either, even though his Pistons coach Chuck Daly was on the sidelines. Isiah certainly deserved to be, talent-wise, but I knew how difficult he could be to some in the league, including with Magic, Bird and Jordan. The Dream Team won gold on August 8, 1992, winning each game by an average of 44 points, without ever calling a single timeout on the floor. Legends.

On October 7, 1992, I signed a short contract with my hometown Pistons. I was waived, though, two weeks later on October 21. After France, I went home for a chunk of the summer. From there, I flew to Oakland

University. Longtime NBA assistant coach, Ron Rothstein, who had worked for the Atlanta Hawks, Miami Heat and Detroit Pistons was holding open workouts in Oakland and he invited me to come by. So, I went and what happened? I played well. I lit it up just about every single day over the course of a few weeks. I played so well, in fact, that the Pistons, who Ron was working for at the time, invited me to training camp at the end of my stint in Oakland. The Pistons asked if I would come to camp and help the coaches work out some of their players. Unlike the Knicks, Detroit was upfront with me about their needs. They told up outright that I wouldn't have a spot on the final roster, but they nevertheless wanted me to come play in camp. So, I went.

Even though I knew I'd be cut for certain, I went out there and played for the entire duration of camp. I even played in the team's first preseason game before they officially cut me. Looking back, I was glad they cut me. I may not have won my second championship ring in Houston years later had they kept me on. But even in the moment, I wasn't mad since they'd been so forthright. Heading into Pistons camp, a few veterans who had found out my plan asked me, "Are you crazy? What are you doing? You're going just to get cut?" But I didn't care. I wanted the workout, the check and I knew every moment I spent playing well under the NBA umbrella was worthwhile. It wouldn't *hurt* me to run a little in camp. I love to play, I love the game, I love to get better. So, I went in, and I did just that. I think it's important to say yes to opportunities.

Around this time in Detroit, I played in some memorable pickup game against the famous collection of college players known as The Fab Five from the University of Michigan. One day me and Terry Duerod went down to play a game against those brash youngsters. For those who've seen the 2011 ESPN movie, *The Fab Five*, you've also seen me there briefly in the footage. Along with me and Terry, John Long and Greg Kelser played against the talented upstarts. We were old, they were young. But beat them! It was the last year they were all together in school, before Chris Webber went off to the pros. We played at the University of Michigan and gave them more than they could handle. We helped show them what the pros can be like, and I think it helped their growth. I've been friends with Jalen Rose of that famous unit ever since. I still play in his charity golf tournaments to this day.

After playing against those young guns and after my quick stint with the Pistons training camp was over, I knew I had to continue to find a landing spot. Without a great NBA opportunity, I decided to head out of the country again. First, I went to South America, to Venezuela, to play in the Venezuelan SuperLiga. Then I traveled to Central America to Mexico to play in the Liga Nacional de Baloncesto Profesional. I didn't spend a lot of time in either place, Venezuela for a couple months and Mexico for about a month, but both were beneficial. Like France, I went for the exercise and to see a bit of the world. I wanted to keep my body, mind and spirit in good shape, keep my game going while I waited for my next NBA opportunity. And earn some checks, on top of it. Both the Venezuela and Mexico experiences, though, had their funny endings.

I went to a team in Valencia, the capital city of Venezuela. I got the idea from a young player I knew, a guy named Antoine, who I was mentoring and who'd dreamed of the NBA but couldn't quite make it. I'd told him to look at teams outside the U.S. and he'd found several. He won championships in Poland and Santa Domingo, and he'd told me about this league in Venezuela. So, I went to check it out, myself. Valencia is in the north central part of the country, near the water. Today, it's an economic hub of the country. I went there at the same time as a few other American professional players, including Tank Collins and Wes Matthews, Sr., I was there for about a month before I was sent home due to an especially odd roster rule.

The team I went to operated strangely, compared to American basketball. At the time, they brought in something like 18–19 Americans to play on the team. That was part of their strategy for winning games, stacking big numbers of players. They'd bring Americans in, sign each to a certain amount of money (they gave me something like $10,000) and the first game you lost, they'd cut you straight up on the spot and you were gone. According to league rules, three Americans could be on the roster at a given time and the team could start just two. For my stint, Wes started and I came off the bench. It was that way as long as we kept winning. The idea was the Americans there would play as hard as they could, wanting to stick around. The threat of being cut always overhead.

But the strangest part of the trip was the team's arena in Valencia. It was elaborate, almost like the L.A. Forum where the Lakers played. But across the street were homeless people lying on the ground. It was quite the juxtaposition.

When I'd first signed to play for the team, I went into the owner's office. He reached into a safe and handed me the $10,000 in cash. Above the safe was a picture of President George Bush, autographed, that read, "Thank you for your generosity." I noticed that framed photo as the owner reached in for the dough. I wondered what business the two had done but I never asked. Playing for the team, we won our first three games in a row and then we went on the road. Of course, every team has to lose eventually, and we lost our second road game. My time was now done, that quickly. I got cut, true to the owner's word. It was a crazy situation compared to the leagues I was used to playing in. But, I thought, *oh well*. I got to see

Venezuela. I'd just gone there to keep sharp. To keep my game instead of sitting around waiting for the telephone.

At the time, traveling to play wasn't something a lot of NBA veterans would want to do. They'd see it as beneath them. Not me, though. I just wanted to play. And it was a bonus to see the world while doing so. The hardest thing for me to do abroad, at times, was find something to eat. I'm an especially picky eater. Like my buddy Oakley, who later became a professional chef. Oak would always send meals back to the kitchen at restaurants, saying they weren't cooked right, or something was off, much to the chagrin of the back of the house staff. Me? I just didn't want to eat anything I didn't know. So, in Venezuela, I stuck to the basics—mostly salads. I didn't want to try anything out of the way. Then, when my time there was over, I flew back home to Detroit to rechange, eat well, see Judith, and figure out my next move.

It wasn't long before I then went to Mexico to play. Before that, though, I linked up with Magic and his famous traveling all-star team. We met up in Memphis, Tennessee, to play some young stars. After Magic's HIV diagnosis, he'd had to retire immediately. But as everyone learned more about his illness, he was able to reintegrate himself into the basketball world again. At first, we didn't know if we could even play against him or touch him. Thankfully, though, we got educated and learned the truth about the HIV virus. Along with the Dream Team, earlier that same year, Magic had been invited to the NBA all-star game. He even won the MVP award in the '92 all-star game after the West beat the East 153–113. (Later, Magic came back to the NBA and played 32 games in the '95–'96 season.)

After the Olympics, having tasted the wonders of international competition, Magic started his touring all-star team, which was comprised of the likes of me, John Long, Reggie Theus, George Gervin, Michael Cooper, Kurt Rambis, Bob McAdoo, Mike McGee, Magic's old Michigan State teammate Greg Kelser and many more former NBA players.

One of our early games was in Memphis against some of the best up-and-comers in the country. A team of college standouts—true blue chippers ready to be drafted—had been assembled like Penny Hardaway, Lindsey Hunter, Allan Houston and more. Magic flew us down to compete against them, to sharpen our skills for his traveling team. A lot of the guys, like Gervin and Cooper, thought the game was something like a charity competition. But Magic wanted to *win*. He always does. So, the college players went up on us at halftime and Magic laid into us in the locker-room. Thankfully, we got it together and managed to beat Penny and the guys. We didn't realize how serious Magic wanted to take it, but he let us know and we came out and showed those college boys what NBA talent looks like. It was fun to see those young guys play, you knew the NBA would be in good hands with people like Penny and Houston.

After the Memphis game, I decided to try out Mexico. My mentee Antoine had told me about that league, too, and I decided to give it a go. So, I flew down. Though I was only there in the country for about a month, it was a wild experience. Thankfully, Judith and I were together throughout it all. I had her to lean on through all these new loop-di-loops in my later career. In Mexico, where I got paid about $10,000 to play for a month, I scored 50 points in one of the league games and, well, immediately after that, I told myself, "That's enough!" Almost as quickly as I got there, I left the country.

When I left, I didn't even really tell anyone, I just hopped on a plane and flew back home. But I'd done down there what I'd set out to do. I'd gotten in even better shape. I dropped nearly 10 pounds and fine-tuned my game. In your 30s, it's easier to get a little out of shape. But if you do and you lose even a quarter of a step, that can close all of the NBA doors. I didn't want that, and Mexico helped me refine myself yet again.

The NBA season in '92–'93 ended similarly to how the two seasons prior had. Jordan and the Bulls took home the championship, beating Barkley and his Phoenix Suns in six games. Jordan had now won three in a row, something Bird and Magic never did. Something only Bill Russell's Celtics had, decades before. Moses never did it, Doc never did it. Wilt, either. Jordan now stood atop the pack, forever now on the NBA's proverbial Mount Rushmore (along with the likes of Russell, Kareem and Magic). Speaking of Magic, I caught up with the legendary floor general after Mexico to play full-time on his traveling all-star team. With them, we had a chance to have fun, play with top talents, see the world and, most importantly, stay in top shape. It was no vacation. Magic was a drill sergeant. He didn't want to lose a game. And we never did. In total, his traveling team all-stars went 55–0.

With Magic's touring all-stars, we went everywhere. We didn't take home huge paychecks (a few grand here and there for each game), but we traveled a lot to places like Israel (which felt a bit dangerous, but everything went okay), Australia, Germany (where I matched up against the NBA great, Detlef Schrempf, and the German National team), New Zealand, Paris and more. Sometimes it was more fun playing with Magic than it was to play in the actual NBA—it truly was a blast, including all those private jets we found ourselves on. Later, the team went to Japan and the Philippines, but I'd gotten picked up by the Houston Rockets at that point, thanks to Magic. I owe Magic a debt of gratitude for bringing me on his traveling all-star team. Without that I might not have made it back to the pros and experienced one of my greatest rewards.

With his all-star team, we played against a handful of CBA teams in the United States, too, along with some good college teams. Against one of the CBA teams, Magic balled out, notching 30 points, 17 rebounds and 13 assists, racking up a signature triple-double (a stat he made famous in the '80s). We won that one 126–121, beating the Oklahoma City Cavalry. For each game, Magic was earning his fair share. But he deserved it, having conceived of, and put together, the whole endeavor. And guess what? People adored him around the entire world. Huge stars like soccer player Diego Maradona embraced him. Fans cheered wildly. It was a scene. That smile of his will always be magnetic.

Magic's popularity began with Showtime, and it went up like a rocket because of the '92 Dream Team. People went crazy for him. He was like a rock star coming to town, Elvis or the Beatles. With the traveling team, we played in smaller venues, but they all sold out. We had our own Magic Johnson all-stars jackets, too! We flew on private jets. Our home base for a while was Buenos Aires in Argentina and we flew to-and-from there. It was incredible. Everyone loved Ervin. They'd shout, "Magic! Magic! Ole, ole, ole, ole! Ole, ole! Magic! Magic!" That's all you would hear. There was paparazzi everywhere. Fans screaming to get a glimpse of him. It was funny for me, I'd known the guy before he was Magic. When he was just Ervin from Michigan. But that's what winning does. The trips were great: we traveled, and we won. But the best part about it was staying in shape. We trained hard. John Long and I pushed each other.

Magic only picked guys for his traveling all-star team that he knew would be dedicated, who would work hard and stay in shape. No lolly-gagging. We didn't want to lose a game and we never did. Magic saw the opportunity during the Olympics to grow his name abroad and this team helped that. I was happy to be a part of it. The ethic resembled the old "barnstorming" days of semi-pro ball. I'm not sure exactly when NBA talent stopped barnstorming, but it must have been around the late '80s. Muggsy did it before he was drafted in '87, we used to talk about that when I was with Charlotte. And even before that, huge names like Magic, Isiah and Mark Aguirre, along with Gervin, Dr. J, Andrew Toney, Dominique Wilkins and many others would go around during the summers and play in different towns like Philly and Detroit for six to ten games, showing their skills and bringing in some extra cash. I'm sure that was something commissioner David Stern wanted to put a stop to. No free opportunities to see the growing league's talent. And no need to risk injury.

Nowadays, lots of professionals have their own summer leagues, like perennial Sixth-Man Award-Winner Jamal Crawford in Seattle. There's no more barnstorming, per se, but players will travel to cities like Seattle and play a game or two in these summer pro-ams. But back in my day, we barnstormed, and it was something Magic brought back in the early '90s now that he was no longer officially part of the league. He brought along with him trusted players who also weren't officially with teams. His traveling all-stars were the talk of basketball summers well into the 21st century. In 2001, he played against his alma mater Michigan State, his first real game in Lansing in 22 years. He had a triple-double then too. Today, there are videos of our games all over YouTube. Check them out to see something that may never be recreated.

Something else that may never be recreated were the basketball trips I used to take to Alaska. For some 15 summers throughout the middle of my career and after, I would head up to the Frontier State in Barrow, Alaska, to teach hoops and gain a little life experience. My friend Rob King from Detroit, a good basketball player in his own right, went up to live in Alaska and he began putting on basketball camps in Barrow. Rob played high school basketball in Detroit, and we were in the same graduating class of '75. Once he made it to Alaska, he began recruiting professional players to come up and coach. A lot of big names came through. One summer, Norm Nixon, Darryl Dawkins and I all went up, coaching a couple hundred local kids. Darryl ate a moose burger and 20 minutes later he was running through the woods to find a place to relieve himself. That was a kick.

Barrow, Alaska, is known as the top of the world, so the air was thin. And boy was it cold—sometimes below 40 degrees! Magic came up to meet the kids one year and Isiah came with him. Others like Jack Skima, Johnny Davis, Antonio McDyess and Brent Barry went to Barrow, too. Up there, we rode snowmobiles, saw nature in abundance and taught local kids the game. It was daylight almost all the time in the summers; I also went up there one winter to coach and it was dark and even colder. There were hardly any roads. We met Eskimos and got to know their culture some and how they lived—they always wanted me to try whale blubber, which just seemed to grow in your mouth as you chewed. They would catch whales and live off them for weeks, using every part of the sea creature, from the blubber to the bones. They made boats out of sealskin to catch fish. We saw polar bears, played cards and stayed in little bed and breakfasts. The area didn't allow alcohol. It was refreshing for mind and body.

Some Americans were up there, drilling oil. But for the most part it was quiet, snow white and frigid. Summers were about 30 degrees. I truly don't know how Rob stayed up there year-round. He must have gotten used to it. One year, Utah star Karl Malone came up for a day while I was there to talk with the kids. He's an avid hunter and he loves to fish, so Alaska was right up his ally. Karl was one of the few guys to win an MVP award in the '90s aside from Jordan, who took home so many. And the kids loved seeing the big fella. He fit in. We all got paid pretty well, but we also did it for the kids. Living in Alaska, you don't see pro players very often and it helps to grow the game and the young kids' confidence to see NBA players. I'd get up there by flying through Seattle and run into some of the SuperSonics players. It was an NBA family thing after a while and I'm grateful for the frosty experience.

Memory Lane: Reggie Theus

"One thing I will tell you about Earl is that he's always been someone you can count on. He's someone that's evolved in himself. He created opportunities for himself. I've just always had an enormous amount of respect for him. Now … he played with some thugs! Those teams he had in Detroit and at the University of Detroit, going back to Dicky V. and them. But I got a chance to travel with Earl, not only in the NBA, playing against him and the Bad Boys and all those guys, but traveling with him with Magic Johnson's all-star teams. We had a great time."

13

Judith and Houston

When Judith and I met I was taking classes in college. After I'd left the University of Detroit for the NBA, I was a few classes shy of graduating. Some of that was because the school didn't accept some of the courses I'd taken at Robert Morris; another reason was because to be a successful collegiate athlete takes so much time that it can be hard to graduate on time like "normal" students. So, in the summers, I'd go home to Detroit and try to finish a class here and a class there, working towards a degree. I'd constantly try to grab a class and complete it, but with my rollercoaster career, trying to stay in the NBA and often having to leave both Detroit and even America to do it, the endeavor was difficult. Nevertheless, I officially graduated some 30 years after leaving for the NBA. In doing so, I'd kept the promise I made to my mother. That was enough for me.

Here I'd like to take some time to talk about Judith. She's my rock, my backbone, and the mother of my daughter, Sari. Judith is about 10 years younger than me. When I met her, she was in her mid–20s, and I was in my mid–30s. Judith is Korean and Black. She grew up in Korea and came to the U.S. when she was 12 years old. She was adopted. We met in a club of all places! Can you believe it? We started talking and one thing led to another. Our first date—don't laugh—was at my house. It was on a day during which there were three NBA games on TV, a triple-header. And we watched all three games together, in a row! She didn't give me a hard time and after the games ended, I thought, "This woman sat here with me through all these, she must be special!" I don't know how she had that patience. She didn't know much about basketball admittedly, but she was curious. That date, which also included lunch and a movie, led to a lifetime more. We've had our ups and downs since, like all couples, but Judith changed my life for the better, there's no two ways about it. I love her to death.

Throughout my career, as I've mentioned, it was hard for me to socialize outside of basketball. I'd tried relationships before, but they always fell apart because, mostly, I didn't have enough time to devote to them. I was wrapped up in my career. And that hurt me, socially. I spent so much time trying to make it that I didn't have time to give to anyone else. Basketball was my life. But when Judith and I met, my career was slowly winding down. When you're in your mid–30s, there isn't much professional time left in the game. So, we got to know one another, and it felt right. She went to France to see me and, 10 years later, we had our daughter. Sari was born in 1999 and, wow, did that change me! What a gift my daughter has been. I must have the greatest daughter on Earth. She is my first and only child. Parenting was one of the toughest things I've had to do in my life. I always try to stay humble, but being a father is *hum-bull-ing!* I'll tell you more about Sari later. Just know I made about as many mistakes as a dad can and still she turned out great.

After France, Judith and I were an official item. She stayed with me throughout my stints at the Detroit training camp, when I went to Venezuela and Mexico. Anyone who is in a long-term relationship will tell you: they can be tough. But the good ones are worth it. And that's the kind of connection Judith and I have always had (as I write this, we've been together for 26 years). Over the years, we grew together. She showed me what love is, what support looks like. And I hope for her I've done the same. It can be hard to be with a guy doing what I do, never knowing what team (or even country) I'd be in at any given time. Yet, she's always supported me. She was there for some of my life's highest highs and lowest lows. And in 1994, that meant being with me in Houston, Texas, with the basketball Rockets.

I owe my shot with the Rockets to three people: Judith, Magic and Joe Ash. Judith, as I've said, was my support system, my source of love, which can't be overstated or looked over. With Magic, his bringing me onto his touring all-star team changed my life, in that it gave me a another chance in the limelight and to be seen by scouts. It gave me a chance to stay in NBA shape, to play with all those legends, and to ball in front of coaches. This was invaluable. My life and career were rejuvenated because of Magic. He pushed us so hard. He helped me shake any rust off that I had after leaving Charlotte. I was nearing the end of my professional career, but he helped me get that last push in, that last lap around the proverbial track. That's the type of leadership Magic brought. And he didn't do it for just me. He did it for all his traveling players.

Sometimes you must truly rely on friends to push you. When Magic's team played in front of CBA teams with professional scouts, I wanted them to remember me, to know I was in the game. So, I worked hard to be able to do just that. I didn't rest on my laurels, content with what I'd achieved in the '80s and early '90s. I wanted more. Magic let me have that chance. And it worked. Now, that's where Joe Ash comes in. Because we'd played so many games against CBA teams, some pro scouts saw me and took notes on where my game was at. Because Magic pushed us so hard to win, we played at our best. That put me in a good position, along with a few others who were getting looks from those same scouts. In fact, if I'm not mistaken, Jack Haley hooked on to an NBA team because of those games, and so did Derrick Martin.

We'd whooped those CBA teams so good, teams from that league started calling me. One such call was from Flip Saunders, a coach for the Sioux Falls CBA team, the Skyforce. Flip would later enjoy a distinguished NBA coaching career with the Pistons, Timberwolves and other teams before he passed away in 2015. In the mid-'90s, though, he was paying his dues and he needed me. Flip recruited me and John Long to play for his CBA team, so we flew to South Dakota and laced 'em up there. We played in some regular season games and then helped the team qualify for the postseason via a play-in tournament. In my time playing in the CBA, I averaged about 14 points, 11 rebounds and 1.5 assists in 25 contests.

But the result of all that was a call from Joe Ash, who was working as a scout for the Houston Rockets at the time. The '93–'94 season was nearing an end and Houston was one of the better teams in the league, led by nimble center, Hakeem "The Dream" Olajuwon. Michael Jordan was out of the NBA at this point, pursuing a career in professional baseball with the Chicago White Sox organization after winning three straight rings with the Bulls. He'd announced his retirement in a big press conference on October 6, 1993. But the result of his absence was that the league was now wide open.

Houston had as good a chance as any to go far in the playoffs and they needed some help on the bench, Joe said. They needed a big man. Yes, they needed me. Thankfully after Sioux Falls (named after the Sioux Native American tribe), where I'd played well and we'd finished third, I kept my conditioning up. Don't laugh, but at the time, I was also playing at a local YMCA in Detroit. I'd been going there with my close friend, Terry Duerod, just to keep my wind up. You can't stay in basketball shape without playing basketball for very long. It was the best decision I could have made because out of the blue one morning, my phone rang. It was Joe and he had an offer I couldn't refuse.

He said the Rockets needed me *that night*. He asked if I would be interested in coming back to the NBA. I played it calm and cool but inside I was thrilled! I told him I'd definitely be interested in coming back. The thing was, he said, the team needed me for the game—yes—that very evening. So, I needed to be on a plane in a matter of hours to make the roster for the required number of games in order to be eligible for the playoffs. The postseason was the main reason Houston wanted to pick me up, for my experience and to back up Dream. I said yes quickly, and we made plans. As Joe talked, I started packing my suitcase, stuffing whatever I could in there, preparing for a flight from Detroit to Houston. It was 10 in the morning when he called, and he said the team would book me a flight and get me in by gametime. Barely. I told him that was just fine with me. I got to the airport and, thankfully, I made my flight.

I don't remember the exact time I made it into Houston, maybe around 3:30 or 4 in the afternoon Texas time. But I was ready. A team assistant coach, Larry Smith, picked me up. His nickname was "Mr. Mean," but he was great to me. After we shook hands, I told him I had to go to baggage claim to get my stuff. He said, "Earl, there's no time to wait for the bags. We have to go now." All I had was my carry-on in my hand. He said, "We'll get someone to get your stuff later. Let's go!" So, I jumped in a car with him, and we went straight to the arena. By the time I made it to the locker-room in Houston, the rest of the team was already on the court warming up. The team had my jersey all ready, name printed on the back and everything, hanging in a locker. I jumped into the uniform, number 35, warmups and all, and I got a quick physical examination from the doctors *right there* in the locker-room.

I was cleared to play, so I made my way out to the court. I went directly to the bench, watching the players as the early minutes of the game ticked away. When the first time-out was called and the Houston players came toward the bench, I came out and high-fived them. They all looked at me like, *"Who is the heck this guy?"* I hadn't even been introduced to anyone yet and I was already trying to bring the positive energy. The team brought me my contract *while I was on the bench* and I turned around and signed it as slyly as I could, trying to avoid any possible TV cameras. It was April 21, 1994, and I was officially back in the NBA.

The team's coach Rudy Tomjanovich asked me if I could give them a few minutes that first night and I said, "Sure can!" After all that, I knew I could give them a few, even if it made me puke in the locker room later. As it turned out, the Rockets didn't need me that game. The team flew out to Dallas for the next game that night after the one we played. But I still didn't have any clothes! So, waking up the next morning and before the next game, I called a lady friend I knew out there in Dallas and asked for some help. She picked me up at 9 in the morning to go shopping so I could get something to wear.

When she picked me up, though, Rudy saw me get into her car and he shook his head as if I was on my way to a booty call or something. I told him, "Coach! I didn't get my luggage! I don't have any clothes, no underwear or anything!" I'd later tell him I was spoken-for, with Judith at home. Rudy had a good laugh about it all. He is from Michigan, used to play at St. Cecilia, so we had a bond even beyond the Rockets. With my lady friend,

I went and got what I needed from the store. And that night in the game, Coach T subbed me in and I got my first run with the Rockets. I played 11 minutes in that game against Dallas, grabbing three rebounds. And even though we lost, playing with the team felt right. In a strange way, it felt like I'd been playing with these guys my whole life. Like the Hornets a few years before, it felt like family.

I knew how to come off the bench, knew how to stick to my role. That's a major way to succeed in the league, especially if you're not a star, and I'd been doing it most of my career, especially in the more recent years. I knew how to box out, stick my elbows into guys and create space. It was what the team needed when Dream was on the bench. For the last game of the regular season, we played in Denver, and I got in the game to play 19 minutes. I grabbed nine rebounds (four offensive) and scored four points, too. Not bad for a guy who was playing in the YMCA like a week before!

Then the playoffs began. In the first round, I didn't play very much—heck, I was still learning the playbook. The team didn't much need me, anyway. We were the West's No. 2 seed, and we played Portland in the first round. We beat the Trailblazers 3–1. The West's No. 1 seed, the Seattle SuperSonics, didn't have it so good. They ended up losing in the first round, which took out one of our top competitors. Basketball fans will remember Denver's Dikembe Mutombo holding the basketball under the basket at the end of that series, lying on his back, in joyous, emotional celebration. Mutombo's Denver squad was the first No. 8 seed to beat a No. 1 seed in NBA history. They did it in five games while, simultaneously, making our route to the Finals that much easier.

Denver later lost to Utah in the next round, their joy ultimately short-lived. In our next round series, we played Phoenix. In that one, my teammate Carl Herrera went down with injury, dislocating his shoulder, which meant I had to step up and play much bigger minutes. Carl was a talented power forward. He was 6'9" and while his numbers were never huge, he knew how to do a lot of things well that helped a team win. Strangely, we went down 0–2 to Charles Barkley and Phoenix, losing the second game in overtime. But we won the next three, to take a 3–2 series lead. We lost to them in game six and then we won in game 7. To be thrown into a playoff series with only two regular season games to get my legs and learn the offense is quite a challenge. Thankfully, Dream did so much for us that most of the guys didn't have to worry too much on the offensive end.

Our plays pretty much involved throwing the ball to Dream and letting him go to work. He was too good and would score nearly every time if the opposing team didn't double-team him. And if they did, we had shooters like veteran Kenny Smith, rookie Sam Cassell, bench leader Mario Ellie, NBA icon Robert "Big Shot Bob" Horry, the fiery Vernon Maxwell and more who could shoot the long ball with the best of 'em. We also had Otis Thorpe, the big fella, who would roll to the rim for an easy dunk if he had the space. Even our backup point guard Scott Brooks could put it in the basket if need be.

Sam Cassell in particular was crucial for us that series. He was a tough guy from Baltimore. I remember before one game in the playoffs that season, he came on the bus in just his sweats. No suit. He was a rookie, but a cocky one. He had a pillowcase with all his gear in it. When he got on the bus, he said to the whole team, all of us dressed in some of our finest threads, "I don't know where the fuck y'all going, but I'm going to *play*. I ain't going to *party*." Sure enough we won that game, Sam hitting huge shot after huge shot. But even with all his work, it was Hakeem who carried us for the lion's share of the series.

With Dream that dominant, all we had to do was make good decisions with the ball and where we cut without it, and he'd do the rest. Dream was so good that he didn't need another all-star on the team to succeed. That season, he won the regular season MVP, Defensive Player of the Year and, later, in the Finals, he would win the coveted Finals MVP. That's an impossibly good season. Maybe the best for a player ever. Thankfully, I was able to come in and fit in and help where I was needed. The team leaned on me especially when Carl went down. I played well against Phoenix, and, against Utah in the Western Conference Finals, I banged bodies with Karl Malone, making him work hard for his shots. We beat the Jazz 4–1. When Dream hit the clinching shot against Utah, I ran to him from the bench and embraced the man of the hour.

I'd played with Moses and other greats. But, to me, in that moment, Dream was the best big man ever to do it. *Sports Illustrated* quoted me after the game when I said, "All Dream's energy was gone, but he knew we needed him to take that shot. And when he made it, I came out to get him, because I knew it had come straight from his heart."

When we got to the NBA Finals, Carl came back from his injury and I was more than happy, for the sake of team chemistry, to let him take back his role in the rotation. When he came back, he told me, "I'm worried about my job." I said, "You don't have to worry, Carl. I want to win this ring." I didn't play much in the Finals against our opponents, the New York Knicks, but I knew I helped the team get there in important ways. In fact, Dream said as much. In a press conference, he told reporters that the team benefited from my presence big time. He gave me a lot of props, which felt incredible to be seen in that way. I was proud, knowing I did all I could to help the Rockets, bringing championship experience and a willingness to contribute. Heck, going into the Finals, I was the only one on the team with a ring.

In the Finals, my old friend Doug Collins announced the series. It's funny how life can come that way. Doug, who let me go in Chicago, was now out of a job, himself, and here he was talking about me in the Finals, talking about how I was one of the oldest players in the league, still doing it. I couldn't help but smile at that one. But beyond anything with basketball that series, one of the biggest things people remember is the infamous white Ford Bronco. During the fifth game in the Finals, on June 17, famed football star O.J. Simpson fled down a southern California highway in that white Ford Bronco, making international news. As much as we didn't want it to affect us for the rest of the series, it was a distraction. Nobody knew what was happening. We lost that game and in the locker-room, we tried to figure out what everyone was buzzing about in the stands. As it turned out, there'd been two murders and Simpson was a suspect. Today, everyone knows now how that all played out.

To that point, Hakeem had enjoyed a long career in the NBA, drafted in the same year as Michael Jordan. He was picked first overall in 1984. He finished his career a 12-time all-star, averaging well over 20 points in his first 13 seasons. But he'd never made it over the hump in the Finals. After getting out of the Western Conference, we met the Knicks. They even went up 3–2 in the series against us. And all the while I was writing a column for the Houston newspaper called "Earl's Pearls," rattling off my thoughts. When the series started, we won the first game 85–78. New York won the second 91–83. We won the third 93–89. Then New York won the next two 91–82 and 91–84. But we won game six by two points, 86–84. In that one, New York's John Starks, one of his team's best players and a former grocery bagger, had one of his best games, scoring 27 points on 9 of 18 shooting.

Spike Lee, the Knicks' legendary fan and movie director, yelled at us the entire series from the sidelines. I'd met Spike years before, introduced to him by the great Knick, Bernard King. We'd met at a restaurant in New York, Jazzabell's Soul Food. At the time he was an up-and-comer. Now, in '94, he was a film giant. But he couldn't do much for the Knicks, except shout from the sidelines behind his big rimmed glasses. Spike had recognized me during the series, yelling, "Earl the Twirl!" Dr. J was around those Finals too, doing some television. I made sure to say hello to him. It turned out, for one broadcast, he'd forgotten his dress shoes. Knowing we wore the same size, 15, he asked if I had an extra pair. I obliged.

Back to the Finals: in the series-deciding Game 7, everything was close, but then, just one game removed from his highlight game six heroics, Starks, the former CBA player, the star shooting-guard for the team, had maybe his worst game ever, going just 2 for 18 and 0 for 11 from three-point range. He just kept shooting and missing. I felt bad for him, but his failure was, in the end, our triumph. We took the deciding game, 90–84, in

Houston, in front of our 16,611 fans. When the final buzzer sounded, I looked for Judith.

Dream, who I'd backed up in the playoffs for about 10 minutes per game, had outdueled the Knicks' star, center Patrick Ewing. Due to his play, we'd won. I'd won my second ring. The first ring came in a sweep, now the second had come in seven hard-fought games. Rollercoasters.

In our celebration, the champagne flowed like water. It was special for me because I knew I'd contributed to a Finals win at a time when I could have easily been out of the league. I hadn't just sat my butt on the bench. I was helpful, especially against Phoenix and Utah, with Carl out. You need players like me to win big. It may not have worked out with the Clippers, Bulls or Hornets, but all those teams weren't ready to win, anyway. With Philly, I was a necessary piece. In Detroit, I helped the team figure out their identity. Now, in Houston, I was the final piece to a championship-winning puzzle. I'd even gotten a call from Magic during the Finals to head out on his touring team but I'd had to decline. History awaited. And for Dream to later say he doesn't know what the team would have done without me made it that much sweeter.

For all those that doubted me, how about that one? Now I had the distinction of being a two-time NBA champion, with rings earned nearly a dozen years apart. Now, I was 36 years old and feeling like a kid again. When we got our rings, they read, "Clutch City." That's right.

Memory Lane: Rudy Tomjanovich

"Earl helped us win a championship. As a team with the Rockets, we were always looking for smart players who were defensive-minded to add to the team around playoff time. He fit the bill there. Plus, he's such a good guy, he understood the situation. He showed intensity on defense. He could block some shots and had veteran savvy. You knew you were going to get good, solid effort from Earl. But then you also knew he fit the bill for a team that could get into foul trouble playing against stars like Patrick Ewing. Earl could fill in valuable minutes.

"When I think of Earl Cureton, I get a good feeling. He's truly a professional and he understood what it was all about. He didn't have these false illusions of grandeur. He knew that every little possession meant something. When he was on the floor, we definitely felt we were going to do well. It's always easy to fit in a good person. When you have a guy with character like Earl, it isn't difficult for guys like him to fit into a team."

14

My First Horrible Injury

Truly, I loved being in Houston. I loved playing for the Rockets. Like Coach Rudy Tomjanovich kept telling me, I fit like a hand in a glove with the roster. But life doesn't always work out the way you plan it. A great example of this is Robert Horry's career. He came in with Houston the year before the team won its first title. But earlier that season, he almost got traded to Detroit. If that had gone through, he wouldn't have been the clutch player he was for us in '93–'94 and Houston may not have gotten over the hump to win. The whole Horry ordeal was especially interesting to me because I happened to be in Detroit the night Robert came into the owner's suite thinking he'd been dealt to the Pistons. The proposed deal was set up to trade Horry to Detroit for Sean Elliott, who had arrived to the Pistons from San Antonio. But Sean failed his physical and the whole transaction was nixed. Before it was cancelled, though, I met Robert. I wasn't then yet part of the Rockets. Instead, I was just in Detroit, hanging out with the Pistons. Robert came in, head down, depressed. I told him about the merits of Detroit, that he was going to be fine, but he wasn't hearing it. He must have perked up when the trade didn't go through, and I know firsthand it benefited Houston to have him on the team for the Finals. No shot to Sean, who was great, but they don't call Horry "Big Shot Bob" for nothing.

I wasn't able to make it to the White House for the '94 championship celebration with the Rockets. Why? Because I'd hurt myself, torn my knee up almost right after our game-seven win. It was the first major injury of my career, and it came, as all injuries do, at a bad time. Not only could I not go to the White House because of it, but I was forced to be on crutches. After the championship series, I should have rested. I had tendonitis in my knee again and instead of giving myself a break, I worked out on it, going to the track to keep in shape. I'd thought about joining up with Magic and going to Club Med to play with his traveling all-stars. I was working out at the time with a trainer, Arnie Kander, who is truly one of the best in the business. Indeed, today if I feel pain anywhere, I call Arnie before any doctors. He was one of the first-ever strength and conditioning coaches in the league. Shane Battier, who was still in high school then was working out nearby, too. I was doing a light workout running when, all of a sudden, my foot got caught on the track, locked in place, and my leg just went out from under me. I screamed with pain.

It hurt worse than anything. I'd torn my ACL, PCL and caused severe nerve damage. A freak accident that would, as it turned out, cause me to miss out on joining the Rockets for the next season, during which they won their second-consecutive ring, sweeping Shaq, Penny and the Magic in the '95 Finals. At the time, the Rockets became the lowest seeded team to ever win a ring (they were sixth in the west to start the playoffs that year). Earlier in the post-season the Magic had beaten the Bulls after Jordan made his comeback from baseball back to the NBA. Nick Anderson famously stole the ball from Jordan in one of the games to help seal the team's series win against the mighty Bulls.

But if I'd been able to re-sign with the Rockets, if I hadn't destroyed my knee, I probably would have made more money with a two-year deal in Houston than in my entire career up to that point. Salaries were skyrocketing with the league's growing popularity—thanks largely to Michael Jeffrey Jordan. But it wasn't meant to be with me in Houston anymore, sadly. Even talking about it now makes me emotional. I loved that Rockets team and not to be a part of the roster for second (or third) season kills me. Especially since they won again! Except for the foot injury early on with Philly, I'd never been severely hurt in my career. Now, I was out for a long time. Another twist in my rollercoaster professional life.

My kneecap dislocated when I'd fallen, too, and I had to knock it back in place while there on the track, in severe pain. When I went to the doctor, they told me I damaged the nerve that runs down the leg and allows the foot to move up and down. My foot itself had just dropped, hanging down. The doctors put my whole leg in a brace. My orthopedic surgeon told me I'd be lucky if I ever walked again. He said I'd almost assuredly never play basketball again. When I heard that news from him, I just looked and said, "You must be crazy, doc! You can't tell me that!" I was motivated by the major setback. In truth, I couldn't wait to start rehabbing with Arnie, my physical therapist guru (today, Arnie is a consultant to several NBA teams despite being officially "retired").

My rehab took a year-and-a-half. In that time, I saw people I know retire from the league, including the great Moses Malone, then the last active player who'd ever laced up sneakers in the ABA. Moses, who came into the league from high school, hung 'em up right before future high school-to-pro players like Kobe and Kevin Garnett came into the league. Personally, I was determined not to let my career end quite yet. Nobody rehabbed like me. I was determined. I went to the rehab facility five hours a day. The entire time, teams were calling me. They'd seen what I did for Houston in the playoffs, and they wanted me. I didn't let on to any of them the severity of my injury. Boston was interested. The Knicks were, too, which was funny since we'd just beaten them, and they'd cut me before that. All these calls motivated me to work.

I wanted to get back to the league for at least *one more* shot. To do that, I had to learn how to run again, how to jump again. For much of my career, I'd relied on athleticism as a player and while I knew that would never come back, I wanted to work my way back onto the court to prove I still had something left. I worked every day. Then, finally, after a long, long comeback, sometime during the '95–'96 season, I was ready to try and play again. I'd done everything I could, even nearly winning a comeback award with the rehab center (though a guy recovering from a spinal injury beat me out for it). The doctor who told me I'd never play again saw me at the end of my rehab, and admitted, "Well, you may have a shot, Earl!"

That's all I needed. I knew I now needed to test myself before looking for a gig in the NBA, so I decided to go overseas again, this time to Argentina. I had an old friend there, Greg Guy, who offered to get me a spot on a team in Buenos Aires in the Liga Nacional de Básquet. I accepted. I'd grown up with Greg in Detroit. A fantastic high school and college player, he was now playing overseas in the middle of a 10-year stint in Argentina and he had local connections. He'd married a girl down there and he spoke Spanish. Greg got me a spot on the team and my old buddy John Long came with me, too. It was comforting knowing John would be there. He was in between teams and agreed to fly down to check it out. We ended up playing in Argentina for about six months, earning about $10,000 per.

One of our teammates was future NBA star, Luis Scola, who was only about 16 years old at the time. Part of my agreement to go down there, along with salary, included some amenities I felt I'd earned. For example, I wanted a first-class ticket for my flight to Buenos Aires. I wanted to stay at a five-star hotel while there. I'd played too many years to get the minimum, I thought. By now I was 38 years old—nearing 40! I also asked for my first month's pay up front. The team fought me a bit, as negotiations often go, but in the end, they granted me what I wanted. Though, at the airport, of course, there were some issues.

I almost turned my butt around at the airport to go home. The ticket the team had sent for me to fly down there wasn't first-class like I'd asked, and we'd agreed upon. But at the last second, the team was able to get me the right ticket and I decided to head down to Argentina in earnest. It was a long flight, but I made it. A team representative picked me up at the airport and took me to an InterContinental hotel. Much like with my joining

Houston, there was a game that night in Buenos Aires. The team rep gave me my first check and I was ready to play. Problem was, I hadn't played a real game since I'd mangled my knee! Since my rehab, I'd been in the gym, getting in shape, putting up shots, but I hadn't played in a real game for some 18 months. Okay, I thought, time to suit up for my first one tonight! Turns out, though some of my athleticism had left me, my skills and intuition hadn't. We played that night, and it was a close game down to the wire. So close, in fact, that I won it at the buzzer with a tip-in rebound!

It was a good first day and set the tone of the next six months. We had a young team. Like I said, Scola was just 16. He would go on to be a major factor, along with the likes of Manu Ginobili, when Argentina stunned the world and won the Olympic gold medal for basketball in 2004. The rest of the team wasn't much older than he was. John Long and I were there as mentors. To talk to the young guys and let them know how to be solid professionals. When the season ended after those six months, I was ready to go. Judith had flown down two weeks before the end of the season. When she arrived, I'd set up a surprise for her. I'd gotten an artist to paint a portrait of her from a photo I had. So, when she got to my InterContinental hotel where I was staying, she saw this giant Judith portrait in the lobby! "This is my hotel," I told her. She loved it. Who wouldn't have?

Judith stayed with me those last two weeks and together we saw the country. We went out to eat often. Unlike me, Judith has always been one of those adventurous eaters. She'd try anything. I won't eat anything unless I know for sure what's in it. But during one meal, she dug into a mystery plate, and when she asked what it was, it turned out to be bull testicles! I looked at her and burst out laughing. I couldn't help it. Other than that occasion, much of her trip with me there was smooth. It was just great to have her by my side. After two weeks, we got on a plane and headed back for Detroit. There, I began working out at a local community center, sharpening my game and building my wind.

With real games under my belt now post-rehab, I wanted to prepare myself for a possible shot at getting back to the NBA for one more chance. The basketball gods must have been smiling on me because soon enough, I had my opportunity. My old pal Isiah Thomas by this time had retired and become a part owner of the new expansion team, the Toronto Raptors. That franchise began its first season in '95–'96 when I was still in Argentina. The Vancouver Grizzlies also came into the league that season. That year, Jordan's Bulls won the first championship of their second three-peat, beating the SuperSonics after going 72–10 in the regular season. Now, in the Raptors' second season, Isiah wanted some veterans to help the team's young core of Damon Stoudamire and rookie Marcus Camby. So, he called me up a few months into the year to join the team.

In that moment, I was in a bit of a conundrum of options. Magic Johnson was still rolling with his traveling all-stars, and he was headed to South Africa to meet the great politician Nelson Mandela. For those that don't know, Mandela was the legendary anti-apartheid activist. After being put in jail for years, he served as the first president of South Africa from 1994 to 1999, the country's first Black head of state and the first elected in a fully representative democratic election. There aren't many more important people in modern history than Mandela. It was going to be an honor to meet him—to be even in the same room as him—and Magic had invited me on that trip. Trouble was, I got a call from Isiah right as I was about to leave, asking me to come up to Toronto and join the Raptors. I was already packed for the trip to South Africa when Zeke called. So, knowing my ultimate goal was to make it to the NBA again, I agreed to Isiah's offer and had to tell Magic I couldn't make it. I unpacked for South Africa and re-packed for Canada.

John Long had also gotten a call from Isiah to join the Raptors. It seemed wherever I went, John was there too, which was great. We even used to work out with his younger cousins, future pros Grant Long and Terry Mills, kicking their butts until they grew and could kick ours! John had already made it to Toronto. And I flew up soon after to meet everyone. Isiah had told me he needed us to help mentor the team, which also included young players like Walt Williams, Acie Earl and Carlos Rodgers. I signed with Toronto on December 2, 1996, for just over $200,000 for '96, after officially being released by the Rockets.

My job was to talk to the star young players, tell them stories about the league, teach them how to succeed, stay fresh, how to prepare, how to manage a long season in the pros, how to focus and stay in shape. I worked with Camby, a promising young big man who had been a star at Dr. J's alma mater, UMass. By putting my name on the dotted line one more time, I'd made it back from my injury to play again in the NBA for the '96–'97 season. I couldn't have been happier. I wasn't 100 percent when the season started but Isiah had given me my shot. And I healed as the year went along. During the year, in fact, when the Raptors played the Pistons in Detroit, all the doctors and nurses who had helped me rehab came to cheer me on. That was a high mark in the never-ending rollercoaster of my life.

I played for the Raptors sparingly that season, lasting just a few months in total. In the end, I was 39 years old when I hung up my sneakers for good. I averaged about one point, and one rebound for the franchise, making it into just nine games and playing five minutes per. But playing time wasn't the point for me. The point was to get back in the league and to help the young guys on the team. I'd now done both. I was at peace with retiring. Later that season, my old team the Bulls won their second championship in a row. This time, they'd beaten the Utah Jazz with Karl Malone and John Stockton. And next year, they'd beat the Jazz again for Jordan's second complete three-peat. He'd finish his career with six rings, going 6–0 in the Finals. But while his arrow was still pointing up, my two-ring career was over. I could breathe a sigh of relief. I'd done what I'd set out to do. Now I had to decide what was next.

Memory Lane: Scott Brooks

"Early in my career, I played against Earl. We didn't play the same position, of course. But the first time I actually met him, we were with the Rockets, and we were making a playoff run. We signed him, I want to say, the last week of the season. And the first time I met him, I was like, 'Man, who is this guy? How is he going to help us? He can barely walk!' But being around him, I said, 'Okay, I know why Rudy Tomjanovich wanted him.' Because of his knowledge, his grit, his toughness, his determination. Those were what we were all about as a team in '94.

"He was the perfect fit and we really hit it off. He was about seven or eight years older; I was in the later stage of my career, and he was in the finishing stage of his career. I remember seeing him: he didn't look too athletic; he didn't look like he could run or jump or shoot! It didn't look like he could defend. But that's the thing: the more you're around him, you realize he can do everything good. The biggest strength I saw in his game was his perseverance. He had a little swagger about him, and you saw his confidence.

"Earl was a dog. He played like a Doberman pinscher. He was just tough. He wouldn't give up any space. You had to fight him for every inch of the court. You need guys like that on your team, especially if you want to win a championship. You need those lunch pail guys, and he brought his lunch pail every day. You knew if you were going to play Earl, you were going to have to play well to beat him. He was a great teammate, too. We shared many meals together. And we've been buddies now for 30 years.

"He gave me great advice one day. Earl was always the wise man. When I was finishing up my career, in the ABA, thinking about getting into coaching, Paul Westhead was our coach. After two days of training camp—if you know anything about Paul's system, you know you're going to run and when you're done running, you run some more. Then when you're down with that, you run even more. So, one day, Earl said, 'Scott, you're too old to play in this system! You need to focus just on coaching.' So, I faked a hamstring injury and ended up being a coach for the team the rest of the year!

"We had great times. Even though none of us got paid anything. Checks bounced so high even Earl couldn't catch 'em. But Earl, on the other hand, is trustworthy. He's a great friend. Truly, Earl will do anything for you and your family. It's been great to see his relationship with his daughter grow over the years. I always tell him these three things: I say, 'Earl, she definitely has Judith's looks, she has Judith's brains, and she has Judith's athletics! But I'm happy to see that she makes you so proud!'"

15

Retired

The official date of my retirement was February 13, 1997. I departed from the Raptors midseason, well, because it was time. I wasn't 100 percent when I started the year with the team and my leg never got much better. I'd come to the new team to help with the young guys, and I did what I had to do over the course of those few months. While I only played in nine games, I had a few where I put up some stats, grabbing some rebounds, getting a few buckets. That was fine by me. I'd made it back to the league after a catastrophic knee issue and I'd proven to myself and to anyone watching that I belonged, just like I always had. That was good enough for me. So, when it felt like the right time that February to hang it up, that's exactly what I did.

When I was ready to announce my retirement, I talked with Isiah to let him know. I also wrote a formal letter to the commissioner of the NBA, David Stern, to tell him I was calling it a day. The news was announced in Toronto, but there wasn't a ton of fanfare, and that was okay with me. No big deal. When you leave the league, you must turn in your official retirement number, which I did in the formal letter to Stern. He wrote back, kindly, saying, "You'll be back, Earl." He was nice about it. But I knew it was the end for me. I was 39 years old and staring at 40. The only thing that lingered was that, if I hadn't been injured, I know I would have been able to play with the Rockets for at least two or three more years. I truly did "fit like a glove" there. But that's life. To this day, I have to wear a brace on my right leg. That's how bad the injury was. I'd come back into the league on just one leg. At least I was leaving with the good one still intact.

The Raptors finished that year 30–52 under coach Darrell Walker. It was the same season the NBA announced its list of the all-time top 50 players. No, I didn't make it, but many of my former teammates did, like Michael, Magic, Moses, Dr. J and Hakeem. Looking back on my own 12-year career, I'd played in a total of 728 games, averaging 18.4 minutes per contest. I'd scored a total of 3,620 points, grabbed 3,172 rebounds, and dished out 678 assists for career averages of 5.4 points per game on 47.3 percent shooting, 4.7 rebounds per game and about 1.0 assists. For you stat-heads, I also notched a 10.4 PER and 14.4 Win Shares. In total, I made about $2 million in salary. A far cry from what was coming up for the league—they say salaries will balloon to some $75 million a year for players before not too long.

The NBA was changing; it's always changing. The 1990s were winding down and the 2000s would soon be upon us. A lockout would happen in 1998, cutting the 1999 season to 50 games. Big, big money was coming into the league. And while it would have been nice to stick around for that, change is inevitable. It was time for my life to change again. No question about it.

But while the end of my career was a big moment for me, it was dwarfed in some ways by another big personal blow. In 1997, my father, Johnny Frank Cureton, was diagnosed with cancer. That was a tough time. It was the end of my basketball career, as a player anyway, and my father was battling lung cancer. I'd been going back and forth from Toronto to Detroit to see him as often as I could while he was in the hospital, and I was with the Raptors. It's about a five-hour drive from the two cities, or an hour-plus in the air, depending on turbulence. But the time didn't much matter to me, I just wanted to be with my dad during his last days as often as I could. Thankfully, at least, we got time to speak before he passed. We were able to sit and talk some days for hours.

Though my parents were separated, my mother was still supportive of my dad to his last days. I was thankful for that. Another thing I was thankful for was my friendship with Isiah. Around this time, he offered me another job, the chance to do radio for the Raptors. I'd always wanted to go into broadcasting and when the radio job came open, I took it. I started the same season I left the team, taking only a little time off to be with my father. I'd also helped the Raptors with some strength and conditioning that season, but when radio became more of a fulltime thing, I switched over to learn the ropes of media.

I was helped in my new broadcast job by having just played in the league. I knew all the players; knew the teams and the plays they ran. My partner on the air was Mike English. He'd go on to have a distinguished career in radio. Before I got there, he was calling games for the Raptors solo. I got the sense he didn't exactly want a partner, but he was kind and taught me a lot. When you jump into new jobs, you need someone like Mike, someone to help break you in. I'd long wanted a career in media, and he helped immensely.

Later, I'd broadcast University of Detroit games and Pistons games, too. I also made appearances on television in Detroit and, after some years, even started a podcast with Oak and Muggsy. That was all thanks to Mike and Isiah and the start they gave me. Doing the job required preparation, flying with the team, and being ready with the right, insightful things to say on-air. It helped to know when to jump in and out of the flow of things. Lots of players want to retire and head into broadcasting, but it's difficult and there are few jobs to go around. Mike was a true professional, organized and structured. He painted an amazing picture. At first, I couldn't get two words in, but it was part of letting me ease into the job, which I appreciated.

Isiah had connected with the Raptors when the league expanded. He had a contract with the team that, after three years, would be reevaluated. If he stayed on, he would become a partial owner with stakes in the franchise. But in the end, after those three years, the team let him go. He'd started them off, but now they apparently wanted to go in another direction. That meant all his people were out, too. That meant me, too. The team brought in Butch Carter as the coach to run the franchise and that, well, was kind of a disaster. Eventually the Raptors got rid of Damon, Marcus

and others and though they brought in Vince Carter and Tracy McGrady, that didn't exactly go as planned either, especially with Tracy leaving for Orlando as a free agent. Butch cleaned house and then, when he left a few years later, the team cleaned house again. That's how it goes in the NBA.

After I left Raptors radio, I got a call from Johnny Davis. A Detroit guy, he'd played in the league from the mid–'70s through the mid–'80s. Now, he had a new opportunity for me. Johnny asked if I'd ever be interested in coaching. At first, I told him no. But Johnny had a way. At first, I didn't want to coach. I just wanted to broadcast. But Johnny was persistent. He said, "Are you sure?" He told me he had a team in the USBL that I could run.

Earl broadcasting with Mickey York of Bally Sports on a night when both his former teams are matched up against one another, the Pistons and the 76ers.

I'd played in the league before and done well. The USBL is played in the summertime. It no longer exists today, but it was a valuable place for the few years it did. Johnny had a team in Camden, New Jersey, in need of a head coach and he wanted me to take the reins. But I kept telling him no. I was still dealing with the aftermath of my father's illness, dealing with the inevitable funeral plans. But Johnny kept calling. "Are you sure?" he asked and asked. "Are you sure?"

Finally, we came up with something of a compromise. He said, "Why don't you help me put together the team for Camden through the draft." I finally agreed to that. I thought it would be fun to see how a team gets arranged. And the 1998 Camden Power would be a good start. The experience could help me if I ever wanted to work in a front office. So, we started thinking about names. Our mind went to our hometown. Detroit. There was a lot of talent there and we were connected to much of it. I looked at schools like the University of Detroit, the University of Michigan, Eastern Michigan, Michigan State and the like. We held informal tryouts in Detroit. A friend Richie McDermott helped. He was a University of Detroit walk-on when I was there and a true basketball freak. He helped me organize everything, as well as evaluate players.

Richie brought in local guys and told me which to go after. He had visions of becoming a sports agent, so he was right in his element. Later, he'd hang up his agent hat and become a lawyer. In the end, though, I took six guys from the Detroit-area to the USBL. It all happened so quickly and right at the time when my father passed away. In fact, the day after his funeral, I found myself in a gym with some 30–40 basketball players for tryouts. Johnny Davis helped, too. He knew people from Philadelphia, and he helped funnel them to me. It was a good system. I felt confident about our chances. We were building something.

The USBL season came up quick, but I was ready for it. One of the players I drafted was Derrick Dial, from Eastern Michigan. I also wanted the diminutive point guard Earl Boykins, but we were unable to get him. Ironically, he was too "big" for us. (Boykins went on to have a 13-year NBA career, averaging more than 15 points per game at his peak.) We also worked out Ya Davis, Derrick Hayes, James Head, Brian Tolbert and more. Eventually we landed Ira Newble, too, from Miami University. We fielded a strong roster. Then, when the roster building was done, the persistent Johnny Davis began working me again. "So, what you want to do?" he asked. I took a deep breath. He'd finally convinced me. I told him, "Okay, I'll coach the team." After leaving the NBA and after my father dying, it turned out working with the USBL as a head coach was the exact therapy I needed. Johnny was right.

There were all these guys in Camden, and they were hungry. I looked at the lot of them and suddenly I was reminded of myself. None of these young men were going to be Michael, Larry or Magic. But they were talented and ready to work, to get better. It was then I realized I might have a future in coaching and Johnny had the correct instincts after all. I'd never coached before, outside some strength and conditioning work with the Raptors, but I took to it well. I knew what it required to earn a roster spot, to fit in, to work and play a role. I'd been doing it all my life! One of the guys on the team that I really took a shine to was Derrick Dial. He was 6'4" and had played much of his college career at forward. But that wasn't going to work for him in the NBA. He had to learn to play point guard if he wanted to go to the next level. I told him so. Dial was extremely competitive, the kind of guy who would run through a wall for a goal. This served him well.

As a team in Camden, we started off great during the opening of the USBL season. I'll never forget it. We had a big win over Hall of Famer Rick Barry, who was coaching the New Jersey Shorecats. We had talent. Many of the players were good enough to make the NBA. Dial was one of them. But he was also a project. I knew he had to work on his ballhandling. So, I set up a special drill for him during our practices. We worked and worked, and it paid off against Barry's squad and a number of other teams, especially in the early going. I made Dial our primary point guard. I knew what a guy had to do to get better, skill-wise. As I continued to coach, the job became more and more interesting. It made me want to get to the next level and for my players to get there, too. I loved the strategy.

When I was a kid, I did the same kind of drill that I'd assigned to Dial. But with Derrick, well, I "dialed" it up. I set chairs up on the court every day for him. And his job was to dribble around the chairs, through the maze. To do so, he had to do crossover dribbles, between his legs, behind the back and spin moves. Ten sets of each, with no mistakes. If he made a mistake on the tenth time in the last drill, he'd have to start all over from the beginning. He couldn't lose the ball once, couldn't dribble off his foot. If he did, he had to start over from the beginning. It worked! He got better and better. And later he earned himself a tryout in the NBA. I was so proud of him for that.

But in a way, that was the problem with the USBL and why it eventually folded. Towards the end of the season, all of the league's top talent—all of *my team's* top talent—left for bigger tryouts in the NBA and opportunities overseas. The NBA starts every year in the fall, so in late summer, the teams get together to evaluate and hold tryouts and training camps. No one with a shot at the league was going to stick around the USBL with that as a possibility, so after we went 7–1 to start the season, we lost a bunch of players, including Dial, and we went on a bad losing streak, finishing just 11–15 for the campaign. Dial left for the NBA pre-draft camp in Chicago,

Others went to the CBA or overseas. But it was all right. To see players like Derrick get a shot was prize enough.

And Dial eventually made the NBA. In 1999, at 24 years old, he made the San Antonio Spurs roster and played with them for two years before going on to play with the Nets, Raptors and Magic for a few more seasons. A few other players of mine got to pro leagues, too. That made me think I had a shot at this coaching thing long-term. It was a win-win, even though our USBL team didn't achieve all it could in the league, it gave us all much-needed experience. When Dial made it, he called me, "Coach, they put me at point guard!" He was so happy. The chair maze had paid off. I knew it would. He'd gotten himself ready. Another of my players Ira Newble later made the Spurs, too. Another success story. He'd go on to play in the NBA for eight years.

Our team also had this tall fella, the 7-footer Ben Gillery. He'd had a cup of coffee in the NBA, playing with the Sacramento Kings for a few dozen games in the '88–'89 season. But he was raw. He wasn't doing much besides hanging around Detroit when I'd called him to come play for us in Camden. When he got to our team, I made him work on just one specific post move. I wanted him to get in shape and improve his conditioning, but I also wanted to pound this one inside move into his head over and over. I knew it was the key to his and our success. I wanted Ben to flash to the post, get the ball, take one dribble to the middle, and throw up and jump-hook. With his size, it was an unstoppable shot. I must have made Ben practice that 5,000 times. My assistant coach kept asking me, "Why are you doing that over and over?"

Well, the answer came at the end of one of our games that season. We were down a point on the last play of the game, and I substituted Ben into the game. I told him to set a screen for one of his teammates, then to flash to the post, get the ball, take his one dribble in the paint, and shoot the hook. Well, guess what? He did just that, made the shot and we won the game! My assistant coach just looked at me and knew in that moment why I'd spent so much time on the move with Ben. We'd worked all that time for those three seconds. That's coaching. Thankfully, my stint with the USBL would lead to more opportunities down the line, in the WNBA, CBA, ABA and more leagues, working with people like Paul Westhead, Scott Brooks and Matt Barnes. But what's important to mention here now is perhaps the most important thing to ever happen to me: the birth of my daughter, Sari Mejah Cureton.

Sari was born on November 1, 1999. And, well, that was a wild day for me and her mom. The Spurs had won the championship in the summer of 1999, beating the Knicks. And I won the lottery in late 1999 with the birth of my incredible daughter. I was in Sioux Falls, South Dakota, when she was born, though, coaching in the CBA. I'd called home the night before to talk with Judith, who was then very pregnant. After leaving the Raptors, Isiah had bought the entire CBA league and he'd given me yet another opportunity, a chance to coach in Sioux Falls for the team I'd played for years prior. I was an assistant coach. And I'd called Judith to see how she was doing, how she was feeling. I was set to come home in a day, or so. It was a Sunday when I called. But I'd heard earlier that Isiah was flying in the next day to check on my team. I asked Judith if it was all right if I stuck around another day or two to meet with him. And I asked if I could fly home on Tuesday.

Judith has always been supremely supportive of me and my career. So, she said it was no problem at all. I remember when I called her, she was cooking dinner. I could hear the pans sizzle over the phone. She told me, "Oh, Earl. I'm doing great. Don't worry one bit. You can stay another day. Go ahead and do what you got to do." She sounded happy, cooking, doing her thing. I told her I loved her; we hung up and I went about my day, ready for Isiah to come by. Then probably four or five hours later, around 11 o'clock at night, I got a call that she was in labor. Her water had broken. Her godparents, who were on call to help her when I was away, went and

Sari with both of her grandmothers, Jung-Sun-Yang and Minnie Mae Cureton.

picked her up and took her to the hospital in Detroit. When they called me, I was freaking out. "Okay," I said, "I got to get home!" I got on a flight as soon as one was leaving Sioux Falls for Detroit, at 5 in the next morning.

When I arrived in Detroit, I was still freaking out. She was still in labor when I got a car to take me to the hospital. But I didn't make it quite in time and my daughter was born right before I got there. Thankfully, everyone was healthy, safe and sound when I arrived. Our daughter's middle name, Mejah, comes from a famous Korean singer. But her first name, Sari, which means "noble," was given to her by her Jewish godmother. After her birth, I stayed at home in Detroit for as long as I could before heading back down to Sioux Falls to resume coaching. And when Sari got old enough after a few months, she took her first plane ride to South Dakota with her mother to come visit. She took that trip and she'll never remember it because she was only six months old, but seeing her was a blessing. It still is. My family is the thing I cherish most in my life. Judith has been my rock ever since we met. She's kept our family together.

Today, Sari is an outstanding young adult. She's a 4.0 student, a graduate of Georgetown University and a four-year player on the school's basketball team. I'd never expected her to play basketball at all. And when she played in high school, I never thought she would continue at the Division-1 level. But she constantly surprises us with what she can do and who she is. Sari is a superhero. Seeing her sometimes makes me think of Kobe and his daughter Gianna. Their death in the helicopter crash remains immensely sad to the entire basketball community. It's sad he didn't get to see her grow up.

With Sari, academics have always been important, which is more than I can say for myself at her age. She also played viola in the orchestra for seven years, studied Spanish for six. She's always had ambition and knew what she wanted from life. Yet, her participation in basketball was a shock to me. I was coaching in the WNBA when she was young, and she never showed interested in the game. But one day when she was in 8th grade, she came home and told me, "Dad, I want to go out for the basketball team."

I looked at her, *Are you crazy?* I'd never thought basketball was her thing. But she started in 8th grade and never looked back, even if some of our training sessions got a little father-daughter intense! Sari has always been tall for her age. A coach noticed her one day in the hallway and asked her to come try out for the team. I could never get her to play, but the coach was able to. I went to some of her practices to watch and help here or there. Sari was really bad when she started! She had to learn to run like a basketball player. In fact, I didn't take her all that seriously until she later got to high school in 9th grade. But she got better each year. I worked with her in high school, helping to train her. Her high school team was one of the worst in the league when she started. But by 11th grade, they were in the playoffs and Sari was playing a big role. She earned honorable mention in the league, too. I went to all her games. But that's not all: Sari was also playing lacrosse and stayed in the orchestra. I don't know how she did it all.

Sari, whom I happily introduced to junk foods like popcorn and potato chips, also gave her class speech at her graduation. It was the culmination of years of work and standing out as a remarkable student. After she was done with high school, she followed her instincts and went to Georgetown. It's a school that's nearly impossible to get into, but she did it on her academic prowess. I was told some 20,000 people apply and some 1,500 get in. I was worried she wouldn't make it (dads always fret about these things) but again she proved me wrong for worrying. She'd done all the extra-curricular things a university wants, from sports to volunteering to music and internships. I was there when she got her acceptance letter. The day it came, I was in the house, just me and her. Judith was at the hospital where she works (for a prestigious kidney doctor). I was so nervous as Sari opened the envelope. When she saw her acceptance, she cried. She broke down in tears, then I did, too. She was so happy. I still have a video of that moment on my phone, which I cherish.

My daughter, who grows in confidence every single day, graduated from Georgetown with a degree in international politics and Spanish and with four years of basketball under her belt. I thought there was no way she could play D-1 but guess what? She did! When she'd enrolled in the school at first, someone from the basketball team saw her and noticed her sports resume, so they called me up and asked if I thought she might be interested in playing. I talked to the coach and said I wasn't sure but that I'd ask Sari. The coach said, "We need her!" Playing D-1 involves a lot of time, travel and work. But I heard the coach's pitch and told Sari about it. She said, "Dad, come on, stop playing around! I'm not playing at Georgetown! What are you talking about?" The school has a long history of success, from the men's team with John Thompson, Patrick Ewing, Alonzo Mourning, Dikembe Mutombo to the women's team, which is solid and boasts big time alums like Rebekkah Brunson and Sugar Rodgers. I told her, "I'm serious!"

Luckily, I still had the voice message from the coach on my phone and I could play it for her to show her I wasn't joking around. Sari looked at me like *I was crazy* when she heard it. She said, "Let me think about it." But she told me not long after, "Okay, dad, I'm going to try it!" It made me so proud. Sari ended up walking on to the Georgetown basketball team and had a four-year career. Sure, maybe she's not the team's all-time leading scorer, but she stuck it out and can say she played four years of varsity at one of the best. Few others can boast that claim. She was an academic and athletic standout at one of the best universities in the world. After she graduated, she stayed at Georgetown to get her master's degree in conflict resolution in international politics. Can you believe it? Now, she's working at the United States Senate in the office of one of Michigan's legislators. Sari recently finished an internship with U.S. Senator Gary Peters (D-MI). Now, she's there full-time. And she's only 23.

Through fatherhood, I certainly made my fair share of mistakes. But my daughter taught me how to be better at everything. Before you become a parent, you don't understand how demanding and how important it can be. Judith has always been an amazing mother, too. She had a natural ability with Sari. It can be harder sometimes for men as parents, especially with daughters. We don't always have that innate sensitivity it requires. But I like to think that, on average, I got a little bit better each day. I supported her through all her endeavors, and she turned out to be a model citizen. Sari has turned out to be the most important person in my world. A close second is Judith, of course, who has been my partner in life for more than 25 years now. I was blessed by both of these strong, beautiful, capable women. Life can involve so many twists and turns, but thanks to them, they've helped to straighten everything out.

Memory Lane: Sari Cureton

"When I got a bit older, I realized how much of an impact my dad had in my hometown of Detroit. It became clear how much his career has meant to people in the city. I'd see people coming up to him on the street. Not just people talking about his playing days, but also talking about charity events, how he met with their kids at this or that camp. It shows how far a career in basketball can take you—it stops being about sports and becomes a way to bring people together, which I find fascinating.

"I studied international politics and now I work in domestic politics, so for me the part that's especially interesting is the fact that sports go beyond just a fun pastime. Having someone in your life who is a living representation of how versatile sports can be is incredible. When I was younger, my dad used to take me out on rides in the city, to visit my grandma, to visit his friends in Detroit. We went to this secret restaurant just off the water, Sinbad's. He'll tell you I was afraid of the calamari there!

"But I think as far as stories are concerned, some things I take away most from my dad's time in the NBA is not just the tales of successes. It's also the tough moments. He talked a lot about navigating the politics of the league. Arguing with teammates. The tough losses. The relationships he built. Those have been the biggest things for me. The good times are great, but I learned a lot more about his story through the tough times.

"I'm definitely lucky to have someone in my life who is as tenacious about his goals as he has been and who doesn't take things for granted. Because I think it's taught me how to be humble and how to appreciate how far I've come. But also, to recognize that I deserve credit for my work. Because if I don't trust myself that I've got it than no one elsewill. Being able to see that has been invaluable."

16

Master P
and Dennis Rodman

After my success with the USBL, I wanted to work with more teams as a coach. I knew I had a knack for player development, and I thought that would serve me well on the sidelines. Besides, what's better than helping someone improve? It had been the story of my life and I wanted to bring that to others on the margins of professional basketball. As mentioned before, my good friend Isiah Thomas purchased the entire CBA for $10 million. He owned the entire league, beginning in 1998. We'd each left the Toronto Raptors after the 1997 season. And he invited me into the CBA as an assistant coach. In sports and business, trust is everything and he and I had a lot of trust working together. It started when I was on the Pistons with him for three seasons and it's continued in our lives through the decades.

In between the USBL and CBA, I did some local broadcasting in 1998 in Detroit for some college games on TV, but when Isiah offered me a gig in Sioux Falls, where I'd played before, I jumped at it. The head coach there for the Skyforce was a guy name Jim Brovelli. At the time, he didn't know me from Adam. But what Isiah said, as the owner of the league, went. So, there I was ready to help Jim for the 1999–2000 season. I'd had my stint playing for a few weeks with Sioux Falls a few years earlier, so I knew what to expect when I went back to the area. The team had a strong ownership group, a good arena and solid fan support. The team had won a CBA ring a few years after I'd left in '95–'96. It was also freezing cold there! Cold like you wouldn't believe. Alaska cold.

Jim Brovelli didn't know me when I arrived and I didn't know him, either. It made for something of an odd situation at first. Usually head coaches like to handpick their assistants, but given Isiah's influence with the league, that wasn't the case with me this time. I knew I wasn't Jim's choice. But he accepted me. We had a good team. Our roster included Monty Buckley, Dametri "Da Meat Hook" Hill, Kenu Stewart, Chris Smith (who was one of the first pros from UConn) and many more. My goal was to come in and work hard right away and do whatever Brovelli needed of me. The CBA was a developmental league, a hoops halfway house. Players either improved and went on to the NBA and Europe or their careers continued downward. For example, we also had Victor Page, a former standout from Georgetown, who was sentenced later to 20 years in prison for assault. Others had reputations. But it was our job to try and help, even mold some of these guys as best we could.

One day at a time, Jim and I got to know one another over the course of the season. We connected, thank goodness. Things worked out. I knew it was a bit of an uncomfortable situation for him in the beginning, but to his credit he accepted me without judgment. I wanted to show that he could trust me, that I was worthy of being there, that I was willing to help the team come together by any means necessary. After a few weeks, he started to take to me. We even had a conversation about it one day. I flat-out told him, "Jim, I know I'm not the guy you wanted. I know I'm not the guy you would have brought in. But I hope you see I'm willing to work. Willing to do whatever it takes." He told me, "Earl, you're right. I wouldn't have picked you. But I'm so happy I have you. I don't know what I'd do without you."

Though we didn't win it all that season, we had a good year with a winning record. We also had a bit of a celebrity on our team. During the year, we added Jimmy King of the Fab Five. He was on that memorable University of Michigan squad with Jalen Rose, Chris Webber, Juwan Howard, and had played in the NBA a bit. Now, he was with us for some games. He played well as we progressed through the year, a guard who could defend and score. Coach Brovelli knew what he was doing, too. He ran the Xs and Os and I handled the personnel and player development. It was a dream combination.

The league was filled with names. Rick Mahorn was a coach, too, heading up the Rockford Lightning in Illinois. It seemed he and I were always meeting in various basketball capacities. It wouldn't be the last time, either. That season, we finished third in the regular season, winning 30 games. We won in the first round of the playoffs but lost in the semifinals. Not a bad year, overall. A few years later, the CBA would close shop and Sioux Falls would be part of the NBA's D–League, the Association's official minor league.

But my next stop was another developmental league. The ABA for the 2000–01 season. Basketball fans may remember the ABA from the '60s and '70s. It was the league with big dunks, big afros and small pay checks. The ABA helped bring in the dunk contest and the three-point line to the NBA. Now, people were trying to bring it back as an alternative to the NBA again. Real money was being invested—at first, anyway. With the rise of the ABA, they were putting teams in California. There were eight teams total, and some top-notch talent was assembled. Paul Westhead, the former championship coach of the Los Angeles Lakers, was hired to run the Los Angeles ABA team. That squad played in the same arena as the Lakers. The Forum. We had NBA legend Jamaal Wilkes in the front office. It was quite an operation. John Wooden was an official Honorary Coach of the team. John Wooden! He has 10 championships coaching UCLA with the likes of Kareem Abdul-Jabbar and Bill Walton.

Personally, I had no connection to Westhead, other than the fact that my 76ers team had faced him often in the early '80s. But I didn't know him at all beyond that. Thankfully, Jim Brovelli recommended me for his staff. Relationships, relationships, relationships. Maintaining good relationships will take you far in this world. I'm example No. 1 of that, for sure. Jim and Paul had coached against each other in college. They remained friends. And Brovelli let Paul know I was interested in coaching and that I'd be a good addition for his staff. So, I went to L.A. and interviewed with Paul and ended up getting the gig.

The ABA started off as a serious league. We had good players, pros like Toby Bailey from UCLA who'd played with the Phoenix Suns. We also had Ed O'Bannon, another former star at UCLA and top draft pick by the New Jersey Nets, along with his brother Charles. Tyson Wheeler, too, who had played for the Denver Nuggets. When I got there, Paul began teaching me his intricate, running system that had been the spark of the Showtime Lakers in the early '80s. We had Corey Gaines on the roster, too. He had a great basketball mind and had played in the NBA in the '80s and '90s. We also had player-coach Scottie Brooks, my former Houston Rockets teammate in '94 who would later coach in the NBA, working with the likes of Kevin Durant, James Harden and Russell Westbrook. Scottie, though, quickly transitioned from a player to full-time coach, taking the reins the following season after Paul left. As a unit, we all learned Paul's system that first year, which focused on the fast break, running and scoring.

The rest of the teams in the league were scattered throughout the United States in cities like Detroit, Chicago and Kansas City. Players were earning about $70–80,000 per season. It seemed like a viable option for those who couldn't crack the NBA. The league had been restarted by businessmen Joe Newman and Richard Tinkham. But soon the ABA began running low on resources. Teams had to find new owners. The Detroit Dogs, coached by George Gervin, won the first league championship, defeating the Chicago Skyliners. The next season, our team made it to the Finals and played against the Kansas City Knights, coached by Kevin Pritchard, who is as of this writing the current general manager for the

Indiana Pacers. We had moved from L.A. to Anaheim for that second season. By now, Paul Westhead had left for the NBA and Scottie Brooks had taken over as our head coach. I was still an assistant.

Scottie and I were friends, former teammates. We had a good connection. It was the beginning of his lengthy coaching career, which also included a stop for a while with the Washington Wizards as the head man. I wasn't sure at first if I wanted to go with the team to Anaheim. They had to cut my salary to keep me. But I decided I would, in the end, knowing I wanted more and more coaching reps to hone my skills for a possible gig in the NBA. Scottie had told me he indeed wanted me there. So, I went. He allowed me to build the team with players I wanted. So, I brought in Derrick Dial and some other Detroit guys. We had new owners. Former Laker A.C. Green was involved in the front office. It was a wild time. Scottie didn't run Paul's system, but we were successful under Brooks' leadership.

After that second season, I coached a summer league team in Vegas, and we won the championship. Reggie Theus was my assistant, my old buddy from the Magic Johnson traveling all-stars. I had some options after that, but I decided to give it one more go in the ABA. For my third year in the league, the 2003–04 campaign, the team moved to Long Beach, and we changed names again, from the Los Angeles Stars to the Southern California Surf to now the Long Beach Jam. Paul Westhead, done with the NBA, returned to the team as the head coach and ran his system. I stuck around, again as an assistant. I also had a bunch of my handpicked guys with us. And Paul brought a few guys, too, including Matt Barnes, who later made a real name for himself in the NBA, and DerMarr Johnson, who had played with the Atlanta Hawks for several years, and Juaquin Hawkins, who'd played for the Houston Rockets. (We eventually lost Barnes and Johnson to the L.A. Clippers later in the season.)

Paul brought in the right players to fit our system. And it worked. We were good. The ABA that year had seven teams, including two in Mexico, and we played 36 games. In total, the teams were spread out, though many of them were in the Southwest. There was us, the Long Beach Jam, along with the Kansas City Knights, Tijuana Diablos, Gallos de Pelea of Juárez, the Jersey Squires, Las Vegas Rattlers and Fresno HeatWave. The league also had a funny rule where, if you lost the ball in the backcourt, the team that got the ball, if they scored, earned an extra point. But thankfully we had a solid point guard, a Japanese fellow named Yuta Tabuse, who racked up assists and could keep track of the rock like it was stuck to his hands with string. He fit in Paul's system, which wasn't easy to learn. Yuta later had a stint with the Phoenix Suns during the '04–'05 season.

By this time, Corey Gaines had become a player-coach with us. We were feeling good as we got out of training camp for the '03–'04 season. We took a trip down to Juárez, Mexico, to play and test our team. It was something of a crazy trip, going through the country. We were shuttled around on a military bus after we flew in from L.A. Paul, who was used to the luxuries of the NBA, knew this was a different scene. It was different for all of us, really. In fact, while we were down there, Westhead got a call. I couldn't make out everything I overheard, but I knew what it was about. He was being asked to come back to the NBA as an assistant coach.

We won our game down in Juárez but when we got back to L.A., Paul called me into his office, saying he needed to meet with me. When we met, he said, "I'm going back to the league. This is going to be your team now. I'm leaving you. We got the players, you helped put it together, it's your team." So, all of a sudden, I was taking over as the head coach of the Long Beach Jam. Finally, I got the head coaching job I'd always wanted.

Corey was a big help since he knew Paul's system like the back of his hand. We were a dominant team in the league that season. We fended off the loss of players to the NBA and other leagues and we kept everything together, winning. We especially had to keep our composure during one game, in particular. We were matched up against Vegas, which had on its roster former rap star, Master P. He will be remembered by NBA fans from his few tryouts with teams in the league. Master P was a solid player, but he was also an overly-confident one, I'm sorry to say. So my guys had to put him and his squad in their place. They were threatening our players *and* the referees. Me and Corey still talk about that game to this day. The referees stopped making calls, scared for their safety.

At one point, Derrick Dial went to the basket and the Vegas team undercut him and took out his legs. He was trying to lay the ball up and they risked his actual life. What made it worse was the officials swallowed their whistles and didn't call a foul. I lost my cool and ran from the bench to half court and took a swing at one of the refs! Thankfully, we ended up winning the game. My team followed my lead. I didn't back down and they didn't back down, either. We beat Master P and his gaggle of guys. We were a bunch of players from Detroit, there was no backing down for us. After the game, I talked to the refs and they said, "Hey, we were just trying to get out of here with our heads." The implication was they were trying to get out of the game … alive. But we proved ourselves.

We had skill and we were on a roll. We sold out arenas because we were playing so well. And our popularity only increased when we brought in the mercurial, talented Dennis Rodman. Basketball fans know his name well. He's the man who replaced me on the Pistons to help cement the Bad Boys. He's the guy who dated Madonna, who dyed his hair all types of colors and who helped the Bulls, with Michael Jordan and Scottie Pippen, win the team's second three-peat. Jordan retired for the second of three times after that. But since those years, Dennis had left the league and he was trying to rehabilitate his image. So, he joined our squad late in the year to get noticed. He'd last played in the NBA in 2000, a brief stint with the Dallas Mavericks. He was with the Lakers before that in 1999 after leaving the Bulls. Dennis joined us for the '03–'04 season and, in later years, he would play for other teams like the Fuerza Regia, Orange County Crush, Torpan Pojat, Tijuana Dragons and Brighton Bears.

Before joining up with us, he'd been working on his film career and on professional wrestling. When he joined the Long Beach Jam, however, he was hoping to get called up to the NBA midseason but that never did happen. Instead, he helped us win a ring. Dennis only played in a few games, but he was impactful. We took him on after we'd lost some of our own to the NBA. He played in the championship for us, which we won against the Kansas City Knights 126–123 at home in an arena on the Campus of Long Beach State University that holds some 4,000 people. We had big time scouts at all our games while I was coaching. And Dennis helped us sell out all the games he played. He came in and everyone went crazy for him—he had that affect. I'd also won Coach of the Year in the ABA that season after taking over for Paul and winning the league. The success made me think I had a coaching career ahead of me. So, I went after it as soon as the ABA championship season was over.

Word was, the NBA was solidifying its own official developmental league, the D–League (now the G-League). They'd seen what leagues like the USBL, the new ABA, the CBA could do to help rehabilitate players and offer coaches and scouts looks at guys that might be useful for NBA teams in many capacities. So, they wanted their own, sanctioned offering. The CBA would possibly become its D–League. And as word of the acquisition circulated, I started to make some calls to throw my hat in the ring as a possible coach. At first, I received positive responses. But soon they turned sour. Why? I'm honestly not sure to this day.

My hope was to get into the D–League and work my way up to the NBA. It seemed reasonable, especially given my success in the ABA. Scottie Brooks had moved up. Paul had moved back up. I thought maybe I had a shot, too. At first officials in what became the D–League told me I was a perfect fit. I had media savvy, I had won a ring and Coach of the Year in the ABA, I had knowledge working in various communities, I was used to travel and the trials and tribulations of leagues, from Europe to the U.S., that didn't have all the amenities the NBA offered. I knew how to develop talent and speak to players. I was a two-time NBA champ.

With all that, I was laying the groundwork, trying to get in. I was hopeful it could work out. But after those calls, once I reconnected with D–League officials again, I was told I had *no shot*. It was stunning. Officials told me they no longer wanted to look at possible coaches from other developmental leagues. They said they couldn't even *interview* me. Thinking about it now, it feels as if the D–League got some edict from NBA overseer David Stern. Maybe it had to do with Isaiah—again, I still have no idea. But since I was "affiliated" with the ABA, my name wasn't considered for coaching in the new D–League. It was crushing, especially since Scottie got his chance. But I knew I just had to keep moving forward.

It's the kind of thing you can't argue. Scottie, who remains a good friend of mine, was "affiliated" with developmental leagues, so was Paul Westhead. But there was no issue with them—and I was the one who'd won the ring and coach of the year! Plenty of players, including Matt Barnes, were in the NBA after being "affiliated" with the ABA. So why couldn't I get a shot? Even as an assistant—anything? Looking to what I could muster next, I had an offer to go overseas to Korea. The Long Beach Jam didn't renew my contract. Instead, they hired NBA legend Tiny Archibald to run the team. I'd put all the players together, but they took the team away from me. I was pissed at the whole situation. Nevertheless, I turned down the offer to go to Korea and I took over another team in Orange County called the Orange County Crush. My ABA ring and Coach of the Year award at least got me that. And out of spite, I took the players we had on the roster for the Jam with me to the Crush.

We had a good year with the Crush. We didn't win it all, but we were solid. I didn't coach the team, though. Corey Gaines did. I was in the front office, officially called the Chief Operating Officer (COO). After that season, I went back and coached in the L.A. summer league and worked at some pre–NBA draft camps, including the camp in Chicago. The legendary Celtic Satch Sanders had helped me out with those positions, giving me a chance. I still had hope I could be a scout or coach in the NBA. In between all that, I had hip replacement surgery, sometimes working and coaching on crutches! But after my stint with the Crush, I left the league entirely. My next gig came from a great friend. Muggsy Bogues.

In August of 2005, Muggs was hired to coach the WNBA team in Charlotte, The Sting. The team was 3–21 when he took over. They'd fired their coach, Trudi Lacey, midway through the season and hired one of the most famous people in Charlotte basketball: Muggsy. When he took over, he went 3–7 and was kept on for the next year. Once he was hired, he asked me if I could come join him to coach and I immediately said yes. I loved the idea of getting back to work with Muggs. He's a great guy and I knew, if nothing else, we'd have fun. It was also another chance for me to test my coaching chops. We were there for a season and a half (going 11–23 in 2006) before the team was sold away from Charlotte. They were supposed to move to Kansas City but instead the organization simply folded.

When it was announced that the team had been sold, I was out on a scouting trip. So much for loyalty and letting the staff know what was happening ahead of time. I was on the road, scouting a tournament when the famed women's basketball player Anne Donovan came up to me and said, "You know your team just got sold, right?" I was in the arena, trying to evaluate players and talent. "That's the word coming out of Charlotte," she said. Well, there goes that, I thought. We'd had a good run, with good players like Helen Darling and Tangela Smith. And our players just adored Muggsy. After that, I went back home to Detroit to figure out what would be next for me.

A couple of years later, I hooked up with my old adversary and friend, Rick Mahorn, who was coaching as an assistant in the WNBA with the Detroit Shock. Bill Laimbeer had been the head coach of the team and had won a title in 2003, 2006 and 2008 (the latter two with Rick as an assistant). In 2009, when Bill left, Rick became the head coach of the Shock for the year before the squad moved to Tulsa, Oklahoma. That's when he brought me in to help his team develop players since I already had WNBA experience.

The Shock had a great squad with standouts like Deanna Nolan and Cheryl Ford. The team also had Cheryl Reeve as an assistant. She'd been in Charlotte but was passed over for Muggsy. Later, Cheryl would go on to win four championships in the WNBA with the Minnesota Lynx. She was an amazing tactician and motivator. We lost in the Eastern Conference Finals in 2009 to the Indiana Fever (Larry Bird bought up any empty seats in the house to pack it), but overall, it was a successful campaign. A few seasons later, my old friend Corey Gaines reached out to me and asked if I could come join his staff with the WNBA's Phoenix Mercury. In 2006, Paul Westhead had gone to the Phoenix Mercury and compiled an 18–16 record, led by star Diana Taurasi, who many consider to be the best women's basketball player ever. The next year in 2007, Paul won the WNBA championship, going 23–11.

Following that, he brought Gaines in to be the head coach, since Corey knew Paul's system and it would be an easy transition with the players. Corey went 16–18 his first year and then 23–11 in his next year, winning the Finals over Indiana, again led by Taurasi, who averaged 20.4 points per game. Gaines went 15–19 in 2010, 19–15 in 2011 (losing in the Western Conference Finals to Minnesota) and 7–27 in 2012. In 2013, the team drafted the center, Brittney Griner, and, under Gaines, the team went 10–11. But he didn't finish the year. Russ Pennell took over and went 9–4, eventually losing in the Western Conference Finals, again to Minnesota. In 2014, the Mercury won the championship over the Chicago Sky.

But for Griner's rookie year, 2013–2014, I was an assistant under Gaines. (Years later, Corey would work with the Japanese national team.

He's had quite a career.) As of this writing, Brittney Griner was recently freed from prison in Russia. It killed me to see her there in those grainy photos. As someone who knows her, someone who worked with her, it was excruciating to see her held captive in a horrible foreign country. When I heard the news of her arrest in Russia due to a tiny bit of THC, I was shaken. Brittney is such a nice woman, she's a beautiful person. Every time I saw her on TV in Russian court, I thought, "Jeez, I can't believe this." I'm grateful I got a chance to meet her, and I'm thankful things finally worked out sooner rather than later for her to regain her freedom and come back to the United States.

I guarded Griner in practice every day. She's 6'8" and we wear the same size shoe! We'd laugh and joke all the time. It was hard looking at her captive on television. I felt helpless. I prayed for her that she could get back home and resume her life. Truly, the situation in Russia was threatening everything for her. She was nothing but a political pawn and it wasn't her fault. Some people in the world wanted to defend Russia and its oligarch Putin saying, "She broke the law." But the American government said she was detained unjustly, and I'd prefer to agree with our homeland on this one.

Beyond those issues, Brittney is a great player. She was one of the few in the league who could dunk, and she did so with authority and gusto! She could run and jump, score and defend. She'd often kick my old butt in practice. And the only reason she was in prison in Russia was because she was playing there in the country in *their* league! She was a guest, bringing in money and interest to the Russian basketball system and look what they did to her. It was totally outrageous. She was caught in the middle at a time when the country decided to invade its neighbor, Ukraine. The whole thing was disgusting from the start.

Another odd occurrence during my time with the Mercury was semi-regular breakfasts with the team's former owner (and former owner of the Phoenix Suns), Robert Sarver. As of this writing, Sarver was recently suspended by the NBA for one year for some horrible comments and actions. That has led him to now sell both teams. But back then, it was normal enough for me to have breakfast with the man. Life is surreal, to be sure.

In between coaching stints, I spent a lot of my free time broadcasting University of Detroit games. I'd go back home to the city in the winters to call college games on the radio for the team—seeing players like future New Orleans Pelicans coach Willie Green—and even some Pistons games when Rick Mahorn wasn't available. Today, I still broadcast both and if Rick ever decides to hang up his microphone, I'm next in line (no pressure, Rick). I also spent more time doing television, until the local legend Mateen Cleaves was hired to take my place. I couldn't even really be mad at that one. Mateen is a local legend a true phenomenon when his Michigan

State team won the NCAA championship in 2000. Mateen later played in the league for a handful of years. His stats weren't as good as mine in the NBA, but he's great on television. He's got a giant grin.

I tried lots of things after leaving the NBA. Not only did I coach in the USBL, CBA, ABA, WNBA but I spent a little time in the NBA as an assistant strength and conditioning coach. Unless there is a XYZ league, I think I've hit the entire alphabet. Isiah brought me in with the Knicks when he took over the team in the early 2000s. He was there from 2003 to 2008 and I helped him some winters working with the players. But after Isiah was gone, the team cleaned house and I was gone, too, just like in Toronto. It was good to get that experience, but it didn't last. To date, the only place I haven't coached is college, though with all my broadcasting experience, I could probably handle a job like that. I get to see all these players day in and day out, watching the University of Detroit. I know I could function well within the NCAA, but I think that ship has sailed. But you never know.

Memory Lane: George Gervin

"It was fun for me to see Earl grow from a kid to a pro and then to play against him as a young pro and me being a veteran. To be able to make it out of that environment of the east side of Detroit, I always compliment him because he figured it out. Earl wasn't the best shooter, wasn't the best scorer, but how many years did Earl end up playing? Twelve? Ain't that something? I was a scorer and a shooter, and I played 14 years and he played 12!

"I always call Earl one of the best utility guys in pro basketball. When I say utility, I mean he came in and coaches and general managers wanted him because they knew he knew his role. I think a lot of other kids and young professionals didn't understand that they wanted to be the man! But Earl wanted to play professional basketball and be a part of a pro basketball team. That's what separated him. For me to see that, it gives me a great appreciation of the man, himself.

"And look what he's doing today. It's all giving back, all changing lives. By him being on all those teams he played for, being in the league 12 years, he motivated somebody else to be better. To have that kind of positive impact on someone else's life, he was greater than just a ball player. I appreciate our relationship. I appreciate how he feels about me. Now I get a chance to let the world know how I feel about him. He's special. That's just who he is."

17

Becoming an Ambassador

Detroit has always been home. No matter where I was employed along my journey, I always returned to the city in the offseason between jobs. After my time was done in Phoenix with the Mercury, that's where I went. More than any specific job, my focus was always to keep going. To find the next opportunity. I've never been afraid to try new things (unless it was a strange food). Over the years, my family probably wished I'd pushed more for college coaching or working on the NBA sidelines. But I did push hard. I just didn't have the response that I hoped for. I still think I'd be good at the gig, developing players. I may not be the best Xs and Os guy on the planet, but I know how to work with hungry players and how to motivate them. How to make people better. Still, it rankles me that no one in the NBA cared about my ABA coach of the year award. But I've had to let that go.

That's what comes with experience. And it's paid off. When the Detroit Pistons brought me in for some jobs, I was more than happy to oblige. At first it was as an independent contractor. But the team quickly saw my value as an employee, and I was hired full time in 2013. I've been working with the Pistons for over a decade, officially now as a team ambassador. In that capacity, I run camps. I hold meet and greets with season ticket holders. I announce games here and there. I'm available for whatever the team needs.

Joe Dumars, the longtime star for the franchise who was there when I played for the Pistons in the '80s, was still the team's general manager when I was hired. It was his last year, actually, when I arrived. He's since moved on to other squads, including a job with the Sacramento Kings. Joe embraced my hire, which I was grateful for. And I enjoy being an ambassador to the team and the community. I've always been able to relate to people and lord knows I have enough stories to tell. My versatility also comes into play on the job. I've been present on days when people were even made nationalized U.S. citizens. A judge came into the arena and performed the service at midcourt, bringing some onlookers to tears.

Of course, that story had another story to it. I met in a suite later that day the judge who did the nationalizing. The legendary player agent Arn Tellem, the former legal counsel for the Clippers when I was on the team, was there (in years later, I'd accept an award on Arn's behalf when Detroit honored him), and he invited me over and introduced me to the judge, who paused a moment and said, "Earl Cureton? You don't remember me, do you?" I said no. And the judge said, "I sued you!" I said, "You did?" He said, "Well, I repped the Italian team that sued you, from Milan!" We laughed about that one. That happened in 2021. It's just one of the many things that can happen in a long career like mine that now includes community outreach.

Truth be told, I'm lucky. My basketball career led me to more and more opportunities in the game. That's not the case for everyone who's laced up sneakers. I remember one great moment during President Barack Obama's time in the Oval Office. He was in Michigan for the Flint water crisis. I managed my way into the reception where he was and when he was walking by, I just shouted, "Mr. President! My name is Earl Cureton and I used to play for the Chicago Bulls!" He stopped right in his tracks. We talked a minute, he told me he remembered me, and we snapped a picture. I'm a people-person and that's helped me immensely. I could always seem to make friends. I'm often in the Detroit Pistons arena now, shaking hands, telling stories, laughing with people. All while my daughter is in Washington, D.C., doing her thing. It's a good life and I'm glad for it. Over the summers, I've been driving all over the state of Michigan, speaking and teaching at camps. In 2022, I coached and spoke with some 2,000 kids and signed some 2,000 autographs. I'm constantly driving back and forth between the suburbs and the inner-city, meeting kids and telling them about the league.

I've been in the city for basketball court renovations, for community events, for Toys for Tots events. I've been a color analyst for the team. And I've earned a great deal of respect from my community. I even got my college degree some 30 years after I left the University of Detroit. I'd promised my mother I'd get my diploma. It may have taken a long time—some three decades—but I managed to keep my word. I'm very proud of that. I got my degree in human services, aided by teachers like Ron Naski and Michael Witkowski, for whom I'll forever be grateful. It was important to me that I keep that promise to my mother, who passed away in 2019 at 102 years old. Before she died, she was able to attend Sari's high school graduation in 2017, too. Mom was 100 that day.

Another big honor for me—well, it's honors, really—was being inducted into both my colleges' halls of fame, as well as my high school's. That's right, I'm in the hall of fame at Robert Morris and at the University of

Detroit, as well as Finney High School. And recently U. of D. retired my jersey, too! I was inducted into the Robert Morris hall of fame while I was still playing in the NBA in 1988 when I was with Charlotte. And in 2007, I was inducted into the University of Detroit Hall of Fame. In 2021, I even called a game between Robert Morris and the University of Detroit, the two schools are now in the same conference, the Horizon League, my two worlds colliding! But there's nothing quite like seeing your jersey and your number-24 hanging from the rafters. That's some *forever* stuff. Detroit has seen its fair share of top talent. And to have my name hanging from the University's Calihan Hall rooftops is a thrill. I wore a royal blue suit and lots of my old teammates were there to help me celebrate. I'll forever remember that day, it was quite an honor. To be remembered is a special thing.

When I was interviewed about the ceremony, I told one news outlet, "I was born and raised here; born on Jefferson Avenue in Lakeside General [Hospital], and I'm a Detroiter. I love this city. I grew up on the east side of Detroit, and had an opportunity to play college basketball here, my high school basketball here and to play in the pros here. Now I work in the community to help the youth—it's just been a great run." Tony Fuller was there that night to celebrate with me, along with his family. Judith and Sari were there. It felt good to celebrated in the place where I left it all on the court. It's these types of acknowledgments that show me I've done some good in my life and they will push me to do more. I take my job with the Pistons these days very seriously. It's an opportunity to help the organization and the city, to connect with and teach younger players, and to honor the game that has given me everything.

Memory Lane: Billy Cunningham

"In Philadelphia, we had a championship team. But to have a championship team, besides Julius Erving and Moses Malone, if you don't have people in the supporting cast like Earl Cureton who come into work every day, to practice at 100% and were supportive of his teammates and did what was needed of him, then you can't win. Earl gave everything he possibly could to us.

"I'm sure there were times he was upset with me and that would be natural with a player wanting more playing time! But he never took that into the locker-room and made it a negative issue for the team. There was a lot he sacrificed in helping the team have success. As long as I live, I can picture putting Earl into Game 2 in the world championships against the Lakers, and he's playing against Jabbar, and he hits that hook shot. I can still see that hook shot going in!

Earl hugging Antoine Davis, the University of Detroit's all-time leading scorer, after Davis's jersey was retired in 2023. The unveiling, in 2020, of Earl's retired jersey and number for the University of Detroit.

Earl, Judith and Sari admiring Earl's retired jersey and number at the University of Detroit. Legendary announcer George Blaha speaks at Earl's jersey retirement ceremony as Detroit Pistons vice chairman Arn Tellem, Derrick Coleman and Ethan Davidson look on.

"How did he hit it? Because he was mentally and physically prepared to do whatever was asked of him. That takes a lot. And to see how he has achieved with his life and with his daughter and family, it doesn't surprise me at all. In fact, meeting Earl for the first time—we used to have a camp in Philadelphia where we brought guys in to make a first impression before the draft. When we brought Earl in, he was just out of the University of Detroit, and he jumped right out to me, his effort and his attitude.

"I've always wondered if I should have played Earl more in Philadelphia—it's part of coaching, second guessing—but I wonder if I should have played Earl more at power-forward alongside Moses or even Darryl Dawkins and Caldwell Jones. *Should I have done that?* I'll always wonder. But Earl—I just love and think the world of Earl Cureton."

18

Final Reflections

Life hasn't always been easy. I've been on top of the world. And I've been aimless. I've been loved and I've been lonely. I've been given big opportunities and I've had them taken away without any real explanation. But I know I'm not unique in this. That's why this story—my story—is applicable to so many other players. That's why I wanted to write this book. It's a field manual to survival. I am an avatar for so many who've walked on the NBA hardwood. If you, dear reader, had gotten a growth spurt like I did in college, you may have had my life, one spent for 12 years in the NBA, and I'd be reading about you. Life is capricious, unpredictable.

While I played with Michael Jordan, Isiah Thomas, Dr. J, Moses Malone, Hakeem Olajuwon and Muggsy Bogues, I was never like them, in terms of my overall skillset. They started the games, and I often contributed off the bench. But teams don't win without players like me. Coaches often play rotations of eight, nine or even ten players in a given contest. Teams were comprised of 12 players when I was in the league, now rosters are set at 15-plus. So, it's not about the stars or even just the starters at any given moment. And as I proved in Philadelphia and Houston, bench players matter. Especially when it comes to earning rings.

When I left the league, I held a lot of jobs. One outside of the game of basketball was even as a car salesman. That's something Michael Jordan has never done! He may have been in ads for cars, but never on the floor of a dealership, gladhanding. I worked at Varsity Lincoln and Mercury in Detroit with my now-good friend John Obied, who taught me a ton about the business. I even sold a few cars to NBA players. I enjoyed the car business, I found it intriguing. I liked the process of putting someone in a vehicle that they loved. It can be a cutthroat business. But so is professional basketball. And I like seeing people happy, sliding into their new leather seats, ready to drive the big highway home.

It's all part of life. All part of my life, anyway. That's what I tell kids when I talk to them at the various basketball camps I attend. There are so few Michael Jordans, Hakeem Olajuwons and Julius Ervings. I should know, I've played with them. It's much more realistic for someone to grow up and be like me—at least when compared to the lives of those stars. Learn my story, digest my blueprint, and you may have a chance at making and even staying in the league. My story is the one they should be looking to for inspiration, at least as much as they look to the all-time greats. It's so hard to be a legend. But it's at least a little more likely that you can live to be a journeyman in professional basketball. Hardly anyone can "Be Like Mike." But it's not impossible to try and "Twirl Like Earl!"

There's a wall up at the Detroit Pistons practice facility today. It's filled with images of the team's past greats, from the Bad Boys to Chauncey Billups to Blake Griffin. Cade Cunningham, the team's No. 1 pick in 2021, will likely have a lasting space there before his career is all said and done. But the wall has filled up over time. I see this wall when I go to work these days. And one of the young men I work with, he must be 34 years old, which is some 30 years younger than I am, has asked me how we can continue the wall for future players if it's already filling up? At some point he said, "Let's just take the first part of the wall down, the old stuff. It doesn't need to be up there, does it?"

His comments floored me. Just keep the new stuff, kill the old? Is that how history should be remembered? He didn't mean anything by it and maybe, in the end, that makes it worse.

Would your mother throw out your baby pictures because you graduated from college, got a job in the big city? Are the present and the future so important that we need to forget the past? No, of course not. Not in my eyes, anyway. But it's very American to forget the past—increasingly so, it would seem. Especially in Florida. It happens all the time. But that's not what I believe is important. In a way, the past is *more* important than the current moment. What do they say? If you don't remember the past, then you're doomed to repeat it? I don't want to be doomed to repeat my or your mistakes. I don't want to forget those who came before me. I don't want my career, my championships, to be forgotten, either. And that 34-year-old young man will likely feel the same as I do when he's in his 60s. He just doesn't know it yet.

Everything has a beginning; everything has a start. History is important. Foundations matter. Without them, houses would crumble and fall. Without offering those early moments the honor they deserve, what are we left with?

These days, I like to think about my life in the game. Between ribbon cuttings and meet and greets, how could I not? All that it gave me, all that it took. I still exercise often, walking on the track for six or seven miles, doing pushups a few times a week. Lifting weights. For the Pistons, I have a busy schedule, especially in the summers. They have me driving all over

Michigan and beyond, working Pistons Academies, going to golfing tournaments, hosting people, chatting and talking about the good ol' days. At home, I spend time with Judith and check in with my lovely daughter in D.C. It's a good life. I spent decades working to cultivate it.

In our living room at home, there's a picture of me shaking President Ronald Reagan's hand. I'm standing right next to Dr. J. If you had told me when I was in high school that I'd have even that framed photo, I wouldn't have believed you. Not for a second. For all the ups and downs, for all the loop-di-loops on my career's rollercoaster, that picture and my family make it all worth it. Of course, there are always regrets. Or, at least, lots of *what ifs*. If I had gone to Michigan State or Indiana State, I could have been college teammates with Bird or Magic. I could have been in that famed 1979 game, which will never be outdone in terms of viewership. Maybe Bird would have beaten Magic if I was there to back him up, grab an extra rebound or two. I missed out on getting rings with Jordan and Isiah with the Bulls and Bad Boy Pistons. Maybe if I had played my cards differently in those years, I'd have my jersey in those cities' rafters. Alas. I managed different dreams. Dr. J and Moses. Hakeem and Kenny Smith. That's good enough.

The other day I was on the golf course for one of Jalen Rose's celebrity tournaments. I've known Jalen, a Detroit favorite son, ever since he was in high school. He later created a charter school in the area and does great work in the community. Grant Long was there, Terry Mills, Calvin Johnson, Ron Harper. Spencer Haywood was there, too. His wife had just passed away and the funeral was a few months prior. Time marches on. Life is brutal, but it's also beautiful. I recently threw the first pitch at Jimmy John's Field, home to a minor league baseball team. I was a guest speaker at the Senior Olympics over a recent weekend. I've also worked with the Special Olympics and been on panels for health and wellness in the Black community. I'm a regular in Muggsy's celebrity golf tournament, too.

Muggsy and I recently got into a good-natured argument about Bill Russell versus Wilt Chamberlin. He tried to tell me about Kareem, and I said, "Muggs, you were a baby when Kareem played!" But that's what makes our friendship great. We can laugh, joke, rib each other. That's what comradery is. That's what love is, really. It's what shared experience can do for two people. It's not something worth giving up. Ever.

Of course, I went to war under the basket with Kareem, too. In the NBA Finals. I was one of many solid backups then. Each of us have stories. We all played our roles. Some backups you know, like famous sixth men like Detlef Schrempf or Jamal Crawford. Some of us, though, aren't nearly as well known. That's why this memoir, to me, has been so important. It's my story but it's the story for so many others. To be in the NBA means you're going to be part of a circus. In a fishbowl, the biggest fish get the most eyeballs, but there are others swimming around, that hear the banging of fingers on the glass walls. In the NBA, we all deal with so much to live the dream of being a professional athlete. So, yes, I've been through a lot, like many before and after me. It's important for fans and consumers of the league to realize and remember that. It's part of the entire dream. Nothing is perfect. But we keep striving forward, one day at a time.

Role players, journeymen have it tough, as I hope I've proven in these pages. Practices are hard, traveling is hard (especially in the days without charter planes). Negativity is everywhere. Like I said, despite being in the top percentile of basketball players, I heard often how I wasn't much of anything. Do you think the 200th best doctor in the world hears he or she is crap? Doubtful. But that's the territory for the NBA too often. But positivity is everywhere, too. With all the people I tell my stories to, I would often hear back, "Damn, Earl, you should write a book!" I always thought, "Maybe one day. Maybe." But now, I've finally done it. Add author to my lengthy resume. It's another nice feather in my cap as we find ourselves around the 40th anniversary of the '83 champion 76ers and the 30th anniversary of the '94 champion Rockets.

And as these milestones continue to approach and pass, it's important to remember those who are no longer with us. I've lost friends, teammates, trainers, coaches and family along the way. People like Moses Malone are no longer with us. It's sad. And one day I'll be gone, too. But thankfully, there's these pages to remember. I made something of my life.

The 1983 76ers Championship team celebrating 40th anniversary in Philadelphia at halftime of a game on March 20, 2023.

Earl, Dr. J and Reggie Johnson celebrating the 76ers 40th anniversary of the '83 championship.

Lately, I've taken to mentoring this one young player. He's 6'3" and his dream is professional basketball. He's having a lot of problems, though, and he doesn't want to go to school. I was able to get him into a junior college, telling him it's his best chance. I know what that's like, of course. His hope is to one day play in the NBA. But I try to tell him there are more options than just the NBA out there. Lots of people don't even know there is more than one option in basketball. That other professional realms exist! I told him when I was his age, I played junior college ball. Told him a growth spurt helped me. Today, we work out together on the track, we talk about life. I tell him that he should focus on getting a degree, that the piece of paper will take him further and for longer than any jump shot. As always, it's a matter of hard work. How much do you want to put into it? Nothing is impossible when you work hard.

Of course, nothing is going to go smoothly all the time, either. Just look at me. I've told you about all the good press I've gotten in my life, some of those articles are in these pages. But one came out not too long ago from the outlet *Bleacher Report* that said I was one of the "worst" players of all time to have won multiple championship rings. Can you believe it? The headline is: *The Eight Worst Players to Win Multiple NBA Championships.* It's comical. No matter how hard you work, someone is there to try and cut down your legs from underneath you. The piece came out sometime in 2010, and the list includes the likes of my old friend Carl Herrera, Will Perdue, Kurt Rambis and others. I want to read the article that's headlined "*The Worst Doctor to Save Two Lives.*"

Recently, I went to a camp in Traverse City, Michigan. Another Pistons academy. There was a large group of youngsters in attendance, all aged between 10 and 16. Of course, these kids didn't know who I was when I showed up. But I told them about my story, told them about people like Muggsy, who triumphed despite maybe the longest (and shortest) odds. I told them about Jordan, Moses, Dr. J, Isiah, Hakeem. Most of them knew *those* names. But they didn't know mine. I joked, "Google me!" So, the next day, they came back, looking at me like I was a hero. It shocked me that they took the time to check out my game. But in so doing, they saw my dunk on Patrick Ewing and the hook shot over Kareem.

I signed a stack of photos for the kids that next day. I told them too

Earl saying hi to Julius Erving with Franklin Edwards and Sari standing nearby during the 1983 celebration.

how I just found out that I'm a character in the popular video game, *NBA 2K*. I warned the kids, though, that they shouldn't depend on me as a scorer in the game, instead they should use me a defender and rebounder. Those have always been my specialties throughout my career—both on and off the court. Focused on regaining the rock for one more shot. For one more chance.

Memory Lane: Judith Pickop Cureton

"We first met at a downtown club. Earl asked me if I wanted a drink and then he asked me to give him a call if I was interested in having lunch, which I thought was neat. So, I called him and the following day we went out. He picked me up for lunch, but it was funny because he was late, and I'd decided that I wasn't going on the date after all. I was just going to eat kimchi and rice. But when he showed up, I changed my mind.

"I remember it was raining and humid outside. And there was garlic coming out of my pores! We went to a movie. But before we did that, we watched a few basketball games and I guess that sealed the deal for him and our first date has, well, never really ended. I didn't know anything about basketball. But he was educating me. I liked the fact that he was straightforward. I wasn't aware of a lot of Detroit history either, but

Dr. J, Earl and Clemon Johnson at the 76ers' 1983 celebration.

he shared that with me. It was interesting to learn so much from Earl, even early on.

"He was funny, too—Earl is hilarious! He was just easygoing. It was very new for me to be introduced to his world. Houston was really big. During the Finals, at the last minute, the team's owner decided to charter a plane so all the wives and family and girlfriends could go to the games. The team's plane took off and then our plane took off. Their plane landed and our plane landed. We were in New York City for a week. It was the most exciting but nerve-wracking and craziest time. I was still new to the environment. Game 6 was crazier than Game 7. I don't know why, but I was just calm for Game 7. I knew they were going to win.

"But more than basketball, Earl is a great father. The day I told him I was pregnant, he just sat there and had the biggest tears in his eyes. We'd had conversations about children, but nothing serious. Because of his job, he was away for months out of the year, but when he came home, he was always hands on. It's funny, Sari would always wait until after I left the house to go number-two! It would drive Earl crazy! But he was very good with her. They would go for walks and car rides. They had their own language!

"We've had our ups and downs, our challenges. But you learn to accept a person instead of trying to fit them into the model you have. We've been through a lot, and you just roll with the punches. It's been great. Earl is terrific with people. I tell him all the time—you know the dog whisperer? Earl is like the player whisperer. He can watch somebody in a scrimmage or a gym practicing, and he call tell you all about that person. He's psychic when it comes to that.

"He can also imitate

Earl with the loves of his life, Sari and Judith, in 2023.

practically anybody. It's part of his awesome sense of humor! He's generous, even in our neighborhood at home in Detroit. He's gracious, too, especially in terms of appreciating other people's successes. Him and Sari have that in common, thank goodness. Even though they may want their dreams really badly, when good things come for others, they're genuinely happy. They celebrate others."

Coda

Earl Cureton

Work, work, work. It seems to be all I do! But I'm more than grateful for it. Working for the Pistons, I travel all over the state of Michigan. I play in a lot of golf tournaments, though I'm not all that good at the game, truth be told. Occasionally, I get a chance to see my daughter. The other day, I flew to Washington, D.C., for a game and to see Sari and her brand-new dog, Roscoe. He's a puppy, just a few months old. I'm even an ordained minister! These days, it's the start of the new NBA season and people are excited about the Pistons, even though they're young. Cade Cunningham, Jaden Ivey, Jalen Duran—these are the new kids in town.

Sometimes I look at these young guys and think to myself: you have no idea what's in store for you, young buck. They train every day, they've worked all their lives, but a career unfolds before you in ways you could never predict. It changes you, tests you. You grow and evolve because of the obstacles your journey presents and because of the gifts it gives you, too. I smile when I think about the number of years ahead for Cunningham and his crew. Who will they be when it's all said and done? What will they be remembered for? What will be their moment? What hardware will be in their trophy cases? And who will be the hard-working role player, the journeyman to help get them over the mountain top?

If they win big, maybe I'll get my third championship ring. Maybe Detroit will honor them like Philadelphia honors the '83 team, or Houston honors the '84 team. Those are the stakes. Recently, I just visited Philly to celebrate 40 years of the '83 team. We're all getting up there in age, but I think I was the youngest-at-heart. Boy, was it great to see Dr. J, Andrew Toney and the fellas again and laugh about old times. Next year, I hope to celebrate with the '94 Rockets anniversary team.

One of my most cherished Pistons family members is the longtime NBA figure Arn Tellem. A former agent of Kobe Bryant's, Arn has seen just about everything in the league, from representing guys like Reggie

Miller, Tracy McGrady and Jason Collins to working with the Clippers and Donald Sterling back in the '80s when I was in Los Angeles. Now he's my boss in Detroit, the vice chairman of the franchise. You know that '90s HBO television show *Arliss*? That was based on his life. Arn is a true legend in the league, a genius behind the scenes. When we talk, he asks me about NBA stories. Arn grew up in Philadelphia and loves to hear about '83.

"One of the biggest joys for me," Arn told me once, "having grown up in Philly, I love to hear all the great 76ers stories. Dr. J, Andrew Toney. Maurice Cheeks and Moses Malone. I could sit all day and hear about them. I realize how special that team was and how close they all were. To be able to hear that—that's something I hope we can build here in Detroit now."

Those who know the game of basketball (and my story) know that the sport is as reliant upon relationships as it is talent. There are only five guys on the court at once, half what there is in baseball, football and soccer. And there are no pads, no helmets like in hockey. You see everyone's emotions, expressions. As the great Celtic Bob Cousy once said, we're all playing in our underwear! So, when Arn talks to me about relationships and building from that sense of interconnected chemistry here in Detroit, I know I'm in the right place.

I'd like to also take a moment to thank the owner of the Pistons today, Tom Gores, who cares as much about the greater Detroit community as he does about fielding a top-talent roster. Without guidance like that from Gores, who is from Flint, Michigan, and others at the top of the team, the Pistons would just be a basketball organization, not the top-flight community beacon the team has become.

From the minute the NBA became a possibility in my life, I always said I wanted to do more than just make the league. For so many, their dream is to just be in the NBA. My hope was always to have an impact on the league, in whatever way I could. To make people remember that I was there. I may have gone about that in a different way than my idol Dr. J or other legends like Jordan and LeBron. But I believe I did just that. I achieved my dream through hard work and a good spirit. Through connecting with people. Some may have said my career wasn't "shit," but those who know the game know that isn't the story.

Memory Lane: Arn Tellem

"Earl is one of the most positive people that I've ever met. To me, so much of life is about attitude. Earl has just the greatest, most positive attitude among people that I know or have met in my life. I'm blessed that we work together. No matter what is going on, Earl always sees the good in

Earl during the 76ers 1983 champion team anniversary in 2023, staring at what matters most.

people. And I think he recognizes the incredible platform that we have with the Pistons. So, he's always striving to make a difference in the community. For us, there is no one better to represent the Pistons family.

"Everyone knows he'll go the extra mile, go above and beyond to help anyone. As big as he is, he has a bigger heart. I think the thing is—the longevity of his career, here's a guy, he wasn't the most skilled player, but was a part of championship teams and very good teams and I think that's because of who he is. It's a testament to him and what kind of person he is. Those kinds of players are essential to winning and culture. He brought that. And it's why he's so beloved by former teammates to this day.

"Earl wears his emotions on his sleeve, so you know he's not coming to you with anything other than a genuineness and sincerity. People see that immediately. But he combines that with an incredible work ethic. Earl works long hours and I wish every person had his work ethic. That's the thing—he has a tremendous sense of responsibility, both to his family and to his former teammates, to the Pistons organization and the city of Detroit. He walks the talk here every day. I love the guy. I truly love Earl."

Index

Printed in the USA
CPSIA information can be obtained
at www.ICGtesting.com
CBHW030739150224
4219CB00113B/964